"Atheists are unpopular religious apple cart. Tha for almost two thousar are coming off and the apples are past their sell by date. Believers are stirred out of their complacency. Their certainties put to the test and found wanting. The religious underlings are being told that their emperors wear no clothes. That their magical castles are built on sand.

They are not turning the other cheek as they are meant to, but are up in arms and go all out to demonise the foe. But where is the evidence for our supposed demonic behaviour? Where are the atheists rioting in the streets. Where are the atheist holy books burning parties? Where are the prisons bulging with benighted infidels? Where are the atheist suicide bombers? Atheists want a quiet life but they are not going to get it unless they stop religion in its tracks. Since we are not the types to resort to violence we can only do it by making our rational voices heard. These messages no doubt will cause offence, particularly to those who secretly know that their sacred beliefs are poppycock.

But nobody has a right not to be offended. You may offend my humanism to your heart's content. Sticks and stones and all that. Rather than act the offended victim I would relish the thought of a good debate, but please don't go burning my book."

HAPPILY
GODLESS

HUMANISM FOR A BETTER WORLD

With best wishes

Tony Akkermans

by

Tony Akkermans

Grosvenor House
Publishing Limited

The right of Tony Akkermans to be identified as the author of this
work has been asserted by him in accordance with Section 78
of the Copyright, Designs and Patents Act 1988

The book cover picture is copyright to Tony Akkermans

This book is published by
Grosvenor House Publishing Ltd
28-30 High Street, Guildford, Surrey, GU1 3EL.
www.grosvenorhousepublishing.co.uk

A CIP record for this book
is available from the British Library

ISBN 978-1-78148-736-5

DEDICATION

This book is dedicated to my partner Seonaid who is the best that a humanist could hope for and who has acted as my rant control throughout. To my children Julie and Richard who have turned out good rationalists without my helping hand. Finally to my grandchildren Zoe and Robert for whose sake I hope that some of my predictions will not materialise.

Contents

Dedication	iii
Introduction	ix
My Path to Humanism	1
Holland	2
Storm Clouds	4
Way back When	7
Bedtime prayer	9
Church	10
Confession and other rituals	11
Priestly respect	15
Mischief	17
Vocation and a Dutch Uncle	21
In Heeroom's footsteps	30
National Service	34
England-Holland-Canada-London-Yorkshire-Shropshire	35
What is Humanism?	39
Humanism – a Potted History	47
Humanist Ceremonies	55
Cremation and Burial – Epitaphs	58
Old hat Religion	62

Omnigod - Blurry God   **64**
Size of the Universe   65
Red in Tooth and Claw   66
Problem of Evil – Free Will   68
First Cause   73
Arrogance   74
Resistance Fighters   75
Agnosticism   76
Teapot in Orbit   78

Atheism is not a Religion   **86**

Religious Gullibility   **89**
Religious Scientists   91
Faith's Comfort Blanket   94

Inside a Believer's Mind   **98**

Faith and Reason   **102**

Guidelines on how to become an Atheist/Humanist   **108**

Cults   **115**
Cult recruitment   119

Toys for Adults   **121**

Jehovah's Witnesses   **123**

Spiritualism   **129**

The Paranormal   **133**
Astrology   136
UFOs and Crop Circles   139
Extra Sensory Perception   141
Ghosts   145
Faith Healing   147
Psychic Detectives   153

Scientists and the God word 159
Nature Programmes avoiding God 161

Timeline of the Universe and
Planet Earth 164

Heavens Above 170

Prayer 176

Women and Religion 185
Abortion 193
The Emerald Isle (that can be vile) 196
Female Genital Mutilation – Forced Marriage 200
Homosexuality 204

Religious Prudery 208

Population Growth 214
Growth Trends and Statistics 216

Multiculturalism 224

Faith Schools 234
SACRE Dieu 243
Compulsory Worship 245
Free Transport 247
Biblical Light Relief 248

BBC (Baffling Belief Crusaders) 251

Church Buildings 258
Remembrance Day 261
Chaplaincy 265

Animal Welfare 267
Animal Testing 273

Nature versus Nurture 275

Menace of Religion 285

Hitler/Stalin Counter Claim 292

Atheist Militancy 297
The tables are turning – Religious
Discrimination on Trial 301
Prayers at Council Meetings 305

Tranquillising the Grizzly Bear 308

Morality 313
The Bible for the Common People 316
The Ten Commandments 319

Religion, Science and Politics 327

Assisted Dying – Euthanasia 334
Euthanasia in the Netherlands 343
Advance Directive 345
Belgium and America 347

Happiness 350

Humanist Utopia 355

My Humanist Wish List 359

INTRODUCTION

What made me decide to write this book? From day one in my life I have been surrounded by religion and its negative effects and I have long had a wish to set down in detail what has bothered me so much all these years and is still bothering me now. The timing has been long delayed. On numerous occasions I have been asked to explain what my humanism is all about. I have usually answered the question in a very few words such as my favourite super succinct : Humanism is trying to be 'Good without God'.

That usually satisfied most of the questioners, because opportunities are rare for in-depth discussions on the touchy subject of religion. Not that humanism is a religion, of course, but that is the heading that we have to put up with. But some people, and I hope my readers are in that group, would have preferred a more detailed reply and it occurred to me that if I put it all down in a book I could refer my questioners to the ready made article and carry on discussing the weather. Since I am well past the proverbial three score years and ten I decided I had better get on with it, before increasing short-term memory loss would make the task much harder.

Another reason why I feel the need to write is that I am very wary of religion. Like Christopher Hitchens,

I believe it poisons everything. I have read a lot of history and the message has got through to me loud and clear: organised religion has always been and is likely to remain, a menace to the peaceful conduct of society. The evidence is all around. It has touched me too. Religion has been unkind to me. Now I am being unkind back. My book pulls few punches. If I offend feelings I apologise, but my feelings too have suffered.

Whereas some people feel that religion has cast off its murky past and is now a force for good, I cannot share this optimism. I believe that as long as there is segregation in society along religious divides there is a real danger of a return to violence and oppression. Not only in the Middle East, the Balkans, Nigeria and Afghanistan but even, perish the thought, in peaceful, civilised Britain and Holland.

I mention both these countries because they are close to my heart. I was born and grew up in Holland and I now live in Britain because my partner and my two children are British. Although Christianity is finally on the decline in both these countries, I feel there are new dangers lurking. If we go on condoning the illiberal demands of fundamentalist, immigrant religion, if we go on adding to the number of faith schools and keeping our children apart in ghetto-like conditions there may come a point when silent hostility can no longer be kept in check. Resulting not necessarily in Enoch Powell's 'rivers of blood', but in lasting deterioration of societal harmony.

With this threat increasingly looming what are caring humanists to do? Of course there is always the easy option of looking the other way and taking the 'après nous le deluge' view of things. 'It will last my time', particularly at my age. There are better things to do than setting the world to rights. Enjoy your family, read a good book, watch TV, keep fit, go on holiday, work in the garden; let the world at large get on with it. I suppose that is the choice a lot of people make and they have my sympathy. But tempting though it is, that attitude is not for me. Nor, I suggest, should it be for others who have children and grandchildren, whose long term future should be a concern.

Our social conscience should not be limited to the pleasures of living in the here and now. There is a duty on all conscientious citizens to work towards a better future for mankind. And if you are convinced, as I am, that a society adopting humanist values will function so much better than any other system, then you are duty bound to do your bit in bringing it about. Being a 'stand up and be counted' sort of person has its price to pay. I dread to think how I would have fared in Nazi Germany. I doubt that I would have been able to keep my head down and I certainly would have given shelter to fugitive Jews, regardless of the consequences. Some evils are too great to ignore. I do think that, at its most extreme, fundamentalist religion stands comparison to the fascist state. The theocracies in Iran and in Afghanistan under the Taliban provide ample proof.

Some of the articles I have written for freethought publications have been criticised for being offensive to the religious. For causing hurt to decent religious folk. This is a frequently expressed concern levied at 'militant' atheists, but I think the distinction between criticising religion and the religious is a spurious one. Religion cannot stand alone. Without people there would be no religion. The only 'dehumanised' artefacts are the holy books. Even they were written by men but because of their anonymity they appear above the fray. The more recent religious inventions and practices can all be related to human beings. How can rationalists be asked to distinguish between individuals and the things they espouse and practise?

In any case few of my attacks in this book are aimed directly at people of unobtrusive simple faith. In places I have poked some gentle fun. My stronger barbs are reserved for the system and its executives. Ayatollahs, Popes, priests, politicians and other assorted manipulators who take advantage of people's humble faith, their efforts and preferably their money; thus turning this army of earnest, well intentioned foot-soldiers, into a major force in keeping religion in power and humanism on the fringes.

Apart from my fear of religion's need to dominate I am stuck with a strong sense of justice. It is not right that state schools should force kids to worship. It is not right that there is a religious propaganda slot at the heart of a current affairs programme on the publicly funded BBC without a right of reply. It is not right that people are denied the choice of euthanasia. It is not right that women cannot have abortion on demand. It is not right that there are unelected Christians in parliament.

And finally I have this thing about logic. I cannot abide illogicality. It is not logical for people to believe without evidence. It is not logical to believe that in a universe made up of billions of galaxies there is an entity concerned with our personal well-being. It is not logical to believe that this being is all good, all knowing and all powerful and to square that belief with the existence of evil. It is not logical that a benevolent god could have created nature red in tooth and claw. Nor is it logical, on a lighter note, for people to believe in the paranormal. That's why I have included a chapter, taking it to task.

All these matters and many more compel me to keep striving on behalf of humanism. In doing so, am I as bad as religious busybodies who bully us, preach at us and knock on our doors bringing the 'good news'? I like to think not. Advocating humanism is a defensive reflex. Without the missionary activities of the religious there would be no need for it. They preach peculiar dogmas; they indoctrinate children. They push for privileges and seek control of other people's lives. Humanists merely try to hang on to our personal freedom and freedom *from* superstition.

* * * *

A note on the main characters in the book: The fact that 'God' gets a lot of mention does not mean that he/she/it gets my endorsement in any way. For me God is as real as Father Christmas. God is only in the script because to a lot of people amongst my readership God will represent a tangible entity, meaning that an extensive discussion cannot be avoided.

The same applies to the Bible, which I have rather dignified with too much acknowledgement. But as long as that collection of self-contradictory, ancient fairy-tales is taken seriously by millions as a guide to moral conduct and keeps appearing in hotel bedrooms around the world, I cannot avoid paying it attention.

The human characters atheists and humanists are indistinguishable as regards God belief. An atheist is simply a non-theist. A humanist is a person with a Godless life-stance. Agnostics I barely mention because it is rarely clear what substance the Agnostic is agnostic about.

A note on sources: My book is an opinion piece, not a scholarly tract. That is why I have felt it preferable not to burden the reader with foot-notes, annotations and extensive source referrals. All my stated facts and statistics have been researched to the best of my ability. The reader is of course welcome to carry out independent checks, nowadays facilitated by the internet.

My path to Humanism

*"Parents can only give good advice and put children
on the right paths, but the final forming of
a person's character lies in their own hands"*
Anne Frank

I have never had a religious bone in my body. Nor a
religious brain cell. I should have had. I was born in
Holland at the start of the war into a deeply religious
Roman Catholic family as the third of seven children
and was thoroughly exposed to every facet of that
religion for the first twenty years of my life. All these
years I spent my time in church and in prayer not
remotely from my own inclination, or for my own
benefit, but always from a sense of duty and a
willingness to do what was asked of me and to please
the adults in charge. So for a long while religion attached
itself to the outside of my head like dandruff, but it
never entered. Years later I discovered a very effective
shampoo. It is called humanism.

From a personal point of view I am of course obliged
to the teachings of the Catholic faith, since if my parents
had been humanists they would almost certainly have
stopped at two offspring and this book would never
have been written. So thank you Pope; it is much

appreciated. Nevertheless I would much prefer to be rid of the Catholic label but that is easier said than done. It is not possible to defect formally from the Catholic Church, apparently once a Catholic, always a Catholic. The Church asserts that "*baptism marks a person with 'a seal of character' that is an ontological and permanent bond, which is not lost by reason of any act or fact of defection*". This hanging on to the punters for evermore doubtless helps to explain why they can keep on claiming that they number 1.2 billion members.

People raised in the Catholic faith can be divided roughly (and if Irish nuns had anything to do with it, it would be roughly) into three categories: a) water off a duck's back escapees, equipped with highly efficient clap-trapometers; b) gullible trusting souls, swallowing pulpit fodder hook line and sinker hence fettered for life; c) sincere agonisers, the head recognises the nonsense but the heart wants to belong and is grievously troubled, leading to a life-time of prevarication. I count myself fortunate to belong to category (a) and this has stood me in good stead on my journey up and away from this oppressive institution. I have been called a lapsed Catholic but that is like calling Terry Waite a lapsed hostage.

HOLLAND

The Holland of my youth in the forties and fifties was a very different place from what it is today. Medieval forces still held our village in an iron grip. The population of some 1200 could have served as a miniature model for Northern Ireland. Half and half Protestant and Catholic, with barely a non-believer in sight. Dictated to by Protestant ministers and Catholic priests, who moved amongst us like gods and who controlled all facets of their half of village life from the comfort of their sumptuous vicarages and fiery pulpits. Protestant churches, Catholic churches, Protestant schools, Catholic schools, Protestant clubs, Catholic clubs, Protestant political parties, Catholic political parties. Tweedle Dumb and Tweedle Dire; an all pervading iron curtain of religious segregation. The only time we schoolboys spoke to members of the other camp was when insults were exchanged. The only physical contact was punches thrown in sectarian battles. Tribal scenes all across the country.

Then something marvellous happened. An enlightened government, tired of petty strife and narrow bigotry began to work towards integration. In our village denominational schools were closed and replaced with a single, modern, well equipped community school where all the children went and where of course the parents congregated too. Soon, to people's surprise, it was recognised that the perceived differences were really no differences at all, but the imagined differences resulting from centuries of partisan manipulation. This process was repeated all over the country. The pooling of resources and the replacement of dogma by open enquiry and free discussion have had a dramatic effect on Holland's harmony and well-being. Standards of education have risen sharply and are now amongst the highest in the world. Christian religious strife is a thing of the past. In my village a new tennis club has opened up. In days gone by it would have had a Catholic or Protestant label. Now they just want to play tennis.

The Dutch Humanist Association enjoys considerable status. The prime minister and half the cabinet attended its 40th anniversary celebrations. There are humanist counsellors in prisons, hospitals and the services. Euthanasia is widely available. There is no unnecessary censorship. Schoolgirl pregnancies are the lowest in Europe. Sixty percent of the population now claim that they have no religion. All this monumental change in just five decades. The Dutch are famous for their outspokenness. (I shall live up to this reputation in this book!) No taboo topics there of sex, politics and religion. I have a private theory that religion was brought low by birthday parties and anniversaries. The Dutch are avid family gatherers and they love a good debate. Add the magic ingredient of a decent education and fusty old religion doesn't stand a chance. People soon discovered that there were vast numbers of closet sceptics who were pleased to discover that they were not the only ones who had quietly put up for years with unwanted religious dominance.

So in Holland Christianity's teeth were rapidly being drawn; not too difficult a job because there were no wisdom teeth. Contrast that with Britain where if faith becomes the topic for conversation, which in everyday discourse is rare enough, suddenly everyone is circumspect. Theological egg shells must not be trodden on. This is because believers know they are on shaky ground and don't like to be embarrassed. So it's back to the cricket and the weather.

STORM CLOUDS

But I must stop waxing lyrical about Dutch progressiveness. Sadly the storm clouds are gathering once again. Ever since the loss of its empire, Holland, like Britain, has nurtured feelings of guilt for the wrongs perpetrated during colonial rule. Since the war the Dutch have operated a virtually open house policy for immigrants from distressed areas around the world. People have been made welcome and given massive social support to help them integrate. It had been naively assumed that incomers would soon adopt the Dutch way of life and fit in seamlessly. But what has been overlooked is that people come with baggage. Their own culture, their own religion. The idea of integration is akin to communism; a laudable objective but extremely hard to achieve.

Failure to assimilate is often blamed on racism but immigrant communities in Holland, as in Britain, live in isolation not because of the colour of their skin but because of their different culture and religion. Not all immigrants are fundamentalists, but they are sufficient in number to cause increasing friction with the progressive secular lifestyle that the indigenous Dutch are now adopting.

It is ironic that just when Holland had got the better of its reactionary Calvinistic and Catholic tradition and was getting close to becoming a model secular society, the envy of the Western world, the clock is now being rapidly turned back because the increasing numbers of immigrants are unwilling to follow the progressive trend.

The alarm was first raised by the politician Pim Fortuyn, not a raving fascist as is often alleged, but a left leaning sociologist, who could see that if nothing were done his beloved Holland would be gone forever. He was murdered for his pains. As was film producer Theo van Gogh two years later.

It is one thing to be lending a helping hand to the third world. But let it be done on their patch. Help raise living conditions locally. To attempt absorption of large numbers of immigrants of different cultures and religions within a single lifetime is a recipe for disaster. Without the religious ingredient it might have been an easier task but for the Dutch to see hundreds of mosques going up, just when the churches are coming down, is too much to take. Islam is not just a religion, it is a way of life, a blueprint for society. No country should be asked fundamentally to change its heritage within a matter of one or two generations. It was wrong what was done in some colonies; it is equally wrong to reverse the roles.

I will return to the bothersome topic of multicultur-alism in a later chapter when I examine the impact it is having in Britain.

WAY BACK WHEN

*"The surest way to corrupt a youth is to instruct
him to hold in higher esteem those who think
alike than those who think differently."*

Friedrich Nietzsche

I remember this worrying development was not
envisaged when nearly sixty years ago, after a
particularly mind-numbing church service, my brother
and I were discussing how much longer the religious
lunacy would last. By lunacy we meant the willingness
of grown-up, ostensibly sane people, to keep on
believing in fairy tales and submitting themselves
uncomplainingly to boring sessions of praise and
prayer to a non-responsive deity. For us the penny
had dropped early. Religion was just silly nonsense
wafted down from the dark ages. As teenagers we were
increasingly amazed that people could be so gullible
as to believe in bread turning into the body of Christ
and similar voodoo rituals. Knowing that most of the
village was still in the grip of medieval superstition,
we realised that it would take a while for sanity to rise
to the surface but I remember us confidently predicting
that within another half century enlightenment would
have dawned.

And sure enough, in Western Europe at least, a lot of progress has been made. I recently returned to the place of hardship where we juvenile apostates had stood and the poor old building looked distinctly sorry for itself. Its once welcoming imposing front door was locked. Gone were the myriad bicycles that used to be strewn about the building and hedges. An eerie silence reigned, broken only by the irreverent cawing of rooks nestling in the bell tower.

I have calculated that I have spent a total of some 5000 hours devoted to the RC religion, made up of time spent in church, religious instruction in school and compulsory prayer at home. The equivalent of three years in an office job. The regime in our household was totally centred around the church. Each morning we would get up at 6.45 to be on time for morning mass starting at 7.30. From the age of seven I was an altar boy, which meant an even earlier start to assist with robing up the priest in the vestry. At least that place was warm in winter, fuelled by a red-hot cast iron stove which one morning, when warming my back, set fire to my surplice and I had to roll the length of the vestry to put out the flames. The rest of the church was unheated and in those far-gone days, when we still used to have severe winters, temperatures could drop to minus 15 C outside and for nearly an hour the congregation shivered, except for the priest, who was wrapped up in multiple layers, able to move about the altar and was fortified by copious helpings of wine before it was turned into the blood of Christ.

The only Latin I recall from my altar boys days is "mea culpa, mea culpa, mea maxima culpa". Which I think means: "I am guilty, I am guilty, I am jolly guilty", but would have been more accurately rendered as: "I am cold, I am cold, I am bloody frozen". A little heat would be provided by the candles I would light, bought by parishioners as an indulgence for deceased relatives who were feared to be still in purgatory. In Catholic doctrine this is a place of suffering, inhabited by the souls of sinners who are expiating their sins before gaining access to heaven. The number and the cost of the candles would count towards the length of remission granted by the Lord. A sort of Celestial Ponzy scheme. The flames in purgatory were said to be less fierce than the ones in hell so that a soul would emerge only lightly toasted, instead of burnt to a cinder. In the middle ages it was possible instantly to spring a dear one from the fiery jail by handing over a hefty sum, but because this led to the schism of the Reformation it must now be done more piece-meal.

As to the exact location of purgatory even the Catholics cannot tell but seeing that heaven is above and hell is below, it must be somewhere here on earth. And sure enough for a rationalist having to put up with all this puerile fatuity, it often feels like purgatory.

BEDTIME PRAYER

In the evening at home, before bedtime, there used to be household prayers, led by my father, in something called the 'Home Blessing'. This was an elaborate concoction of prayers at the heart of which was the dreaded rosary. For those readers not familiar with this instrument of torture, which I hope for your sake is all of you, let me explain. It involves going round a vicious circle of beads each one of which requires the recital of a 'Hail Mary'.

After every fifth there is a larger bead which signifies an 'Our father', after which it is back to 'Hail Mary'.

If you are looking for mind numbing tedium the Catholic church is there to lend a helping hand. We used to kneel on the carpet, except in a family of nine we could not afford a carpet, and we were on coconut matting. Physical agony to compound mental torture. For hours afterwards your knees resembled grid irons. This, I suspect, is where the first seeds of humanism were literally embedded.

Then to cap it all there were individual bed time prayers. The boys bedroom was above that of the parents and if we failed to kneel down on the boards and say our prayers they would be aware of us shirking our duty and shout: "I don't hear anything". We would then go "rhubarb, rhubarb" and one of us would dangle a leg out of bed and simulate the required kneeling noises.

CHURCH

On Wednesdays, as well as morning mass, there was evensong or vespers from 7 pm to 8 pm. This meant a lot of singing and more dreaded Hail Marys. Sometimes in a supreme act of sadism, when you least expected it, the priest would start up the litany of All Saints. I can still recollect the surge of acute despair this would induce. There would be dozens if not hundreds of saints and they would all get a mention. The priest would list the saints and the congregation would answer 'pray for us'. Holy St. Joan, 'pray for us', holy St. Antony, pray for us. On and on it went.

When we were older we couldn't stand it any more. My brother and I devised a cunning plan. Since my parents occupied the front pew and we used to skulk at the back, it was easy at the start of the service to sneak out of the building and repair to the local speak-easy. Timed to perfection we would be present once again at the church exit to be re-united with our parents. We feared our father, if not God. He couldn't prove that we had skived because we knew the proceedings by heart. What's more, so as not to give the game away we had been drinking orange juice.

On Sundays there used to be an orgy of church activity with two masses and more evensong. There was an agonising choice between Early Mass, which was shorter but meant you couldn't have a lie-in, or High Mass, which gave you a bit longer in bed but was a much longer service. There was no escape; you were caught between a rock and a hard place.

CONFESSION AND OTHER RITUALS

The weirdest thing of all was the confession. This grotesque Catholic snooping ritual takes place inside an enclosed booth called a confessional or oratory.

The priest and penitent are in separate compartments and speak to each other through a grid or lattice. A crucifix is sometimes hung over the grille. The priest will usually sit in the middle and the penitents will enter the compartments to either side of him. The priest can close off the other compartment by a sliding screen so that only one person will be confessing at a time. Kneelers are provided in the compartments on each side of the priest. Confessions and conversations are usually whispered.

Sometimes a confessional will be built into the church walls and have separate doors for each compartment;

other confessionals can be free-standing structures, like portaloos, where curtains are used to conceal penitents (and even the priest in some confessionals) from the rest of the church. Many modern confessionals have moved into the electronic age and are equipped with two or three lights outside, which can be controlled by the priest from inside, or are automatically activated by the penitent by kneeling on the kneeler.

In the more common two-colour system, a green light above the priest's location shows that he is in the confessional and he is available for confession, whereas a red light above the penitent's area shows that it is already occupied and that parishioners should keep away from it so as not to overhear something. In the less common three-colour system, a white light above the priest's location shows his presence and there is both a green and red light above the penitent's compartment: green to show the area is free or red to show it is occupied.

High-tech confession, putting many a pedestrian crossing system to shame. Who says churches don't move with the times. If it is necessary to walk by a confessional, it is considered polite to cover one's ear with one's hand, to show respect for the sanctity of the confessional. This is a pious practice even when no-one is in the confessional. None of this electronic gadgetry was available in my time. Just as well since I am red/green colour blind and might have walked in on a penitent in mid-flow.

Kids as young as seven would be lined up for this blatant child abuse and our biggest challenge was to think up sins. There was a choice between venial sins and mortal sins. We weren't quite sure of the difference although in catechism at school much time was spent to get us up to speed in the niceties of good and evil. I always decided to play it safe and would produce a standard shopping list of heinous crimes including such favourites as pulling my sister's hair, teasing my other siblings and stealing biscuits from my mother's larder. The adult on the other side would have to listen to this rubbish with a straight face but often he would be asking leading questions about naughtier things. At a younger age these would fall on deaf ears but when we got older this would be more embarrassing.

One day my older brother, always a fearless rebel, when he had had enough and planned never to darken the confessional door again, decided to get his own back and let the unfortunate father confessor have the full works. He unloaded heinous crimes of a sexual nature in spectacular detail to such an extent that the bachelor priest was driven from his box with a head the colour of a ripe tomato. It is truly mind-boggling how thinking adults could have fallen, and for all I know are still falling, for this obvious priestly ploy of keeping abreast of the local gossip and getting their fill of sexual excitement.

Another ritual of a less prurient nature was holy communion. As a child you were first introduced to this holy 'sacrament' at the age of just six. It involved sticking out your tongue, receiving a white thin wafer and swallowing this without biting on it. You must not bite on it because the wafer, by some mysterious priestly hocus-pocus, had turned into the body of Christ and of course you are not going to sink your gnashers into Jesus. Also before receiving this unwanted treat you had to endure a period of fasting probably so as to avoid causing Jesus to get mixed up with the detritus in your stomach. There are a couple of interesting philosophical conundrums here. If Jesus came back would he be expected to take holy communion and if he did, would he explode? And how do vegetarian Catholics deal with the transubstantiation of wafer into meat? Does God know and give them a lentil gentle Jesus instead?

Yet another freakish custom was inflicted upon us on Ash Wednesdays. This is the first day of Lent, a forty day period of fasting in preparation for Easter. It was to commemorate Jesus' fasting in the desert for this length and being tempted by the devil. It also involved our forehead being smeared with ash, supposedly obtained from palm branches, blessed the previous year. Sceptic that I am, I suspected that the Pastor's ashtray might have been a more likely source. He did smoke a lot of large cigars. The accompanying words were: "remember that you are dust and to dust you shall return". Just the sort of thing that trips lightly off the tongue when talking to an eight year old. The mark was in the shape of a cross. We were never told how long this imprint was meant to keep us branded, so some worried kids used to wash around it. In those post war years the fasting wasn't a big deal; it was the default position. But rare treats of sweets and chocolates were ruled out and had to be preserved in tins until Easter was upon us. Then the whole lot would be wolfed down and ghastly sickness would be the result.

A couple of other occultist practices merit a mention here. They were the wearing of scapulars and St. Christopher's medallions. St. Christopher is the patron saint of travel and he is depicted equipped with a walking stick, carrying little baby Jesus on his shoulders. Scapulars consist of a couple of black cloth squares connected by a ribbon, worn permanently around one's neck under the clothing. These were the preserves of adults who were lay members of monastic orders such as the Benedictines, Franciscans or Dominicans, also known as oblates. The scapular was intended to protect against the suffering of eternal fire in hell and the more elaborate ones were inscribed accordingly. St. Christopher's medallions were mostly intended for children and were worn pinned to one's vest with a safety pin. In play these sometimes would become undone and give you a nasty stab. As they were intended to protect you from harm this would be rather counter-productive.

PRIESTLY RESPECT

Religion used to pursue us into school too. Endless learning and reciting of catechism, scripture studies and weekly harangues on morality from the parish priest.

I remember he had a thing about warning us about body parts 'above the knees and below the shoulders'. 'Sins committed against the body.'

All this in front of ten year olds. We hadn't the foggiest what he was on about.

Goodness knows what that man would have downloaded if there had been the internet.

Priests, as God's representatives on earth, were held in high esteem. They were not above bolstering this esteem themselves. I remember our village pastor coming to our school lecturing us on the manner this respect should take. One aspect involved removing your headgear should you encounter him on his regular house visiting tour of the village. (Mostly for the purpose of berating reluctant mothers for not breeding fast enough). Sure enough on a cold winter's day I was on my bicycle wearing my tight fitting balaclava, lovingly knitted by my mother, when I spotted the priest on foot, coming towards me. Remembering the respect injunction I desperately tried to remove the balaclava, but this being a two-handed job I soon lost control of my bike and landed in an untidy heap at the pastor's feet, still tugging at my reluctant head-cover. He looked down on me in disdain and sternly announced: "balaclavas are exempt". Another rule involved tipping one's hat when passing the local church. I remember my uncle who passed the church on his way to and from work, had to tip his hat twice because the church was on a corner.

Even our rare, much prized, spare time was hi-jacked in the cause of religion.

We were pressed into a fund raising scheme which involved collecting waste paper and cardboard from all around the village. For two whole years we spent our precious Saturdays sorting this detritus and at the end of it we had amassed the princely sum of 400 guilders. How we remember statistics from our youth! And what was this hard-earned money put towards? Cancer research?; save the children? Animal welfare, perhaps? Sadly no. It went towards the purchase of a hardwood, carved statue of the blessed virgin Mary. This still adorns the church today, although hardly anybody darkens its door to see it.

MISCHIEF

All these duties and inconveniences brought out in us boys a need for revenge. This would take a number of forms, mostly centred around the bane of our existence; the local church. The church tower housed a massive bell which punched considerably above its weight. It attracted our wrath because its persistent peeling would summon us towards the building of doom. We were intent on silencing the culprit. This was ingeniously achieved by knocking a six inch nail through the bell rope just above the hole through the ceiling. Pull as he might the verger failed to produce the required din. We also conspired to stop it from striking the hour. On the first occasion we got this hopelessly wrong, naively believing that the hourly chimes were achieved by the mechanism tipping the bell. We wrapped a blanket around the clapper. Lying in wait and come the hour, we were amazed and disappointed that the clock happily performed as usual. Could this be divine intervention? On further inspection we red-facedly discovered that the mechanism drops a hammer on the side of the bell and after a suitable wrap up job this time all the bell could produce was a very doleful muffled thump. The sort of noise to match a miserable sinner's mood. We rolled about in hysterical laughter and for quite a while the more po-faced villagers were in high dudgeon.

Of a more sacrilegious nature was our tampering with holy water. Easter was the time when the annual supply of this highly prized liquid was created. After the Easter service a large tub of water was placed at the back of the church. With the help of some appropriate mumbo-jumbo by the priest this water would become holy and acquire highly beneficial properties. Afterwards the parishioners would line up, armed with assorted bottles and vessels to claim their share of the sanctified fluid. In the course of the year this water would become a cure-all for a very wide range of woes, surprisingly not available on the NHS. It would be used to bless houses, protect buildings from lightning strikes and be administered to the sick for all manner of conditions. Rumoured successes would boost the number of applications. The water would be spooned into ailing cattle and evil gossip would allege that some of it was applied as a forerunner of viagra. Its most common usage though was as a fill-up for the holy water stoups in church, used by the congregation on leaving the service by dipping their fingers and making the sign of the cross. A mind-bogglingly unhygienic procedure. Yet for all I know it may well have contributed to a highly developed adaptive immune system from which I am still feeling the benefit today.

One year my friend and I decided to carry out a test on the efficacy of this magic liquid by tampering with its content. My accomplice was a bit of a rogue who happened to be looking for urgent relief at the time and could only just be restrained from seriously compromising the integrity of the water. Instead we decided on complete replacement. Hurriedly the tub was overturned and replenished with clean water from a nearby pump. Shortly after, the first customers arrived and the not so holy water was soon carried away by grateful recipients. Our sceptical expectations were fully met when village life that year carried on pretty well as normal with the occasional report of a miraculous healing of a sick goat whose owners had been thoughtful enough to add a spoonful of holy medicine to its diet. There is a story of the village priest sprinkling holy water around a peasant's home. Peasant: "why are you doing that?" Priest: "To keep the devil away". Peasant: "There is no devil here". Priest: "Told you it would work".

Another target of misconduct was presented by the well stocked wine cellar in the parsonage. This was the biggest mansion in the village, built next to the church and connected to it by a corridor. In it lived the parish priest catered to by two housekeepers. As altar boys we had developed a taste for the wine, taking furtive swigs in the sacristy, when nobody was looking. Now we wanted more and we knew where to get it. During evensong when the priest and his housekeepers were at church we used to climb in through the priest's study window, swipe a few cigars off his desk and make our way to the staircase leading down into the cellar. And there, as far as the eye could see, were row upon row of the best wines and sherries that parishioners' money could buy. Many a merry night was thus enabled and we never failed to drink a suitable toast to his holiness the Pope.

The Pope featured in another bit of mischief that I perpetrated upon my old Gran. I feel guilty about this now but at the time we thought it was quite a hoot.

She was even more devout than my parents and for her the Pope represented the pinnacle of human virtue. So I showed her a picture of Pope Pius the Twelfth as a young man, in military uniform. Holding my thumb over the caption I told her that this was a photograph of the dreaded Stalin. She was duly horrified and said "yes, look at the evil in those eyes". Then I said "Oh dear, now you have called the Pope evil" and showed her the caption. Not a good day in family relations.

There were a few good things attached to religion as well. At first communion, when you were six years old and later at confirmation when you were aged twelve, a lot of fuss was made of you. You were kitted out in new clothes and a special effort was made to provide nice things to eat, even in those post war years of austerity.

At Easter and Christmas, mother, who was a very good cook, excelled herself and put on sumptuous feasts, a marvellous treat to come home to after suffering cold and boredom at midnight mass.

VOCATION AND A DUTCH UNCLE

*"Each of you has a personal vocation which
He has given you for your own joy and sanctity.
When a person is conquered by the fire of His gaze,
no sacrifice seems too great to follow Him and give
Him the best of ourselves".*

Pope Benedict XVI

And then my parents got vocation for the priesthood at my expense. I was deemed suitable material to follow in the footsteps of my Uncle Wout, who was a Roman Catholic priest. This man, although considerably younger than my father was much admired by him because he had been 'educated' and therefore he was on a pedestal and his word was law. When he was ordained my father gave him a gold plated chalice, which cost a thousand guilders. Bearing in mind that at that time, just before the war, a house could be built for four thousand guilders, it will give you some idea of the sacrifice he made. In front of us my father used to refer to him as Heerbroer, (Sir Brother) and we were not allowed to call him Uncle Wout but must address him as 'Sir Uncle' ('Heeroom' in Dutch). But because we thought his name was 'Heeroom' we called him 'Oom Heeroom', (Uncle Sir Uncle); an early example of double Dutch.

As was the custom at the time, he was held in almost Godlike esteem. Aware of his exalted status Heeroom, at family gatherings, used to hold forth on matters moral and theological. In his company we children were allowed to be seen but not heard. But we did hear him and I recall an occasion when Heeroom treated us to a detailed biography of Jesus, including a physical description. Apparently he was of athletic build, stood 6 ft tall and was 12 stone in weight. Bearing in mind that no contemporary historians ever gave him a mention and that to this day scholars of the period are undecided whether or not Jesus ever existed, this was taking conjecture to new heights, even for a church where conjecture is seen as a vital virtue. Heeroom did not live to a ripe old age. Rich food and drink plus good cigars took a heavy toll. He died at the early age of 62, the same age as Christopher Hitchens. Proof that not only the good die young. It has always been a regret that I was never able to 'have it out' with him. To have a heart to heart to find out what really went on above and below that pristine white collar. Heeroom was a pulpit pilot in an era when religion in the Netherlands was still dominant and brooked no challenge.

Now that the winds of change have blown to the farthest reaches of the land and have cleared a path to rationalism, it is tempting to imagine a retrospective dialogue with Heeroom from the grave:

Tony: In days of yore you strutted around the village like a feudal Lord and we weren't allowed a word in edgeways; do you think we can now have an adult chat on equal footing, without you doing all the talking and me in the role of the nodding donkey?

Heeroom: Of course, times have changed and we priests are past masters of the art of furtively moving the goal posts. We move with the times so as not to lose the flock. In the old days there was less need for that, thanks to the church's rock solid position, we were comfortable with dogma. You would have to have been superhuman not to have taken advantage. In those days the cowed masses were kept in line through fear and ignorance. Nowadays my successors must use popularity and gimmicks to achieve the same result. But even modern marketing methods are hard put to keep the clients sweet.

Tony: To turn the clock back a bit: what made you choose the priesthood?

Heeroom: There were a number of reasons: in large Roman Catholic families it was tradition for one of the younger sons to be put up for the priesthood. So you might say that my parents pushed me in that direction. On top of that, from an early age, I was the sort of person who likes the sound of his own voice, relishes status and, last but not least, personal comforts. I also felt unsure about my sexuality and the company of men felt attractive.

Tony: I don't hear anything about serving the Good Lord.

Heeroom: Oh, that one. To be honest that bit came a long way down the line. A handy cover for the real motivation. Fortunately it always worked a treat. For example I have known several chaps who turned missionary in order to lay their hands on cute brown boys in darkest Africa, but because it was done under the guise of saving souls, nobody had an inkling. That was in the days before the paedophilia scandal broke. That particular gravy train has been derailed, hence the huge drop in vocations.

Tony: I appreciate that you are now telling it like it is. Pity that you didn't do it earlier. That would have saved my father quite a packet. Do you remember that once, out of his hard earned money, he bought you a gold plated chalice?

Heeroom: Yes, your father was my greatest fan. It was pitiful the pride he took in me. He was very disappointed that you declined to follow in my footsteps. I do have a few qualms about that chalice but he took great delight in making the sacrifice and no doubt thought it would stand him in good stead at the pearly gates.

Tony: I know you once slapped my sister hard because she contradicted you on abortion. Why did you pick on her and not on me?

Heeroom: Because you are bigger than she is and you might have hit me back. Besides you are a man and she is a woman. And you know what we think of women in my church. No doubt you will go into that subject later in your book. By the way, why didn't *you* want to join the priesthood?

Tony: Although my parents tried very hard; it was always a non-starter. I am a natural-born sceptic. From an early age I have always asked 'where is the evidence' before taking things on board. And if it's evidence you want religion isn't the place to go. In your case it seems clear that your lifestyle and attendant status formed your chief motivation but what exactly was your stance towards religion?

Heeroom: Similar to that of most of my colleagues. I found the romanticism attractive but also saw religion as a vehicle towards the acquisition of comfort and status. In my time priests hob-nobbed with the great and the good and lived in the largest mansion in the village. Priests, in my view, may be roughly divided into three categories: 1) the less bright, credulous types who have had religion and priestly vocation spoon-fed from the cradle and who have had no option but to swallow. They go through life sacrificial and duty-bound. They genuinely do their best to make sense of a confusing doctrine, try to lead good lives and help others. They agonise over their sexuality and are naive enough to think that all other priests are suffering alongside in good faith. 2) the smart manipulators, in the style of American televangelists, who selfishly seek to extract the maximum in personal benefit from their privileged position; their so called faith is the smoke screen that makes it all possible. These are the clerical wideboys, using religion as a God-given tool for self-gratification. 3) the ostriches: a mixture of categories 1 and 2. Men who appreciate a pleasant lifestyle, wish to do some good in society but who prefer, when it comes to the tenets of their religion, the existence of God and the hereafter, to bury their heads in the sand for fear that intelligent reflection might undo their cosy make-believe. I imagine that most of us can be found in this last category, including myself.

Tony: Not a strong launching pad, wouldn't you agree, for leading the flock heavenwards.

Heeroom: No, but fortunately the flock was not very well informed. A Bishop once remarked to industrial magnate Frits Philips "I will keep them stupid so you can keep them poor". These days, in the Western world, it is becoming almost impossible to join the priesthood without negative repercussions. Respect and deference are hard to come by. All your actions are scrutinised. Secrecy and hypocrisy no longer protect. The papers are bulging with scandals.

Tony: According to revelations everywhere but particularly in Ireland and America, the priestly cassocks are bulging too. It appears that abstinence makes the church grow fondlers. Is it not time that your successors were released from the duty of celibacy?

Heeroom: This celibacy business is much overrated. Haven't you read Clochemerle? For a lot of priests the sap rises but slowly, many are homosexual and the heteroes usually manage to find a discrete outlet among understanding parishioners.

Tony: Just as well my dear departed mother doesn't have to hear that. You used to honour us with the occasional visit and my poor mother would get into a dreadful state with worry about her level of hospitality. Father appeared in his Sunday best and we children were sometimes allowed around the table to form a respectful audience. This was the philosophy hour, Rowan Williams style. I remember that you proved the existence of God with Anselm's knock-out ontological argument that if it is possible to think of a perfect being, that perfect being must exist. (I have just thought of a perfect idiot, but let's move on).

You also explained the role of Jesus and his immaculate conception, followed by an insight into transubstantiation. It is obviously difficult for me after all these years to recall your explanation of these momentous proceedings but I will try. I will skip the immaculate conception as this could become embarrassing but I'll have a stab at the process of transubstantiation: 'During transubstantiation, the simple molecules of the wafer instantaneously convert into the familiar double-helix of Jesus's DNA, and the wine transforms into hemoglobin, platelets and plasma. Vibrations from the odd words and gesticulations of the chanting priest act as the chemical catalyst for these reactions. Despite this well-known process, however, careful microscopic observation of the wafer and wine will reveal no traces of anything having taken place. This is due to what is known as the 'Heisenberg Theology Principle' which states that no religious truth, when actually examined by the scientific method, will reveal its properties to the observer'. You will notice that I may have twisted your words a little here but I am trying to hint at what you should have said.

While we're at it can you remind me how the church explains the conundrum of God being simultaneously all good, all knowing, all powerful alongside the existence of evil?

Heeroom: Well, it was so easy then. There were very few lateral thinkers and people accepted the first super-ficial explanation that came along. Few people had enjoyed a proper education and philosophical problems were left to the specialists and that was us, or so people thought. Because we were not under any pressure we did not give such difficulties much thought either. Why give yourself a headache on top of the discomfort that might follow from the many gins and tonic and cigars in prospect?

Tony: You haven't answered my question about almighty God and the existence of evil.

Heeroom: Why would I change the habit of a lifetime? You atheists had better get used to the idea that there are certain questions we theologians tend to skirt around.

Tony: Talking of skirts; what are your views on the current Pope?

Heeroom: In my time I had mostly to do with Pius XII the Nazi pope. Fortunately I have always managed to keep the fascistic side of the Catholic faith from your parents because they had a hearty dislike of Hitler. All Popes including the current one, clearly have a problem with women. As far as they are concerned the only thing women are good for is to function as church membership creators. Earlier on I didn't have much time for women either. You probably remember that you used to be my altar boy when at a side altar, after hours, women who had given birth crept in to be 'churched'. I remember looking down on them with great disdain. In my final years when I shared a bed with my housekeeper I looked down on her from a different perspective.

Tony: Yes, that really shook my father to the core. If you could have your time over, would you be a priest again?

Heeroom: No, definitely not. Many advantages we then had can now be enjoyed outside of the priesthood. Nor do I think that I would have died aged 62 from a drink and smoke related cancer.

Tony: According to the British cardinal Basil Hume one's whole life is a preparation for the hereafter. Where are you now?

Heeroom: Cardinal Hume will now know, as I do, that he has sacrificed the whole of his precious life to backing a chimera. Like putting all your money on a single horse only to see it stumble at the last. Not only have we wasted our own lives but the lives of countless of our dupes. I am nowhere. In other words I am where I was before I existed and I must say that it doesn't really surprise me. For which, even semi-rational human being, could seriously believe that it is possible to carry on, fully functional, in an unspecified place, minus body and brain, as if nothing had happened.

By the way, I have to disappoint you. This discussion only took place in your brain. My brain, along with the rest of my body and soul (couldn't resist that last bit) is lying here, keeping the grass greener on the other side.

In Heeroom's footsteps

*"Unhappiness in a child accumulates because he sees
no end to the dark tunnel. The thirteen weeks of
a term might just as well be thirteen years."*

Graeme Greene

What following in Heeroom's footsteps would entail first came home to me when my father called me in for a father to son talk and with a grave expression on his face told me that unlike my brothers and sisters I would not now be permitted to use the communal swimming pool in the nearby town as I might come into contact with girls. The long term effect of this has been that I still cannot swim and have always had a healthy appreciation of women.

Next thing I knew a place was booked for me at a Roman Catholic boarding school for boys which doubled as a seminary. I was twelve years old. In hindsight the three years I spent at the school seemed to have lasted forever. I never really settled, always was a fish out of water. Homesickness stands out as the greatest trauma. That and the tedium of frequent worship in the college chapel.

There seemed to be two distinct categories of pupils: those who were part of cosy 'boys own' coteries and those who were stand alone individualists, inappropriately inserted into an alien environment. The coterie types could not wait to get back after term breaks, the lone wolves would return in a state of utter gloom. I was in the latter category. Amongst the in-crowd there was a great deal of homosexuality, often taken advantage of by the teaching staff, who except for a handful of lay members, were all ordained Catholic priests. I was never personally involved. I probably wasn't cute enough. Some of my prettier friends would be invited after hours for 'exam prep' by a friendly tutor. Next day there would be a good deal of gossiping and sniggering. I must say in defence of the priests that the boys involved, usually aged 13 to 15, knew perfectly well what they were doing and were quite prepared to allow favours in exchange for higher marks.

I am aware that this is a highly controversial observation but that is what I witnessed and I am now largely sceptical of ruined lives claims by 15 year old boys with similar experiences. One wonders about the incentive of compensation. Not that I am too sorry about the fact that the RC church in many countries is having to fork out substantial sums. Their massive wealth ought to be spread around instead of being squandered on more churches and perks and palaces for the clergy.

Despite these distractions I did well enough academically, managing even to win a form prize or two. On the whole the school life, when the homesickness subsided, was quite bearable. I particularly enjoyed the well organised sports activities. It was the religious component that made it such a trial. There used to be days of retreat when you were not allowed to speak and had to wander about the place in a zombie like state, pretending to meditate upon matters spiritual. I have never needed much sleep and lights out at eight thirty for years one and two was quite an ordeal. The school manual gave clear instructions about one's conduct in bed. 'Adopt a decent posture, preferably lying on your side, with arms folded across your chest, being quiet and still, concentrating your thoughts on Jesus on the cross'. I know you won't believe what you just read. I know you think I have made this up for special effect. But I've still got the quote in print and I have given you an exact translation. That kind of thing the Catholic church has always done to children and probably still would do, if 'militant atheists' would let them. Because the whole atmosphere was so alien I should of course have rebelled at once and demanded to be removed but that is not how it works when you are aged thirteen. Children are pathetically trusting and willing to please and as a dutiful perfectionist I did my level best to justify the considerable fees my parents had to pay.

But three years later, at almost sixteen, which seems to be the age when teenagers start to think independently, the situation became untenable. I had never been a true believer but like all young children had gone with the flow, without thinking much about the reasons why. This now changed and very soon the questioning process became unstoppable. To my parents deep disappointment I insisted that I could not go on and this is how my brush with the priesthood came to an end.

I asked to carry on at teacher training college but this would have meant similar expense, which my parents, I suspect slightly out of pique, were unwilling to finance.

So instead I ended up at an engineering college. (In hindsight this was a very fortuitous move because the practical things I learned there have stood me in very good stead all my life, much more, I dare say, than any further academic studies I might have followed instead. I am now convinced that education generally is too biased towards scholastic pursuits and too little towards useful life skills).

This too was denominational but religion played a very minor role. We had one hour of RE a week taken by a Franciscan monk. The only thing I remember from that was his passionate liking of classical music. What it meant to him was not what it did for me. A perfect analogy to religion, I suppose. Ever since I have tried to emulate his enjoyment but it is still a work in progress.

At the age of eighteen I was subjected to one more attempt at keeping me on board. To keep the peace at home I agreed to join a course run by the village pastor in preparation for the holy state of matrimony. The irony in this will not escape the reader. A celibate priest dispensing advice on matrimonial matters is behaving like a neutered tomcat, making a lot of noise, but only in an advisory capacity. By now I had applied some serious thought to the theological arguments and found them hopelessly wanting. I was quite keen to cross swords in debate and whilst others on the course were prepared just to listen I would ask a lot of troublesome questions to which of course there are no good answers. Before too long the disruption became too great and I was quietly asked to leave.

NATIONAL SERVICE

My next hurdle, and being young seems to exist of taking lots of hurdles in succession, was National Service. Even then the long tentacles of religion kept attempting to pull me back because at that time there wasn't as yet the strong presence of Humanism in Holland that there is today. Nowadays as well as chaplains and padres there are humanist counsellors in the army, hospitals and prison service, but in my time it was still mostly geared towards religion. Admittedly there was also a 'none' category but you could not be exempt from religious exposure because the 'nones', which by this time included me, had to choose between the Catholic 'padre' and Protestant 'chaplain'. Mullahs, at that stage, were yet unheard of.

Fortunately by the early sixties the sharp edges of religious dominance had gone. RE became little more than a social break from army duties, in fact something to look forward to. We used to play football and God was left in an off-side position.

At the end of my two year stint I was keen to have a break from Holland and purge myself from the bad taste left by all the religious baggage. I wanted to improve my English and one sunny day in June 1963 I found myself on the ferry heading towards Harwich. The relief of being free of religious obligations was palpable and it took a long time for the elation to subside.

England-Holland-
Wiltshire-Canada-London-
Yorkshire-Shropshire

"To travel is to live"

Hans Christian Andersen

In those days of work permits I had a choice between work on a farm or becoming a bus conductor. Pounds, shillings and pence were far too much for my decimally indoctrinated brain so cow-herd I became. There were some seventy of them, none spoke English, so at night I attended evening classes. English for foreigners along with twenty five Au Pairs. Nothing to complain about there. Back on the farm, religion simmered in the background. The farmer was a vicar's son and very high church of England. So high in fact that when I was invited to their church service I thought I was back with the Catholics. At the dinner table they regaled me with religious argument. I had to sit and take it. My English just wasn't good enough. If only we could have another round today! I joined a youth club theatre group. My role was an Italian nobleman. The adjudicator said my attempt at an Italian accent was commendable. I was only trying to speak English. When I had finished at the farm I was offered lodgings with the drama teacher's family. They were Quakers. The religion was getting softer. When I went along to one of their meetings I met my future wife. She wasn't a Quaker either.

We were married at a registry office in The Hague. My parents didn't come. Religion is very unforgiving. We returned to England, lived in Wiltshire and West Yorkshire. When our family was complete we emigrated to Canada. Four years later our marriage broke up. Sadly these things happen. We settled back in England. I took up employment with the Dutch Chamber of Commerce in London.

All these years I had been non-religious but like so many fellow travellers I didn't think I could be alone. There must be others like me. People who had worked out for themselves that religion has wafted down from ignorant times and is merely an instrument for wishful thinking, a ready vehicle for manipulators to take advantage. One day passing a second hand bookstand I picked up a copy of '*Individual Morality*' by education-alist *Dr. James Hemming* who later wrote one of the earliest outright atheistic books '*Instead of God*'. That's how I finally discovered humanism and knew I had found my philosophical home. I joined both the National Secular Society and the British Humanist Association as a life member.

In my job as trade counsellor I would sometimes be asked to suggest business introductions for companies supplying religion related or homeopathic products. This would test my neutrality but I would always manage to stay professional. Less restrained was I on one occasion when I represented the Dutch Chamber at a luncheon hosted by the Manchester Chamber of Commerce in honour of the Belgian Ambassador. When grace was said out loud: *'for what we are about to receive may the Lord make us truly thankful'* I felt this was a liberty too far and I said "I wish to be exempted from that prayer". A stunned silence followed. The man on my right whispered, "well said". The one on my left never spoke to me again. I don't enjoy unsettling such a gathering any more than anybody else, but if we go along meekly condoning all the liberties taken by the relatively few practising Christians left, just because they once were the majority and have tradition on their side, then we might end up with a tiny tail wagging an ever larger dog. Well this dog barked and I have a feeling that next time Mr. Graceman might suggest a moment of silence instead of unilaterally embarking upon mission humble before God. To some this kind of protest may seem petty. But ready assumptions made by the religious that everyone else is like them should be countered at every turn. Otherwise these assumptions will only be re-enforced. When I retired I decided to step up my bit for humanism. I joined local humanist groups as newsletter editor, first in Leeds and later in Shropshire, where for seven years I was chairman of Welsh Marches Humanists.

I have called this chapter 'my path to humanism' but in truth the humanism had always been lurking in the background, I just couldn't put a name to it. Religion, though it tried its damnedest, never got under my skin. I knew I wasn't, never had been, religious but I didn't know what I was instead. What terminology would apply to me? Many people having torn themselves away from religious shackles, face a similar question. What is the right label? Are we unbelievers, apostates, infidels, atheists, agnostics, secularists, nullifidians? All these terms are merely a counter to religious belief and what I required was a designation that would define a life stance rather than narrow opposition. This is what I found in humanism and it is time that I explained what that is all about.

What is Humanism?

*"I use the word 'Humanist' to mean someone
who believes that man is just as much a natural
phenomenon as an animal or a plant; that his body,
mind or soul were not supernaturally created but are
products of evolution, and that he is not under
the control or guidance of any supernatural being,
but has to rely on himself and his own powers".*

SirJulian Huxley, First President of
the British Humanist Association

It is a remarkable fact that in 2014 the word humanism
should still be so little known. People who knew
that I was writing a book and asked what it was
going to be about were almost invariably none the
wiser when I told them that it was going to be an
explanation of humanism. Some confused it with
humorism, thinking that it might be a book of jokes.
In deference to this thought I have indeed tried to
keep the tone as light and mischievous as possible.
The irony is of course that since the latest polls now
tell us that the majority of the British population no
longer profess a religion this means that all these people
are unaware of their own philosophical status.

Many people coming across humanist literature readily recognise their own outlook on life. It is quite straightforward really: if you are non-religious, nor superstitious in other ways, look to science, reason and compassion in order to live an ethical and meaningful life, then you are a humanist. People's intelligence, common sense and acquired wisdom tell them that our golden rule: *'do as you would be done by'* or *'don't do as you wouldn't be done by'* (the latter version to avoid G.B. Shaw's objection that other people's tastes may not be the same as yours) has been a recipe for successful human interaction ever since mankind evolved.

The most succinct definition of humanism is expressed in just three words: *'Good without God'*. Another three word summary could be: *'Morality without Mythology'*. And to squeeze the last drop out of alliteration: *'Sanity without Superstition'*. A somewhat broader definition says humanism is a way of life based upon shared human values. Because humanists do not rely on the existence or help of a supernatural power, we accept that it is up to us to make sense of our lives through living responsibly and caring for other human beings, the animal world, our community and our environment, not just for us here today but for future generations. Humanism does away with false hopes, delusion and dependence on imagined deities. It attempts to solve mysteries, not revel in them. As freethinkers humanists are open to all questions about our existence. There are no guidelines, no precepts imposed from above. This freedom to explore is much more exhilarating than slavishly following the dubious notions of others, particularly if these others happen to be bronze age desert tribesmen.

The *IHEU* (International Humanist and Ethical Union) official definition reads:

"Humanism is a democratic and ethical life stance which affirms that human beings have the right and responsibility to give meaning and shape to their lives. It stands for the building of a more humane society through an ethics based on human and other natural values in a spirit of reason and free enquiry through human capabilities. It is not theistic and it does not accept supernatural views of reality."

Another brief way of putting it slightly more poetically is:

"A believer is a bird in a cage, a humanist is a bird in flight exploring the world with an open mind." And more sarcastically: Humanist: 'a benighted creature who has the folly to worship something he can actually see and feel.'

For good measure some dictionary definitions:

"Humanism is an active ethical and philosophical approach to life, focusing on human solutions to human issues through rational arguments, without recourse to gods, sacred texts or religious creeds." (*Wikipedia*)

"Humanism is an appeal to reason in contrast to revelation or religious authority as a means of finding out about the natural world and destiny of man, and also giving a grounding for morality. Humanist ethics is also distinguished by placing the end of moral action in the welfare of humanity rather than in fulfilling the will of God." (*Oxford Companion to Philosophy*)

I should point out that in the past and to some extent still today, the term humanism has been used in a bewildering range of contexts and meanings, the complexity of which is beyond the scope of my book. An extensive treatise on the etymology of the term can be found in *'Humanism what's in the word'*, written by Nicolas Walter and published by the Rationalist Press Association in 1997. The use of the term throughout my book is strictly in the modern sense as described in the above definitions. Scientist and author Isaac Asimov has left a good summary of what humanism meant to him: *"I certainly don't believe in the mythologies of our society, in heaven and hell, in God and angels, in Satan and demons. I've thought of myself as an 'atheist,' but that simply described what I didn't believe in, not what I did. Gradually, though, I became aware there was a movement called 'humanism,' which used that name because, to put it most simply, humanists believe that human beings produced the progressive advance of human society and also the ills that plague it. They believe that if the ills are to be alleviated, it is humanity that will have to do the job. They disbelieve in the influence of the supernatural on either the good or the bad of society. I am not responsible for what other people think. I am responsible only for what I myself think, and I know what that is. No idea I've ever come up with has ever struck me as a divine revelation. Nothing I have ever observed leads me to think there is a God watching over me".*

Because theists are in the habit of referring to non-believers not as humanists but as atheists I should make it clear that, like Asimov, humanists tend to be unhappy with the atheist label. It simply means 'without God'. That's all there is to it. It is not a world-view nor a life-stance. There is more to life than living in denial of someone else's imagined entity in the clouds. In that way the term 'atheism' dignifies theism and gives it undeserved status. There are no similar words for a denial of other imagined beings. There is no such concept as 'afairyism'. That is why 'humanist' fits the bill much better. Then atheism, or in some cases agnosticism, is just an aspect of someone's philosophical position and lifestyle. Humanism encompasses a person's whole outlook on life and concerns itself with many issues. That is why it could be called the executive arm of atheism. Humanists are individualists and there are no prescribed tenets for them to follow. Yet there is probably more common ground amongst humanists than amongst the faithful, whose holy books are short on clarity and big on contradiction and confusion, ripe for a plethora of schisms. Humanists by contrast need only bring to bear logic and common sense to their concerns and base their conclusions on the evidence produced. To the humanist the miracle is in the here and now. It is the miracle of the natural world, there is nothing supernatural about it.

Because humanists believe that this life is the only life we shall ever have, it is vital to make the best of it. For humanists the afterlife is what you leave behind in other people. Humanists are anxious to make the world a better place to live in, not only for the present population but for future generations too, particularly since the lives of their descendants represent the only sense of immortality that humanists recognise. Humanists can also be described as rationalists because they consider human reason as the best guide there is in facing life's questions. In their social concerns humanists are secularists because they want to free society from the stranglehold that religious beliefs still have on it. Humanists are freethinkers because they refuse to surrender their minds unthinkingly to any church or creed but remain free to think for themselves. Humanists rely on the scientific method not only to explain nature but in every aspect of life to safeguard against accepting anything unquestioningly. They pride themselves on their ability to distinguish between the metaphorical and the real. Humanists are materialists, lacking belief in souls and spirits and any 'ghosts in the machine'. They are empiricists in their approach to knowledge, evidence being the key feature always.

Humanists derive their morality from an understanding of our nature as social beings who like to co-operate with one another and show sympathy and compassion for our fellow creatures. They don't feel that life owes them anything because they themselves take responsibility for it. They consider that every responsible human being should be free to make his or her own choices and conduct their own life-style, as long as they don't unfairly restrict the freedom of others. Humanists are more than usually candid: 'this is what I think, this is the evidence I rely on, this is how I mean to apply it: show me where I am wrong'. They are ready to counsel and to be counselled, to accept themselves as one among many, each to count as one and no-one as more than one.

Because they are not afraid of pleasure they are not puritanical; they would rather make love than war. That's why humanists tend to get on well. Yes, there is endless discussion and debate but because there is no gospel truth and dogma written in stone, humanists are not likely to go to war or split up into factions.

'Open' is a key word for humanists. It is essential to have an open mind and an open society. By an open society is meant one in which individuals are confronted with personal decisions as opposed to a magical or tribal or collectivist society. The actions of individuals can be freely assessed and monitored and subjected to criticism in liberal and democratic debate. It would be impossible for humanists to force humanism on others or to persecute non-humanists, for if they did they would no longer qualify as humanists. Unlike theists humanists see no virtue in blind faith, unmerited obedience, meekness, unworldiness, chastity or pointless self-denial. The most valued humanist virtues are: a regard for what is true, personal responsibility, tolerance, sympathy, public spiritedness, concern for the environment, leading a good and useful life.

In terms of politics there is no obvious consensus amongst humanists. But with honourable exceptions it may be said that people who are irreligious and sceptical in outlook tend not to be conservative. Neither is there a great deal of affinity with politics on the far left. Although there may be sympathy for the various socialist systems, pragmatists amongst us have come to realise that socialism and particularly communism fit uncomfortably with human nature, which sad to say is as yet unready for the share and share alike mentality that collectivism demands. For all we know it may never be. That is regrettable for in theory at least, socialism is a much more humanitarian system than capitalism. Personally I have long since taken the easy way out and now describe myself as a 'golden rule libertarian', trying to keep out of politics as much as possible. It is when politicians start interfering with personal freedoms that don't impinge on anybody else's, that I am inclined to take up the cudgels. However the menace of political machinations in our semi-democratic society is as nothing compared to the damage done by power in religious hands. Give me Castro in preference to the Taliban every time.

The humanist agenda, although undefined in prescriptive terms, tends to encompass the following topics of interest: a lack of belief in a supreme being; the pursuit of science in order to understand how things work and how life can be improved; the importance of free speech and absence of censorship; the need for population control and sex education; equal rights for women and other groups who tend to get a raw deal from religion; the right of women to control their own fertility; opposition to all forms of superstition and the paranormal, particularly all oppressive aspects of religion; a right to assisted dying in case of unbearable suffering; provision of ceremonies to mark significant events in life; opposition to faith schools funded by the state; animal welfare; personal freedom, as long as it doesn't impinge on the rights of others; scepticism about prayer and miracles; the importance of evolution and genetics, in short all matters that focus on the betterment of life on earth for all its creatures without a sense of sin or fear of punishment in a supposed hereafter.

All these issues will receive further attention in the course of the book but first I will give a potted history of the origins of humanism.

HUMANISM, A POTTED HISTORY

Because of the world-wide dominance of religion these last 2000 years, unbelief has had to exist unobtrusively in the shadows. But the philosophical ideas underlying humanism go back much further than that. In Greece, around 500 BCE, there were Protagoras ('man is the measure of all things'), Democritus and Socrates all sceptical about the existence of the gods. Later came Epicurus, a materialist philosopher, who found everything explicable without supernatural causes and taught that the purpose of life is pleasure. In the next few centuries an Epicurean inspired epitaph appeared on the graves of many of his followers throughout Italy, Gaul and Roman Africa: '*I was not, I have been, I am not, I do not mind*'. The sort of stoic pragmatism humanists appreciate. Later still came the great Roman poet, Lucretius (99-55 BCE) who popularised the Epicurean philosophy in its full application to human life and nature in his famous Latin poem *De Rerum Natura* (Of the nature of things).

During the six hundred years following the break-up of the Roman empire there was so little education in Christian Europe that this period is known as the dark ages. For centuries Christianity, armed with the omnipotence of the Church and State and opposed by no competition, was able to control the mind of Europe. It had no competitors, because outside the Church there were few thinkers nor educated persons. The revival of learning was very slow but gradually started to blossom into what is now referred to as the 'renaissance' or rebirth. This can be seen as the long drawn out transitional period between the rigid, oppressive authoritarianism of the religion plagued middle ages and the enlightened freedom enjoyed in some parts of the world today. The renaissance 'humanists', particularly Erasmus and Thomas More were not humanists in today's meaning, because they were still Deistic. The great artists of the period, da Vinci and Michelangelo, still mostly used religious subjects for their artwork because no other sponsors were available.

It is often argued that we have to thank Christianity for the progress made in art and science in bringing Europe out of the 'dark ages'. Examples given are the magnificent medieval cathedrals, abbeys and religion inspired music, art and sculpture. True enough, these specimen of medieval architecture and visual art are beautiful, awe inspiring and still mightily appreciated in our time. The observation to make here of course is that we will never know what might have been achieved if religion had been absent. Rather than concentrating exclusively on works for the greater glory of God there might well have been great strides made for the more practical benefit of mankind. Magnificent libraries, schools, laboratories, theatres and sports facilities spring to mind as better examples of more usefully directed enterprise.

With more emphasis on science, advancement would have been more rapid and by now we might have been streets ahead in all areas of human achievement. Particularly since the religious hierarchy has had the nasty habit of incarcerating scientists and in some cases burning them at the stake. So instead of giving credit to religion for having been a force for progress, its narrow focus will have had a stultifying effect. Now that religious influence in the West is fading, research, science and technology in all fields are speedily making up lost ground.

The next period was the 'Enlightenment'. The philosophers of this modern science, beginning with John Locke (1632-1704) were called 'Empiricists' from the Greek word 'experience'. This held that all knowledge of reality comes from observational experience. Empiricism was a very important step towards modern humanism, although most of the 17th century empiricists were still Christian, or pretended to be so. Those of them who denied Christian beliefs, such as Irish born John Toland, were persecuted and their books were burnt. The best known philosopher of this period was the great Scottish empiricist, David Hume (1711-1776) whose rational analysis of religious dogma left theologians floundering. One of his best known observations is that extraordinary claims (i.e. miracle claims) require extraordinary evidence.

A contemporary philosophical movement known by the French name 'philosophes' was started in Paris with amongst others the great writer Voltaire, the famous encyclopedist Diderot and the philosopher Baron d'Holbach. These eighteenth century sceptics did not go so far as to call themselves atheists, although many of them were. It was still too dangerous to do so. Nor had science, before Darwin's time, made enough progress to readily rule out God. Most of them called themselves 'Deists' meaning believers in an undefined supreme being. Other names they used were naturalists, rationalists and freethinkers.

In the emerging United States of America the inventor and statesman Benjamin Franklin was one of the several pioneers of thought and political action who were also deists. Others included George Washington, Thomas Jefferson and later Abraham Lincoln. In fact the fist six presidents of the USA rejected the Christian creed which makes it highly ironic that today no one has a chance of being elected president of that country unless s/he claims to be a Christian. But fortunately the 'founding fathers' did ensure that in America there is separation of church and state. The most outstanding of the English deists was Thomas Paine (1737-1809) a self-educated man who wrote three very important tracts: '*Common Sense*', which helped bring about the American War of Independence; '*Rights of Man*', a defence of the French revolution and '*The Age of Reason*', a devastating polemic against the Bible. He helped establish both the French and American constitutions but his native country Britain is still waiting.

Moving now to the 19th Century we encounter the philosophy of 'utilitarianism' first put forward by Jeremy Bentham and James Mill, later developed by Mill's son John Stuart Mill, Herbert Spencer and Leslie Stephen, the father of Virginia Woolf. The utilitarians said that moral law is based on utility i.e. on the practical consequences of particular actions. These consequences must be judged in terms of human happiness. This was really a throwback to the Epicurian ideal but the return had to be made in modern philosophy before humanism could be accepted as a moral system of thought. Several new words for labelling people in the humanist tradition now came into use. In 1840 freethinker George Holyoake coined the words 'secularism' and 'secularist' based on the French for 'worldly'. These terms are still in common use today. Secularists say that religion ought not to interfere with the law, education and other ordinary worldly matters. In 1859 Holyoake used the word humanism in today's meaning for the first time.

As for the difference between the labels atheist and agnostic, I will discuss these separately later in the book. In the first half of the twentieth century there were many outstanding humanists in science and public life but perhaps the foremost of all was an English Earl, who was a mathematician, a philosopher, a social reformer and a political activist. This was Bertrand Russell (1872-1970). He was a prolific writer on mathematics, philosophy, ethics and international affairs, completing some 70 books, many articles and writing tens of thousands of letters. In 1950 he was awarded the Nobel prize for literature. He co-operated with Albert Einstein in combating the threat of nuclear war.

The British humanist movement first known as the Ethical Union, was gradually built up after the second world war, largely through the work of its Secretary Harold Blackham, who later became the first Secretary of the International Humanist and Ethical Union which was founded in 1952. Ten years later he became the first Executive Director of the British Humanist Association (BHA), whose first President was T.H. Huxley's grandson Sir Julian Huxley. The humanist movement in Britain was given a big boost in 1955 as a result of the hysterically hostile reaction of some sections of the public and press when the BBC allowed the humanist viewpoint to be put very moderately by an Aberdeen lecturer in educational psychology, Margaret Knight, in a series of three radio broadcasts for parents. The extent and fury of the outcry seem almost unbelievable today. Yet it seems to have had a lasting effect on the BBC for even now no humanist opinion is allowed on the 'Today' slot 'Thought for the Day'.

In our own time unbelief has become much more widespread and open discussion goes on in the press and the internet, fuelled by best-seller books by leading atheist authors Richard Dawkins, Christopher Hitchens, A.C. Grayling and by Sam Harris and Daniel Dennett in America. As a result the BHA is thriving, increasing its membership and influence. There are some 40 affiliated local humanist groups spread throughout the country, organising monthly gatherings at speakers' events and providing humanist ceremonies to mark major life occasions.

Because humanism has an independent outlook most humanists see no particular reason to join a humanist organisation. It is sometimes said that organising humanists is akin to herding cats. This has the unfortunate consequence that the membership of the various humanist organisations is only a fraction of the total numerical strength of humanism in the population at large. This low head count is then held against it when it comes to giving the movement recognition. Generally it matters more for organisations to be able to point at membership numbers rather than to the number of people who agree with their aims.

A side effect of this is the accusation often levied at humanists that they do a lot of talking but not a lot of doing. This overlooks the fact that humanists (not necessarily members of a humanist organisation) are disproportionately involved with charities such as Unicef, Voluntary Service Overseas, Médecins sans frontières and Oxfam. Small local humanists groups regularly donate sizeable chunks of their funds to charity. A survey of BHA members in Humanity 2000 recorded that humanists give money and/or time generously and regularly to an average of 6 charities each. Humanists tend to plan their giving rationally and selectively, but most also respond generously to emergency appeals and street collections. The most popular causes were those connected with social welfare (27per cent) and international development/aid (21per cent). Only 2 out of 676 responses did not support charitable giving. For comparison: according to a Mori survey for Nestlé Family Monitor in 2000, just under ½ the British public undertook voluntary work that year, and 92 per cent had given money to at least one charity. 1 in 5 gave regularly, and 1 in 5 was a member of a charity, though the most popular forms of giving were to street collections (55 per cent) and to door-to-door collections (50 per cent). Only 36 per cent of the general public contributed to 5 or more charities. Children's charities and medical research charities were the most popular.

Some humanists also contribute to society through their work as celebrants, helping the non-religious to mark important occasions in their lives through humanist ceremonies for baby namings, weddings, affirmations and funerals. Others perform other voluntary humanitarian work, such as in hospital visitor or chaplain roles. In recent years there have been humanist peace groups, most recently the Humanist Peace Forum, and there is now a web-based group 'Humanists for a better World', formed to encourage and enable humanists to take action to help create a more peaceful and sustainable world.

Apart from the BHA there are two national humanist organisations, the National Secular Society, founded in 1866 and the Rationalist Association (1899). There is also a London based humanist society (Conway Hall Ethical society), who own the Conway Hall Humanist Centre at Red Lion Square.

The National Secular Society has a very interesting history. In 1877 its founder Charles Bradlaugh, who was a parliamentarian, writer, editor and famous public orator, was sentenced to six months imprisonment plus a large fine, along with his collaborator Annie Besant, for the offence of publishing a family planning pamphlet. He was involved in many other court cases, several of which established important principles of civil liberty. In 1880 he was elected as MP for Northampton but his request to substitute a secular affirmation for the religious oath taken by MPs on entering Parliament, was refused. When he then agreed to take the oath this was disallowed because he was a known atheist! He was arrested by the Serjeant-at-Arms and imprisoned in the cell under Big Ben in the clock tower. His seat was declared vacant but each time a by-election was held in Northampton Bradlaugh was re-elected and he was finally allowed to re-enter parliament in 1886. Two years later, he secured the passage of a new Oaths Act which enshrined into law the right of affirmation for members of both Houses, as well as extending and clarifying the law as it related to witnesses in civil and criminal trials. Sadly he died before he had the opportunity to use the new option himself.

Humanist publications are the quarterly magazine 'New Humanist', the BHA News, the Ethical Record and the Freethinker which is associated with the NSS which also has its own Bulletin.

Internationally most countries have their own humanist organisations, all applying general humanist principles to their own situation. Many of them are federated through the International Humanist and Ethical Union which was founded in Amsterdam in 1952 and is now head-quartered in London. IHEU is an international non-governmental organisation with representation on various United Nations committees and other international bodies. It seeks to influence international policy through representation and information, to build the humanist network and let the world know about the worldview of humanism. Its vision is a humanist world; a world in which human rights are respected and everyone is able to live a life of dignity.

HUMANIST CEREMONIES

Humanists are divided about the need for specifically humanist ceremonies to mark births, weddings and funerals. Because religions have always surrounded these events with ritual, humanists have been somewhat reluctant to follow suit. But for many of us with no religious belief it's important that we too can mark these occasions with honesty, warmth and affection, using words and music that are appropriate to the lives of the people involved.

Church conducted weddings are in steep decline, dropping from 70 per cent in 1963 to 30 per cent in 2012. Any couple in the UK can choose to have a humanist ceremony, but outside Scotland marriage must also involve a legally recognised registry office confirmation. Since humanist weddings have acquired legal status in Scotland, in 2005, the demand for humanist wedding celebrations has increased rapidly, overtaking the Catholics. In 2011 they numbered 2486, compared to 1729 for Catholics.

It allows a couple to express their love and commitment by telling their story in front of their relatives and friends in their own words rather than those of a church or state. People are attracted to the idea that marriage vows can be exchanged in a setting of their own choice be it a beach, a castle, a grand hotel or even one's own back garden. But the biggest demand for humanist ceremonies centres around the funeral. Most humanists choose cremation and the British Humanist Association has a network of celebrants who have been trained to lead a funeral, taking the place of a minister of religion. A humanist funeral differs from a religious one in that the attention is on the life that has just ended rather than a forward look to a purported future life. Commemorating the life of the deceased often involves favourite music, poetry readings and tributes from friends and relatives. I recently attended the humanist funeral of my brother-in-law over in Holland and it was a most moving and poignant occasion. Very different from the all too many church funerals I have attended in Britain where even the non-religious are in danger of going out on a wave of hymns and praise the Lord. The one advantage that such services have for me is that the cold impersonal approach and all the God talk tend to make it easier to control the emotions. Gritted teeth are an anti-dote to tears. Perhaps one day some smart cleric will claim that is exactly what it is for.

My first experience of a Christian funeral was at the age of ten at the death of my grandfather. The service was conducted by his son, my uncle 'Heeroom'. All the words spoken around the coffin were in Latin, accompanied by much wafting of incense and sprinkling of holy water. Not a single mention of anything personal, no celebration of his long life. The choir just singing a requiem. Even at that very young age I thought it strange and callous.

The worst such funeral I ever experienced as an adult was in Canada where I was friendly with a family of Mennonites. They were delightful people, the absolutely acceptable face of religion, but when it came to the funeral of the father of the household, not a single word of personal tribute to this saintly man was allowed to be spoken. Like for my grandfather the Good Lord was fully centre stage. It was not my place but I was sorely tempted to walk to the front, push the incantating minister aside and say a few words of appreciation about my friend, this kindly person, now reduced to a non-entity before the Lord.

Gradually in Britain the churches are cottoning on. In fear of losing business they are beginning to copy the popular humanist approach.

Here's a challenge to the religious: compare the two poems below to any of your favourite hymns and admit that unless you have a heart of stone, only Frye and MacColl will move you to tears. This poem by Mary E.

Frye is an example of the type of poetry favoured by Humanists:

Do not stand at my grave and weep;
I am not there. I do not sleep.
I am a thousand winds that blow.
I am the diamond glints on snow.
I am the sunlight on ripened grain.
I am the gentle autumn rain.
When you awaken in the morning's hush
I am the swift uplifting rush
Of quiet birds in circled flight.
I am the soft stars that shine at night.
Do not stand at my grave and cry;
I am not there. I did not die.

And this one by Ewan MacColl:

Take me to some high place of heather, rock and ling
Scatter my dust and ashes, feed me to the wind
So that I will be part of all you see, the air you are breathing
I'll be part of the curlew's cry and the soaring hawk
The blue milkwort and the sundew hung with diamonds
I'll be riding the gentle wind that blows through your hair
Reminding you how we shared
In the joy of living

CREMATION AND BURIAL – EPITAPHS

Humanists usually ask to be cremated but there is also a growing demand for 'green' burial. The essence of a green funeral is age-old elemental simplicity. It rejects the so-called traditional funeral with its stuffy, Victorian, urban look, in favour of a homespun, back-to-nature look. It prefers an unspoilt landscape to that of a regimented conventional cemetery. Coffins or shrouds are locally made from natural sustainable materials. Usually no markings are allowed but some sites permit a small simply-worded stone marker laid flat. It is not the grave that commemorates the life lived, it is the entire site. My partner wants her ashes sprinkled on her beloved vegetable plot at home. So I will join her there. Or she will join me.

Burial sites are very moving; I mention war cemeteries elsewhere. When coming across graveyards on our walks we always have a look around. Its sobering experience puts life into perspective. What is the point of making so much noise in our three score years and ten when the last word falls to eternal silence. All the human emotions are represented there: love, grief, piety, wisdom, humour and sadly, even hatred. The epitaphs tell their tales. I pass up on the cliched ones. 'Here lies ….beloved father, grandfather, husband….may the Lord have mercy….at peace in the arms of Jesus'. These are as instructive and dull as the messages on Christmas cards. It is the originals that strike a chord. I find it difficult to reconcile humour with a churchyard setting but the less solemn will have no difficulty with such gems as Spike Milligan's "I told you I was ill". My partner will certainly like this horticultural tribute found in Searsport, Maine:

'Under the sod and under the trees,
Here lies the body of Solomon Pease.
The Pease are not here, there's only the Pod;
The Pease shelled out and went to God.'

Death as the great leveller is reflected in this inscription:
'Here I lie, at the chancel door,
Here I lie, because I am poor
The farther in, the more you pay
Here I lie as cold as they.'

The cruelty of enforced bondage in 'till death do us part' religious marriages finds vindictive expression as in this example:

'Underneath this tuft do lie
back to back my wife and I.
Generous stranger, spare a tear,
For could she speak, I cannot hear.
Happier far than when in life,
Free from noise and free from strife.
When the last trump the air does fill,
If she gets up then I'll lie still.'

And how is this for an example of Christian charity:
'Here lies my poor wife
without bed or blanket,
but dead as a doornail
the Lord be thanked!'

The biscuit for gross callousness must go to this, found in Burlington, Iowa:
'Beneath this stone our baby lays
He neither cries nor hollers.
He lived just one and twenty days
And cost us forty dollars'.

A very salutary thought comes from Broughton, Northants:
'Time was I stood where thou dost now,
and viewed the dead as thou dost me;
Ere long thou 'lt be as low as I
And others stand and look on thee'

The prize for succinctness, which would appeal to humanists, goes to:
'Once I wasn't
Then I was
Now I ain't again'

I somehow find this sideswipe at the need for rhyme quite amusing:
'Here beneath these churchyard stones
lie the bones of Mary Jones
Her name was Smith, it was not Jones
But Jones was put to rhyme with stones'

And finally what would I choose if I were to be buried?

'Here lies Tony Akkermans and he is miffed that he can't tell you that he was right about no heaven'

OLD HAT RELIGION

Today's religion will be the future's mythology

When it comes to religion there is nothing new under the sun. Contemporary believers tend to think that their Christian and Islamic faiths were original inventions but if you dig further back into the history of human superstition it turns out that it has all been done before many times over. If religions were businesses they would be sued for copyright and plagiarism. There is a great deal of similarity for example between Christianity, Islam and Judaism: all worship the same god; all believe in angels; all believe in prophets and divine revelations; all believe in the resurrection of the dead, a day of judgement and in heaven and hell; all regard Jerusalem as a holy city; all pray on a daily basis; all have fasting as a part of their doctrine; all have mandatory rules about what they can or cannot eat; all allot subsidiary roles to women in the conduct of their religion. These similarities are not surprising since they are all derived from the same primitive, mythological beginnings, all copied from Egyptian, Greek and Persian folklore. I won't bore you with the details here, but it is widely recorded that there many gods, sons of gods, immaculate conceptions, virgin births, resurrections from the dead, walks on water and other miraculous events, long before Jesus and Mohammed appeared on the scene. The great monuments to Isis and Osiris still stand but no person believes in them anymore though it was a faith that lasted a thousand years longer than the religion of Christ so far.

There is an amusing cartoon depicting a bunch of crucifix waving dog collars laughing heartily at a red Indian native on his knees before a totem pole. They personify all the short-sighted people in the world who fail to see that what they believe in as sacred, is totem pole material to others. Instead of making war they should congratulate each other on having found common ground in childish moonshine. It is a great pity that the fables contained in scripture have been used as the moral basis for both the Christian and Islamic religions when there was a much better source available at the time in the form of Aesop's fables. Aesop is believed to have been a slave and story-teller and to have lived in ancient Greece between 620 and 560 BCE. Attributed to him are the well known stories: The Goose that laid the Golden Egg, the Tortoise and the Hare, the Boy who cried Wolf and many more. The morals of these tales are much more inspiring and relevant to modern times than the crude and contradictory fare obtained from holy books. While many gods have come and gone we, in the West at least, are still saddled with a particular resilient specimen who, I am sad to say, will have to be given top billing in this book.

OMNIGOD - BLURRY GOD

"I can't feel anything but sure that when men form ideas about God, creation, eternity, they are making no more sense in relation to what lies beyond the range of comprehension than the cheeping of sparrows"

Author Diana Athill

Once upon a time there was, in the Western world at least, but a single god. Closely defined with clear-cut attributes. Omnipotent, omniscient, omnipresent, omnibenevolent. In fact so many omnies that from here on in I shall refer to him as Omnigod. I am talking, of course, about the god of the Bible and the Koran, the creator of heaven and earth. A hands on god who controls every happening here on earth, who is compulsorily worshipped in school assembles, who is at the heart of church services, who hears prayers and who, if they cross themselves in good time, makes footballers score goals.

For some two thousand years this father figure god has had a very good run for his money. He has been feared and worshipped unfailingly and his every capricious move has been meekly documented and accepted. But things are changing. All is not well with Omnigod. Wicked, troublesome rationalists have started ganging up on him. They have been pointing out major weaknesses in his lifestyle, such as the total lack of evidence for his existence. This is greatly worrying his self-appointed representatives on earth. All the great minds in the churches have got together in a telephone box and have racked their brains over a proper line of defence. After Herculean metaphysical labours, laced with much prayer, they have come up with the solution: Omnigod must be given a makeover.

A collection of brand new words and phrases have been brought to bear. Out goes the Omni and in comes the obfuscation. God is now the 'Ground of all Being' he is the 'Ultimate Reality'. He is unfathomable, ineffable and unknowable. He is woollier than a champion sheep. Let Dawkins try and shear him now. The trouble is that if rationalists can't get to grips with such an elusive customer, then his befuddled apologists can't either. As Freddy Ayre has said in '*Language Truth and Logic*' if things are unknowable there is no point in entering into further discussion. After all unknowability and nothingness have much in common. So 'Blurry God' as I shall dub this ineffable creature won't let the religious off the hook. Nice try Don Cupitt, Paul Tillich and the rest, but it must be Omnigod or nothing.

SIZE OF THE UNIVERSE

But boy, oh boy is Omnigod on thin ice these days! When he was the idol of the desert tribes his fiefdom was restricted to the sun, the moon and pancake earth. The size of real estate a god worth his salt could manage. But, it turns out, the acreage has grown. Let me give you two remarkable statistics: there are more stars in the universe than there are grains of sand on all the beaches of the earth. And more staggering still: light from the exploding star GRB 090423 has taken 13 billion years travelling at the speed of light to reach us. (To give you an idea of the magnitude of 13 billion you would not reach that number if you counted uninterruptedly for more than 400 years). Bearing in mind that a single light-year represents a distance of 6000 billion miles this would tend to hint at the insignificance of our otherwise so self-important little planet earth.

Within this mind-numbingly huge universe there must be many other civilisations that would demand God's undivided attention. Think of the trillions of prayers that must be answered or arbitrarily ignored; and if you are a football fan think of the all the wonderful goals scored with God's help on all the pitches in the galaxies. The theologians have the answer (if they don't they always make one up): God is Omnipotent and moves in mysterious ways. But so does Santa Claus in his annual toy deliveries. For centuries men of God have been explaining the unknowable in terms of the not worth knowing. There is a choice here: resort to increasingly contorted explanations or simply conclude that God is imaginary.

RED IN TOOTH AND CLAW

All creatures great and small the Lord Omnigod hates them all. Witness the unmitigated suffering in creation. If on a large screen in a stadium people could witness even a fraction of the appalling suffering that at any moment is going on in the world: the murder, rape, torture, illness in the human world and the unrelenting cruelty bestowed on animals, within minutes all of us would breakdown in total distress or have to flee the building. You don't have to travel far to witness what is going on, particularly in the tragic animal world. The rabbits in our garden don't have a minute's peace, they are constantly vigilant and frightened. Couldn't they have been given an easier life without being the target of everybody's lunch? The ducks on our pond start out with families of twelve, only to see them reduced to two or three by a variety of predators. Pigeon feathers are piled up on the lawn. Their owners hacked to death by sparrowhawks.

From time to time all of us are confronted with direct examples of nature's cruelty. I was in the kitchen, washing up, when my attention was drawn to an unfolding drama right in front of me. A tiny spider had spun a web suspended from the wall light. A fly had flown into the web and got ensnared. The spider approached but the fly being twice its size was struggling mightily and at first managed to keep it at bay. But gradually and relentlessly the spider got closer and started to spin the hapless fly into a cocoon. The victim struggled pitifully but at last it became immobilised and the spider fastened onto it and started to suck it dry. Before long it had grown to more than twice its original size. This whole sadistic process took almost an hour of unabated cruelty. It brought it home to me once more that similar dramas must be taking place simultaneously in hundreds of thousands of other places in nature, unobserved and unpitied. The thought of that often causes me sleepless discomfort at night. If I had a switch at my disposal that would painlessly eliminate all predators, including human ones, from mother earth, I would flick it in an instant.

I have given these graphic examples of nature red in tooth and claw, not to be ghoulish, but because I have always thought that nature's viciousness is a major reason for doubting the existence of an all powerful, caring God, comfortable with his handiwork. Man's inhumanity to man is explained away by believers as free will but spiders, brutal carnivores, viruses and all the rest of the horrors that inhabit this earth, instinctively follow the way they have been programmed (by God they say) and if their god is unmoved by the mayhem this causes, then so much for his compassion.

We are further reminded of this gruesome state of affairs whenever we are shown nature documentaries where zebras are torn apart alive by packs of hyenas and wildebeests are ambushed by crocodiles at river crossings. Is this the best that the supposed omnipotent designer could manage? The religious don't seem to worry much about animal suffering. In fact they happily add to it with their ritual slaughter and gory sacrifices. But it is unimaginable that a caring god should have created an animal kingdom that functions entirely on the principle that one half survives, solely by killing and eating the other half. The only proper explanation for this ghastly state of affairs is that the natural world is the result of dispassionate evolution and that Omnigod is imaginary.

PROBLEM OF EVIL – FREE WILL

Omnigod's biggest bugbear of course is the problem of evil. For human induced catastrophes such as murder, mayhem and war, Omnigod's apologists think they have found a clever get out clause: free will, it's the people's fault, God is off the hook. This expedient may be sufficient to mollify the unthinking flock but cuts no ice with rationalists, who are in the habit of thinking things through. The free will idea goes as follows: God is in charge of the boardroom decisions while we, the minions on the shop floor, may decide the petty detail. If we get it wrong we must carry the can because God is too busy with the bigger picture. But this convenient division of responsibility must have its limits. There must be a point where certain misdemeanours by the workers are of such a magnitude that they endanger the corporation's survival and can no longer be ignored by the MD. Free will and Omnigod's overall control are mutually exclusive. If Omnigod allows the Germans the free will to vote for Hitler and He also allows Hitler the free will to murder six million Jews, then Hitler is running the show and Omnigod is a cowardly bystander pretending not to notice. Would it not have been the decent thing to zap Adolf with a heart attack? That is what my sister suffered recently and she has done no harm.

To crank this up a little further I have devised the ultimate freewill test. Suppose a deluded Ayatollah, wishing to meet his 72 virgins in paradise or an Armageddon-crazed redneck fundamentalist, hoping to be raptured soon, managed to get hold of an arsenal of nuclear weapons and employed his acolytes to plant devices in all population centres of the world and that all the bombs were connected by mobile phone signals to his hideout, where he is sitting with his finger poised over the button. Ready to blow God's beautiful creation to smithereens. (a fanciful scenario I admit, but you get my drift). The ultimate moment of truth. Would God strike him dead or would he have to shrug his shoulders and say: "well, I have granted this person free will – do your worst; no exceptions to my scheme, nothing I can do about it"? At that point theologians must stop waffling and make up their mind. Either they must say that God would act to stop the destruction or they must allow that a mere human being has become more powerful than God. If, as I suspect, they would argue that God would act, they would have to face the follow-up question: if he can act now, why not in Auschwitz, why not in Dunblane? Why not in thousands of other dreadful scenes of human suffering? And if God cannot or will not act, where is the justification for all the centuries of worship and prayer?

Worse still for Omnigod is his inability or unwillingness to stop earthquakes and tsunamis, regularly killing hundreds of thousands of innocent people. Now the lame free will excuse is more pointless still. To square this one the apologists are working overtime. Soon the explanations will be found. Brilliant theories are unveiled. The Lord is testing people. He is testing them to death. He is calling them to him for their own good, kicking and screaming all the way. Meanwhile in the case of the New Orleans flood it was the fault of homosexuals. Evangelist John Hagee linked hurricane Katrina to a gay pride event known as 'Southern Decadence Day'. Louis Farrakhan's explanation was 'God's way of punishing America for its warmongering and racism'. Faced with this same question, Archbishop of York John Sentamu said he had "nothing to say to make sense of this horror", while another clergyman,

Canon Giles Fraser, preferred to respond "not with clever argument but with prayer". Less reticent was the American evangelist Pat Robertson. He suggested Haiti has been cursed ever since the population swore a pact with the Devil to gain their freedom from the French at the beginning of the 19th Century. This seems the daftest theory yet, because even if it were true the question must be asked why would a loving deity allow such a pact to seem necessary? Why wouldn't he have freed the Haitians from slavery himself, or prevented them from being enslaved in the first place? And why, in particular, would he punish today's Haitians for something their forbears supposedly did more than two centuries before?

The second century saint, Irenaeus, and the 20th Century philosopher, John Hick, appeal instead to what is sometimes called soul-making. God created a universe in which disasters occur, they think, because goodness only develops in response to people's suffering. To appreciate this idea they say: try to imagine a world containing people, but literally no suffering. Call it the Magical World. In that world, there are no earthquakes or tsunamis, or none that cause suffering. If people are hit by falling masonry, it somehow bounces off them harmlessly. If I steal your money, God replaces it. If I try to hurt you, I fail. So why didn't God create the Magical World instead of ours? Because, the soul-making view says, its denizens wouldn't be - couldn't be - truly good people. It's not that they would all be bad. It's that they couldn't be properly good. For goodness develops only where it's needed, the idea goes, and it's not needed in the Magical World. In that world, after all, there is no danger that requires people to be brave, so there would be no bravery. That world contains no one who needs comfort or kindness or sympathy, so none would be given. It's a world without moral goodness, which is why God created ours instead.

But here again there are questions to ask. Even in a world where nothing bad happens, couldn't there be brave people - albeit without the opportunity to show it? So moral goodness could exist even if it were never actually needed. And, anyway, suppose we agree moral goodness could indeed develop only in a world of suffering. Doesn't our world contain a surplus of suffering already? People do truly awful things to each other. Isn't the suffering they create enough for soul-making? Did God really need to throw in earthquakes and tsunamis as well? Suffering's distribution, not just its amount, can also cause problems. A central point of philosopher Immanuel Kant's was that we mustn't exploit people - we mustn't use them as mere means to our ends. But it would appear that on the soul-making view God does precisely this. He inflicts horrible deaths on innocent earthquake victims so that the rest of us can have the moral benefit.

I have dipped briefly here into the theologians' murky world of moral philosophy. I don't know about you but it has left me none the wiser. I would rather listen to a taxi driver. To me there is no escaping the conclusion: either Omnigod is criminally incompetent or much more likely, he is imaginary. Humanists who are pragmatic bods remain untouched by the problem of evil. For them pointless human and animal suffering doesn't make God evil, it just makes it crystal clear that such an entity does not exist and that at bottom there is no design, no purpose, no evil and no good, nothing but blind pitiless indifference.

FIRST CAUSE

*"Or how do you Mystics, who maintain the
absolute incomprehensibility of the Deity, differ
from sceptics or atheists who assert that the first
cause of all is unknown and unintelligible?"*

David Hume, Dialogues Concerning Natural Religion

The most obvious justification for a belief in a god for
most people is the need for an explanation of matter.
The earth is here, we are here, where does it all come
from? Everything must have a cause; the cause of all
existence is God. This cropped up on a walk in the
woods with my ten year old son. He said "Dad, they
told us at school in RE that everything must have a
cause and therefore there must be a God. But I think
that if everything has a cause then god too must have a
cause. How did he come about". Impressive for a ten
year old and yes, the boy done well; he ended up
with a doctorate in Chemistry from Oxford. But for an
adult this should not be rocket science. The causal
argument is not merely invalid but self-contradictory:
the conclusion, which says that something (God) does
not have a cause, contradicts the premise, which says
that everything must have a cause. If that premise
is true, the conclusion cannot be true; and if the
conclusion is true, the premise is not. Many people do
not at once see this, because they use the argument to
get to God and then having arrived where they want to
go, forget all about the argument. If the conclusion
contradicts its own premise, we have the clearest
indictment of an argument that we could possibly have:
that it is self-cancelling. So if everything must have a

cause then God can't be an exception and we are no further ahead. It just moves the problem up one notch. It becomes a case of infinite regression; who created whoever created God? So somewhere along the line something had to be just there.

The idea is similar to the ancient Hindu belief that the world rested on an elephant and the elephant on a giant tortoise. There was no answer to the troublesome question as to what supported the tortoise. Much more honest and sensible to admit that we simply do not know and might never know. So why not just skip the idea of God and concentrate on planet earth. Believers rush in where sceptics fear to tread. That is the difference between humanists and theists. We are willing to admit we haven't got all the answers. Science is a work in progress. To posit a creator god is no solution, we must not worship a hypothesis. God remains imaginary.

ARROGANCE

There is an interesting irony involved in the God debate. Believers tend to accuse sceptics of arrogance. How dare mere people with their limited intelligence question the miracle of creation. They ought to show some humility and bow before the might of the Supreme Being. But arrogance is exactly the term that sums up the religious proposition. What religion is saying is simply this: here we are faced with a mighty mystery that we cannot comprehend. As this is rather disconcerting we will invent an answer that we shall call God and then the mystery is sorted. It is like saying the answer to a problem is X and then working backwards to arrive at the problem. As Ludwig Feuerbach was the first to put it: Man has created God in his own image.

He viewed Christianity as an example of extreme objectification of a particularly destructive sort, in that it was the best human attributes that were projected onto the objectified God, whereas the most undesirable human attributes remained with the human being in the form of original sin. God became the source of love and God's will became the issue rather than man's ability to love, to will and to think. Feuerbach once said that his principal aim was to change *'the friends of God into the friends of man, believers into thinkers, worshippers into workers, candidates for the other world into students of this world, Christians who by their own definition are half animal and half angel into whole human beings'*.

RESISTANCE FIGHTERS

In making all these points against a deity it may readily leave the impression that humanists like me are protesting too much, that by paying so much attention we are giving credence to the existence of such an entity. Nothing could be further from the truth. God to me is an alien concept. I had rather spend my time marvelling at nature and making the best of my brief time in the sun. I and others like me, are only having to confront the God notion because in this demon haunted world there is no escaping him. At public gatherings, at national events, at funerals at weddings, even in schools he is omni-present. God this, God that, God the other thing. So criticising humanists for bothering about God is like accusing resistance fighters of worrying about the Gestapo. Or saying that Martin Luther King was intolerant when he demanded civil rights. We would rather put our time to better use but god and religion are like unwanted visitors. They keep knocking on your door. Humanists could of course pretend not to be at home and hide quietly in the cellar but that strategy has failed to work. Our doors are battered down and the cellar is invaded. Our last resort is to come out fighting but then we are branded 'militants':

For more on this topic see the chapter: 'Atheist Militancy'.

AGNOSTICISM

"The trouble with Agnosticism in the God debate is that Agnostics don't know what entity to be agnostic about"

T.A.

There is in humanist circles a good deal of deliberation as to whether one should style oneself an agnostic or an atheist. Choosing the agnostic label holds obvious advantages. It suggests a number of attractive attributes: open-mindedness, tolerance, reasonableness. Atheism, on the other hand, gets the demon treatment: itself a religion, aggressive, intolerant, arrogant, immoral. If some believers had their way they would replace the 'athe' in atheist with 'rap' or 'sad'. The word agnostic was first coined by Darwin's bulldog Thomas Huxley in 1869. On joining the Metaphysical Society Huxley started using the term agnosticism because he found so many people there talking about things as if they had knowledge on the topic when he, himself, did not:

'The one thing in which most of these good people were agreed was the one thing in which I differed from them. They were quite sure they had attained a certain "gnosis" - had, more or less successfully, solved the problem of existence; while I was quite sure I had not, and had a pretty strong conviction that the problem was insoluble.

So I took thought, and invented what I conceived to be the appropriate title of "agnostic." It came into my head as suggestively antithetic to the "gnostics" of Church history, who professed to know so much about the very things of which I was ignorant.'

Some would argue that Huxley's agnosticism was not a theological position concerned with addressing the existence or non-existence of God, but merely a general statement that when faced with any proposition one should always retain an open mind. Although in his writings defending the agnostic position Huxley strongly attacked and undermined many of the assertions made in the Bible it may well be true that in his day, 150 years ago, Huxley intended his agnosticism to be no more than a newly coined expression for the scientific method, i.e. not jumping to conclusions until all doubt is removed and even then keeping all conclusions under constant review. But unfortunately that is not what agnosticism represents in present day theological debate. Here are three dictionary definitions, taken at random. Collins English dictionary: *Agnostic: A person who holds that only material phenomena can be known and knowledge of a supreme being, ultimate cause etc. is impossible.*

The New Shorter Oxford: *Agnostic: a person who holds the view that nothing can be known of the existence of God or of anything beyond material phenomena.*

Longman Synonym dictionary: *Agnostic: sceptic, nullifidian, unbeliever, disbeliever.*

It is clear that the contemporary meaning of the term, far from conveying an all purpose impartiality in the absence of evidence, specifically addresses uncertainty about the existence of a higher being. If Huxley had wished to use a term merely to indicate his desire to keep an open mind in general, non theological terms, he could have styled himself a scientist, logician, rationalist, sceptic, empiricist or syllogist. For humanists, today, to accept the dictionary defined agnostic label merely serves to give religious belief more credence than it deserves. If outrageous religious dogma such as the resurrection or immaculate conception can only be countered by a statement of neutrality which is what agnosticism amounts to, then the religious can be forgiven for drawing the conclusion that their assertions, however bizarre, deserve serious consideration and equal status. Agnosticism places a person with one foot in the religious camp.

TEAPOT IN ORBIT

To borrow an analogy from Bertrand Russell we must then be equally agnostic about the theory that there is a teapot in elliptical orbit around the sun. It is impossible to disprove but that doesn't grant the existence or non existence of the teapot equal credence. It could of course be argued that there are good reasons for finding a Supreme Being more plausible than a celestial teapot but that would necessitate presentation of a proper scientific case which should be evaluated on its merits. There should be no protection from scrutiny behind a screen of agnostic tolerance. If religious arguments are superior to Russell's teapot proposition then let us hear about them. In their absence let those who call themselves agnostic about god belief, admit that they are equally agnostic about orbiting teapots.

The teapot proposition stands for an infinite number of things whose existence is imaginable and cannot be disproved. There are the ancient gods Zeus, Apollo, Thor, Wotan and more frivolously, the tooth fairy, Santa Claus and the Flying Spaghetti Monster. The fact that they are unfalsifiable is not felt by any reasonable person to be of great consequence. None of us feels an obligation to disprove, or be agnostic about, any of the numerous far-fetched notions that a deluded or facetious imagination might dream up. Why make an exception for the last remaining god? I have come across an amusing paragraph, set in rhyme, which neatly sums up the illogicality of such god belief:

"There is no God but our God The humble Christians say. There is no God but our God, to Him alone we pray. What of the others by the score, Gods just as great and mighty. Of Allah, Odin, Jove and Thor, Venus and Aphrodite. If to the one alone we pray, and He is just a faker, there surely will be Hell to pay when we meet our maker. So, good Christians take my advice: don't be so egotistic. And on occasion in your prayers address some other mystic. Remember there have been a score, a hundred, thousands, maybe more. To say there is but one God might make the others sore. Good Christians believe in one God. Myself,

I must confess, am not so very different. I believe in just one less".

There are of course legitimate cases for agnosticism. Carl Sagan was happy to be agnostic about the probability of life elsewhere in the universe. Agnosticism about what caused the end-Permian extinction or the later extinction of the dinosaurs is reasonable. But agnosticism about God is another matter. Richard Dawkins distinguishes two kinds of agnosticism. TAP or Temporary Agnosticism in Practice. This refers to legitimate fence-sitting where there really is a definite answer, one way or the other, but where the evidence is as yet unavailable. TAP would be a reasonable stance towards the Permian extinction. There is an answer which one day may be found. The other kind of fence-sitting, which Dawkins humorously has dubbed PAP (Permanent Agnosticism in Principle) is appropriate for questions that can never be answered, no matter how much evidence is gathered, because the very idea of evidence is not applicable. Many people, including some scientists, place the question of God's existence in the forever inaccessible PAP category. Dawkins, however, argues that agnosticism about the existence of God belongs firmly in the temporary or TAP category. Either he exists or he doesn't. It is a scientific question which one day may be answered. But the fact that we can neither prove nor disprove the existence of something does not put existence and non-existence on an even footing.

This is particularly so when a definition of the God concept is taken into account. It would be perfectly acceptable to be largely agnostic about the existence of a cosmic force or laws of physics and chemistry, hitherto undetected by mankind, possibly beyond our reach and understanding. Even the most hardened sceptics might describe themselves as agnostics when faced with such a nebulous definition. But then of course we are no longer talking about a concept that could even remotely be given the god description. We are then merely talking about an unknown aspect of science, unrelated to the God question. The dilemma of detecting such an illusive entity is neatly illustrated by a story first told by the philosopher John Wisdom: *"Once upon a time two explorers came upon a clearing in the jungle. In the clearing there were growing many flowers and many weeds. One explorer concludes 'Some gardener must tend this plot'. The other disagrees, 'There is no gardener'. So they pitch their tents and set a watch. No gardener is ever seen. 'But perhaps he is an invisible gardener.' So they erect a barbed-wire fence. They electrify it. They patrol with guard dogs. (For they remember how H.G.Wells's Invisible Man could be smelled and touched though he could not be seen.) But no howls ever suggest that some intruder has received a shock. No movements of the wire ever betray an invisible climber. The guard dogs never bark. But still the believer is not deterred, 'There is a gardener, invisible, intangible, insensible to electric shocks, a gardener who has no scent and makes no sound, a gardener who comes secretly to look after the garden which he loves'. At last the sceptic despairs, 'But what remains of your original assertion? Just how does what you call an invisible, intangible, eternally elusive gardener differ from an imaginary gardener or even from no gardener at all?!'*

There is another analogous tale that I could use to illustrate the point. Say I am putting it about that there is a fire-breathing dragon living in my cellar. People who hear me allege this will want to see him. Dragons are not an everyday occurrence. I take them downstairs. There are some bottles down there, some old boots, some bric-a-brac but no dragon. "Where's the dragon", they ask. "Oh, he is here alright, but I neglected to mention that it's an invisible dragon". The visitors suggest spreading chalk on the floor of the cellar to show up the dragon's footprints. Good idea, I reply, but this dragon floats in the air. "Then maybe use an infrared sensor to detect the invisible fire". Good thinking, but the invisible fire is also heatless. "Why not spray-paint the dragon to make him visible"? "That can't work because this is an incorporeal dragon and the paint won't stick". And so merrily on, much as one would want to answer a child's searching questions about the whereabouts of Father Christmas. I counter every physical test that is proposed with an ingenious explanation of why it won't work. This is what philosophers refer to as 'death by a thousand qualifications'.

This scenario begs the question, of course, what is the difference between an invisible, incorporeal, floating dragon, who blows heatless fire and no dragon at all? If there is absolutely no way to disprove my contention, no conceivable experiment that could discount it, what does it then mean that my dragon exists? Your inability to invalidate my hypothesis is not at all the same thing as my proving it true. Untestable claims, assertions immune to disproof, are philosophically worthless, whatever value they may have in inspiring people or exciting our sense of awe and wonder. What it boils down to is my asking others to believe me simply on my say-so.

The only thing that is obvious from my insistence on the dragon's presence is that something funny is going on inside my head. Substitute God for the dragon and the idea of God, which in the first books of the bible has very clear and definite meaning, becomes ever vaguer until in the minds of some modern believers little is left but an empty word. If you hypothesise that there is a God, but that there is nothing sure and definite you can point to as a reliable pattern of things that God actually does, how does a state of affairs where a God does nothing, functions in no discernible way, differ from a state of affairs where God is just a chimera?

It would be highly inappropriate to ascribe the same degree of agnosticism towards a definition of a god, which I have dubbed Omnigod, as an all powerful higher being in benign control of all events here on earth. Faced as we are with complete lack of evidence of any such being existing and with an enormous amount of evidence suggesting its non-existence, as exemplified by nature red in tooth and claw, the exis- tence of disease, huge death tolls in natural disasters, the holocaust, the random vicissitudes affecting believ- ers and non-believers alike, the absence of response to prayers, it is entirely reasonable for humanists to aban- don their agnostic stance and in the theological debate refer to themselves as atheists. After all atheism does not concern itself with providing proof that a god does not exist. It is a wide-spread misunderstanding that an atheist tries to prove the non existence of God. For one thing it is impossible to prove a negative, for another the burden of proof rests squarely on the theist; for s/he is the one making the assertions.

In her poem 'Good God', Barbara Smoker, ex president of the national Secular Society, brilliantly deals with the futility of god belief.

"The ground of being" has a grand
and philosophic ring-
but theists who would take their stand
on abstract "ground" tread shifting sand:
it doesn't mean a thing.

If common-sense were common, no
religions would arise:
Old Occam's razor, to and fro,
would cut them down to size.

Why "Blessed are they who have not seen
and yet believe"? Why should
such purblind faith the Nazarene
extol, as something good?
And worse, he would to Hell consign
those men who dared to doubt
the marvels of his market line -
who tried to work things out.

A God of Love I cannot square
With Hell - not fact, nor in the air -
nor yet with hell-on-earth.
Less sickening, for those who care,
if naught but neutral chance be there
to bless, or blight, our birth.

ATHEISM IS NOT A RELIGION

*"Atheism is nothing more than the noises reasonable
people make when in the presence of religious dogma"*
Sam Harris

To all theists out there this is a real 'read my lips'
statement: **'atheism is not a religion'.** This is the
mantra atheists must put up with time and time again.
This is probably due to the fact that believers cannot
imagine anybody not subscribing to a religion. It's
the 'there are no atheists in foxholes' insult. Atheism
as a religion is a ludicrous idea. It is the absence of
religion. Calling it a religion is calling abstinence a
sex position or describing baldness as a hair colour.
Dictionary definitions almost invariably define an
atheist as "one who denies the existence of God".
In reality there is no notion of 'denial' in the origin of
the word (a = Greek for 'without', Theos = 'god'. Hence
atheism = without god) and the atheist who denies
the existence of God in any form is by far the rarest
type. Most atheists would agree with the statement of
Charles Bradlaugh who said, in the *Freethinker's Text
Book:* "Atheism is **without** God. It does not assert no
God. The atheist does not say there is no God, but he
says I know not what you mean by God. I am without

the idea of God. The word God to me is a sound conveying no clear or distinct affirmation. I do not deny God because I cannot deny that of which I have no conception and the conception of which by its affirmer is so imperfect that he is unable to define it for me". And d' Holbach, author of the '*The System of Nature*', the first openly atheistic work ever published, said: "*All children are atheists, they have no idea of God. The idea that a child not yet exposed to theism would be an atheist can only be true if atheism means 'without a belief in God' as opposed to denial of the existence of God*".

Lest I be accused by inveterate atheists of uncalled for even-handedness, let me hasten to state that I do not grant theists equality of proposition in the God - no God debate. If I and the Vicar are sitting opposite each other and he asserts that behind me he can see a purple, three horned cow and I tell him that behind him I can see an angry man wielding a cricket bat, we both have to take these two statements on trust because without looking round we cannot be sure what's there. I contend, however, that the vicar would be sorely tempted to take a peek, since men with cricket bats have been known to exist and that they should wish to take a swing at a vicar is a distinct possibility. I, on the other hand, would not take his three horned purple cow very seriously, for such a creature has never been reported. No need for me to turn my head. Equally his assertion of the existence of a God, for which there has never been any evidence, is a poor match for my scepticism. For whilst the Vicar cannot produce God supporting evidence other than laboured hypothesis I, taking a more pragmatic approach, can point at plenty of evidence, perhaps not for his non-existence but certainly for his non intervention.

However, If theists stray beyond their remit and start encroaching on unbelievers' turf as they are inclined to do, then the 'a' in atheism is entitled to turn into 'anti'. Equally, if someone started a religion in worship of, say, the Great Widget in the sky, collected a lot of proselytising followers, built churches and mosques, disturbing peace and quiet, causing divisions in society, had schools pressured into Widget creationism and worship, pronounced the death sentence on authors because the beloved Widget did not like the contents of their books then I am sure our vicar and his people would be the first to declare themselves anti-Widget.

Religious gullibility

*'Religion is an advertising campaign for
a product that doesn't exist'*

If to a rational person it is so blindingly obvious that
Omnigod is a figment of mankind's imagination why
is it that after a couple of centuries of modern science
the god illusion still has such a powerful hold on
people's minds? How is it that people manage successfully to outgrow the childish notions of tooth fairies and
Santa Claus but get stuck for life with the adult fanta-
sies of religion? It is of course tempting to argue that by
and large religious belief is restricted to, how can I put
this politely, people who are not in the habit of thinking
things through. Who are quite prepared to let other
people do the thinking and go along with whatever is
put before them by people whom they consider superior
thinkers. Clear evidence of this is the strong correlation
between the beliefs of parents and that of their offspring.

A child born to Catholic parents in Dublin would
grow up a Muslim if s/he had been born to Muslim
parents in Karachi. Jesuits famously claimed 'give me a
child till the age of seven and I will show you the man'.
The almost universal opinion that one's own religious
convictions are the reasoned outcome of a dispassionate

evaluation of all the major alternatives is demonstrably false for humanity in general. If that really were the origin of most people's convictions, then one would expect the major faiths to be distributed more or less randomly or evenly across the globe. But in fact they show a very strong tendency to cluster, which illustrates what we suspected all along: that upbringing and social forces are the primary determinants of religious belief for people in general.

A study funded by the Economic and Social Research Council, carried out by Manchester university, concluded that even in Britain, when it comes to religion, parents are the most important influence. The research found that only one child in twelve is likely to opt for a denomination not adhered to by either parent. The problem is that rigidly conforming children have a way of growing up to be rigidly conforming adults. They are not educated; they are moulded. They are not trained to think, but to defend. They are not asked to reflect, but to memorise. As I grow older the mystery as to why people entering the 21st century are still able to believe in the contrivances served up by ancient desert tribes is ever deepening. Two thousand years ago religious belief was very understandable. Science was in its infancy and in their eagerness to understand, people were willing to jump to unsubstantiated conclusions. But time has moved on, mankind has had the benefit of Galileo, Einstein, Darwin, Russell, Attenborough and Dawkins.

By now we should have reached the point where amongst intelligent people religion has become extinct. A relic of more ignorant times. But somehow the antiquity of religion gives it enhanced status. At what point did people start to conclude that the ancientness of this or that religion somehow gave it extra kudos? Religions with relatively modern origins are almost always described as 'cults', the implication being that new religious nonsense is somehow more nonsensical than old religious nonsense. Paradoxically, the more absurd the claim, the more grandiose the dream; the more incredible the mystery, the more committed and devoted the true believers are likely to become. As Hilaire Belloc said: "Oh let us never, never doubt what nobody is sure about!" If religion were restricted to the uneducated, the gullible and the frankly stupid, then this conundrum could be solved. Educate the ignorant and leave the stupid with the comfort their religion might bring.

RELIGIOUS SCIENTISTS

But here is the dilemma that makes us humanists scratch our heads: research examining religious belief amongst scientists still reveals substantial percentages of believers. Exact figures are hard to come by, but US surveys amongst university educated scientists average a one in three for god belief. As might be expected the percentage is lower for eminent scientists (members of the National Academy of Sciences). For them a1998 poll returned the much lower figure of 7 per cent, confirming that the higher the calibre of scientist, the lower the belief in superstition.

A similar study amongst NAS scientists, held in 1914, produced a 28 per cent belief in God, showing that progress is being made. Improving trends or not, the fact remains that even in these modern, more enlightened times a substantial proportion of educated people retain adherence to a religion or a belief in a higher power. This is where we rationalists remain baffled. What is it that sets us apart? It can't be just intelligence or else there would be no religious scientists at all. So why is it that some of us have readily concluded that it is unlikely that amongst the billions of galaxies in immeasurable space, little planet earth has been earmarked for special attention. That it is fanciful to believe that humans survive in an incorporeal state after death. That prayers have as much chance of being answered as a random throwing of the dice. That miracles and apparitions only happen when witnessed by peasant children and hallucinating adults. That nature red in tooth and claw is grotesquely incompatible with a benevolent creator. That human suffering can only be alleviated by other humans.

How come that people who are high achievers in certain intellectual tasks can come across as supremely naive in other fields? It must be because a crucial ingredient is missing. Defining this ingredient has been the subject of many learned and not so learned articles in freethought publications. I will venture my own attempt. To escape superstition the necessary mindset is rigorous scepticism. Particularly towards memes. Dawkins has defined memes as viruses of the mind. Beware of attitudes that result in turning baseball caps the wrong way round. Avoid bandwagon jumpers of all descriptions. People who readily adopt clichés. Sheep who run with crowds. Me too, copy-cat behaviour, comes naturally to most humans. Just watch footballers celebrating goals or tennis players in doubles games touching after every point. Similarly, addictive belief systems become so much part of the identity of some people that it is often impossible to determine where the individual being ends and the religious group think begins. The rationalist must stand alone, fiercely independent, always prepared to examine the facts before coming to conclusions. Most people, including the religious, are rational enough in the everyday affairs of life. But where the bigger questions are concerned, in matters of life and death, they readily begin to wobble. When, for example, the facts point to ignominious demise then for many people that is too much to take. For the majority resignation in the face of one's personal oblivion is one rational step too far. The emotions rise up to stifle the horrid thought.

Religious scientists would do well to heed the words of Poet Brian Blackwell:

"No reason; no justification; just arcane dogma. No debate. Freakish fears of breaking rank.

That is why religions do not connect, do not evolve. Superstition has to operate.

It must not be questioned. The antithesis of science.

In science there is no banality, no furtiveness, no fanciful solemnity, no jarrings and discordances, no purposeless emotion or ritual, no ritualised pomp, no ceremony".

I have often thought that although people are dubious about their own belief they assume that most people around them do believe. This makes them think that they are on their own and must be wrong. Hence the tendency of religious people to gather in groups. Because when you are being told something really fantastical like God had a son who was really him and he sent him on a suicide mission and he survived and you are eating his flesh, when you are really eating bread that was obviously bought in a shop; if you are going to swallow all that, you need somebody standing next to you swallowing it too. A classical case of mass delusion. Surely millions can't be wrong? Well yes, they can be. Muslims think millions of Christians are wrong and Christians think millions of Muslims are wrong. They can't both be right.

As Bertrand Russell said in Marriage and Morals *"The fact that an opinion has been widely held is no evidence whatsoever that it is not utterly absurd. Indeed in view of the silliness of the majority of mankind a widespread belief is more likely to be foolish than sensible"'*

FAITH'S COMFORT BLANKET

The primitive fear and uncertainty built up over hundreds of thousands of years in the human psyche and the desperate need for comfort cannot readily be eradicated. If science cannot console then something else must. So in the brain an attic door is kept ajar. It leads to a secret room of promising delight. No deep thought may enter here just pleasant notions of make-believe. Thus anaesthetised the religious go through life guiltily aware that hoping it is so, doesn't make it so, but not having hope at all is simply too much to bear. It enables even scientists to pull off the remarkable schizoid feat of reconciling transubstantiation with the basic laws of physics. Such people seem to require the solace offered by faith to such an extent that their emotional demands trump their rational conclusions. Thus an intellectual giant may be turned into an emotional pygmy. A case of watertight compartments in their brains. Perhaps there are glandular, even genetic factors that predispose some people to crave security in belief, whereas others are able to cope with ambiguity and live with uncertainty.

So the most formidable opponent of rationalism is not theology but the pitiful frailty of the human condition. It takes a hardy soul who can contemplate oblivion with equanimity. So strongly held is comfort faith that when asked what they would do if scientists were to disprove a particular religious belief, nearly two-thirds (64 per cent) of people say they would continue to hold to what their religion teaches rather than accept the contrary scientific finding, according to the results of an October 2006 Time magazine poll. What's more, in a May 2007 Gallup poll, only 14 per cent of those who say they do not believe in evolution cite lack of evidence as the main reason underpinning their views; more people cite their belief in Jesus (19 per cent), God (16 per cent) or religion generally (16 per cent) as their reason for rejecting Darwin's theory.

This reliance on religious faith may help explain why so many people do not see science as a direct threat to religion. Only 28 per cent of respondents in the same Time poll say that scientific advancements threaten their religious beliefs. These results also show that more than four-fifths of respondents (81 per cent) say that "recent discoveries and advances" in science have not significantly impacted their religious views. Remarkably, 14 per cent reply that these discoveries have actually made them more religious. Only 4 per cent say that science has made them less religious. All findings quoted here are US based. Faith surveys are common there. In

Western Europe religion is in rapid decline. In Britain just 18 per cent of the public say they are a practising member of an organised religion. Only 33 per cent describe themselves as religious and 40 per cent claim to believe in a god. The proportion of religious scientists is minuscule at less than 2 per cent. This is readily in evidence when time and again we see the same few religious scientists wheeled out in defence of superstition.

I have sympathy for religious people, even if scientists, who need invented crutches to cope with the vicissitudes of life. But I have to be honest here and admit that I can't bring myself to consider religious scientists as well rounded people. The religious bug gets in the way of full respect. In the same way that I might admire a brilliant sportsman's skill only to wince when he crosses himself. Or a professor of horticulture who believes in fairies at the bottom of his pristine garden. I could respect such people's beliefs only in the sense and to the extent that I would respect their notions that their wives are beautiful and their children clever.

The loss of respect for god believers is proportionate to the type of belief involved. There are the die hard Omnigod disciples, people who don't believe in evolution, who do believe in such oddments as transubstantiation or immaculate conceptions, personal favours obtained by prayer; in short the whole panoply of strange beliefs. For humanists this category really is beyond the pale. If as adults in this scientific age they are still in thrall to all that archaic ignorance, then there is no escaping the conclusion that such people are a sandwich short of the rational picnic. The blurry God subscribers are a more slippery bunch. Perhaps a banana short. They are very hard to pin down. If pressed they seek refuge in increasing amounts of fuzziness. It is touching and yet infuriating to witness the contortions and acrobatics the blurry god believers will go to, to hang on to their once firmly held beliefs. But eventually such people are ripe for the humanist harvest. One more heave and they are ready for a plunge into the clear blue water of personal freedom. Ready to board the good ship 'Freethought' where there is no captain to tell them what to do or threaten a keel haul for sinful trespass.

Inside a believer's mind

*"Faith may be defined as an illogical belief
in the occurrence of the improbable.
Faith does not give you the answers,
it just stops you asking the questions"* T.A.

Not everything we believe has been urged upon us,
either by reason or by the collective know-how
around us. Most commonly we take things on board
because we have seen or sensed them. In such instances
we trust our own experience and our own feelings
rather than rational arguments. We believe that the
world exists, not because we are persuaded by argument,
but because we have experienced the world. Perhaps
that is how it is with God belief. We cannot actually
see God, but many of those who believe in him tell
us that they have had personal experience of his
existence. Is it really likely that they may have
experienced him in some way and is it reasonable for
us to trust what they say they have experienced? You
cannot get inside another person's mind and know
for yourself what that person has felt. Equally you are
not convinced when he says he can feel, or in some
other way experience something which you do not
experience. If your friend says he can see a tiger in a

cage and you do not see it after looking closely, then you won't believe the tiger is really there. You will assume your friend is imagining things.

Sometimes he really does experience something which you can't experience. That will happen, for example, if he has a headache. Then you can remember having experienced headaches in the past, so you will agree that what he claims is likely to be true and in any case it is not at variance with what you otherwise know about the world. But if your friend tells you that he can experience something that is very unlikely to be true, then it is sensible for you not to believe him. When you tell me that you have seen a cow in a meadow, then it is reasonable for me to believe you. But when you tell me that you have seen a cow jumping over the moon, it is reasonable for me not to believe you. I may allow that you did see something but it was not likely a cow jumping over the moon. Although I cannot know your experience in either case I can assess whether what you say you experienced is likely or not. The occurrence of God's presence is not an ordinary thing, like cows eating grass; it is extraordinary, like cows jumping over moons. That is a very good reason for believing that what your friend tells you he has experienced was not really the presence of God. Things that people say they have experienced are not always what they seem to be. For one thing, it is possible to have hallucinations.

Drugs can produce vivid hallucinations and the sensations that follow are very real to people who have them. People may also 'see things' when they are very upset, or when they are short of food (for example, the saints, who kept having visions of God, used to fast for protracted periods and most religions have periods of fasting).

People who claim they have personally experienced God are often emotional people who might be expected to have intense feelings. Another factor is wishful thinking.

People who encounter God are usually people who already believe in God or who are trying very hard to make themselves believe. They hope that God exists. They would like religion to be true, so they persuade themselves that it really is. Eventually they start to feel it is true deep inside and they become aware of the presence of God. The process is not always deliberate: it may be sub-conscious but that does not make it any less real. If the presence of God is really there to be encountered, why do most people not notice it? You would expect that God would give the religious sense to everybody, so that we could all experience his presence and hear what he has to say, rather than select a chosen few. Why should he wish to keep his existence a secret from the rest of us? People of different religious faiths often say they have experiences of God, but those encounters very often do not agree with each other. When God reveals himself to Hindu believers he may be Krishna or Shiva, the God whom Muslims experience is Allah and even the Christian God can have many interpretations.

Even if you say that it is the same God whom the Muslims experience as Allah, the Christians as Jesus and so on, it is still hard to explain why this God says quite different things to Muslims and to Christians. At one time he used to tell Christians that they should burn witches and start wars against Muslims; he tells Muslims not to eat pork and to start wars against Christians and he tells Hindus not to upset cattle. God was always appearing to saints and the prophets and telling them things which nobody would believe today. Are people going to argue that the personal experience of God which the saints, the crusaders and the witch-hunters had was not real, while the experience of God which some people today say they have is real? How are they different? The man who says he has experienced God already had the idea of God in his mind. When he felt a deep emotion, he assumed it was the presence of God.

A humanist who had the same kind of experience might have called it 'awe' or 'wonder' or something else. It might be the kind of excitement you feel when you are stimulated by poetry or music; you may have felt something like it when looking at a mountain range or at the stars or when marvelling at the mind-boggling size of the universe or other wonders of nature. All the believer can really say is that he felt something and he thought it was the presence of God. What he claims as an encounter with God is really his own interpretation of some experience. Research carried out by Oxford University in 1970 collected details of religious experiences which people said they had undergone. Apart from noticing that many of the people who had these experiences were, to say the least, rather odd, they came up against another problem: some of the things they experienced did not agree with their religion. A lady said she had seen her dog in heaven. But Christians are not supposed to believe that dogs have souls and go to heaven. Another thing which the survey revealed was that about one third of the people studied, appeared to have had a 'religious experience'. That means that the other two thirds had not. But if religious experiences are real, why don't we all have them? Could it be that all of us are sensitive to feelings and experiences and one third of the people concerned, interpret those experiences as religious?

FAITH AND REASON

"He that will not reason is a bigot;
he that cannot reason is a fool;
he that dares not reason is a slave"

William Drummond

Martin Luther stated in no uncertain terms what is the greatest enemy of Christianity: '*Whoever wants to be a Christian should tear the eyes out of his Reason. Reason must be denied, blinded, and destroyed. Faith must trample underfoot all reason, sense, and understanding, and whatever it sees must be put out of sight and ... know nothing but the word of God. Reason is the devil's harlot, who can do nought but slander and harm whatever God says and does*'

When religious people die their eulogies often mention their 'tremendous faith' as if this was some form of supreme achievement. The American author Maya Angelou has died. When writing she used to take inspiration from the Bible and Roget's Thesaurus in equal measure. (I too use the indispensable thesaurus and possess a copy of the Bible but I keep it on a shelf next to Dawkins' 'God Delusion'. Poison and its anti-dote). The media report that her good deeds were inspired by her 'deep faith'. Are we to conclude that without it she would have been a selfish failure? Not likely, but it would suggest that like others of such faith she lived her whole life taking things on trust without evidence. Not an accolade I would be proud of. Believers often claim that faith is not contrary to reason. But if faith were rational it would tell us to believe the same things as reason tells us to believe. That would render faith redundant. Faith is only pressed into service to help us believe the kind of things that are unreasonable to believe. If you choose to use faith then you are believing in spite of the evidence.

The very fact that we need faith to help us believe in God proves that reason will not lead us to that conclusion. The answer that reason shows us is the opposite to the answer of faith, because faith is contrary to reason. It says so in the Bible "Faith is the substance of things hoped for, the evidence of things not seen." (Hebrews 11,1) Faith may have a positive value in helping people to deal with their emotions. It may offer them solace, it can give them support in coping with disease or grief. It can give some people great joy and elation. But the questions that are being asked in my book are not a matter of emotion: we are after the facts. Faith may help with emotional problems, but reason is the only tool we have for evaluating and testing evidence, for weighing arguments and for deciding which of our ideas are likely to be true.

Even religious believers who say we should have faith prefer to use reason when it suits. It is only when they reach a position where reason is against them that they say we must turn to faith. The philosopher John Locke noted that as long ago as 1689 when he wrote: "I find every sect, as far as reason will help them, make use of it gladly: and where it fails them, they cry out: It is a matter of faith and above reason". *(Concerning Human Understanding")*. For as long as it was possible Christians tried to prove the existence of God by logic. If you want to give yourself a head-ache then take a look at the musings of Aquinas. But now it has become clear that these proofs do not work, (I have stayed clear of dealing with these 'proofs' in my book, they really are too torturous and facile to be taken seriously) most Christians do not use them anymore: they find it convenient to say that the facts of religion are beyond reason and you have to accept them on faith.

Reason is the finest tool we have for testing our beliefs and arriving at the truth. Theists believe that God gave it to us. Why should God give us this power of reason if he meant us not to use it, but instead to trust in faith to show us what is true? Faith is said to be a good thing. It is the best crutch a believer can have. When doubting Thomas, touched Jesus's wounds to see if he had really been crucified and had risen from the dead, Jesus (according to the gospel story) chided him and said that "those people are more blessed who have believed and have not seen" (John 20,24). Jesus is often angry with those who will not believe until they have seen the evidence: "Oh ye of little faith!" (Matthew 6,30; Luke 12,28); "Oh faithless and perverse generation, how long shall I suffer you?" (Matthew 17,17). That belief is essential to salvation is also accepted by all schools of Muslim theology. "It is the faith of the individual that decides his fate on the Day of Judgement; whether he will enter Paradise or Hell".

Theists cannot avoid saying that faith is a virtue because they know that nobody would believe their religion if they looked at the evidence in the light of day. They tried reason for long enough but it has become a losing battle so they now tell us we must have faith. When theists say you ought to have faith we should ask them: "Why must I have faith in what you tell me, rather than have faith in what somebody else tells me? Why is it good to have faith in your beliefs but not in devil worship, the Easter Bunny or the Loch Ness monster? If I ought to have faith in Jesus, shouldn't I also have faith in Apollo or in Santa Claus? (After all there is repeat evidence every year for his existence). If you are going to have faith in the miracles of Jesus, should you not also have faith in the miracles of Krishna, or the miracles of Jupiter? If it is bad to disbelieve why do Christians and Muslims disbelieve in the gods and scriptures of the Hindus? Christians and Muslims refuse to believe in hundreds of gods. Why is it bad for an atheist to disbelieve in just a couple more?

Believers are sorry for people who lose their faith and hope they will recover it. They take for granted that faith is a desirable attribute. The word faith is sometimes synonymous with 'trust' and trust can be a good thing. I like people to trust me and life is more pleasant if they do. But trust is not always a positive thing. It is not good to trust a dodgy used car salesman, or to trust –instead of taking care – that things will turn out all right. Trust is not good in itself; it is a matter for our rational judgement whether we should trust a particular person or turn of events. We should not 'trust in God' (regardless of what is stamped on American coins) unless we have good reason to think he exists and is worthy of being trusted; it would hardly be a virtue to trust someone who does not exist or is not trustworthy.

We also use the word 'faith' to mean 'faithfulness', 'honesty' or 'integrity' as when we say something is done 'in good faith'. In that sense too faith can be desirable (especially if the people we keep faith with are decent people rather than crooks). These are possible meanings of the word 'faith', but they are not what theists mean when they are talking of their religions. When they say that god exists and the bible or the Koran are true and they tell you to have faith, they don't mean that you should trust honest people, or be loyal to good friends, or be honest with yourself and tell the truth. They mean that you should forget about your doubts and persuade yourself to believe. This is where they urge the non believer to accept Pascal's Wager.

Blaise Pascal was a French mathematician and philosopher who famously argued that the potential benefits of faith in God were so vast that it would be wise to opt for it. If you are right you are saved, if not you lose nothing. This may appear a sensible plan at first but a small dose of logic will strangle it at birth. God, who is omniscient, knows your every thought and would recognise that this kind of calculating faith was merely an expedient. In matters of religion the word 'faith' means the determination to believe that there is a god regardless of any supporting evidence. Can it really be a virtue to have faith, rather than to apply reason to the evidence? The French philosophe Denis Diderot satirised the idea: "*I was lost in a great forest at night and I had only a tiny light to guide me. A stranger came and said: 'My friend put out your candle, so that you will find your way better'. That person was a theologian*".

It may be true that reason does not illuminate everything and at times it is only a dim light. But even a little light is better than no light at all. Sometimes we have to accept that our knowledge is limited. That limitation may be irksome but you cannot get reliable knowledge by turning to faith. You could have faith in any number of ideas, but there is nothing except reason that can test those ideas objectively and show you which of them is more likely to be true. Faith does not tell you what to believe. It is either reason or prejudice that determines which ideas you are going to have faith in. If you choose to have faith in irrational ideas, then reason will make you doubt those ideas and faith will help you persist. If your faith is not strong enough to suppress those doubts then you will suffer what believers call a 'crisis of faith', a crisis which they try to overcome by re-strengthening their faith. Conquering your reasonable doubts and having faith means believing something in spite of what your mind is telling you. It is lying to yourself.

Humanists believe you should do your best to discover the truth, taking account of whatever evidence there may be. If the evidence does not justify belief then belief would be irrational and wrong. If you are seeking emotional strength or consolation then it may be helpful to have faith. But if it is the truth you are after then it is unwise to suspend the judgement of your own mind and believe irrationally. Reason should never be abandoned for the sake of faith.

Guidelines on how to become an Atheist/Humanist

Come take your place in our pews
And hear our heretical views.
You were not born in sin
So lift up your chin
You have only your dogmas to lose.

Readers of my book will of course bring with them their own existing beliefs and/or philosophies. For those of you who still think of yourselves as believers, but who are unsure and curious as to what it would take to become an atheist/humanist, I am listing a number of considerations which may help you towards making up your minds. But first let me summarise why it is that so many people are inclined to feel a need for religion. Underlying this need are just three basic thoughts: 1) there must be something out there responsible for the creation of all that we can see. 2) human life is so superior to any other form of life that it cannot just end in extinction. 3) Hence life must have a special meaning and purpose.

From time immemorial there have been religious leaders who have homed in on these sentiments for reasons good and bad. Some have been well-intentioned others have been manipulators and advantage takers. Between them they have created a vast empire of religious control which has left few people unaffected. If you feel you are one of these it may help to do the following:

- Examine your current beliefs. No matter what you previously believed, if now deep down you find no belief in god, your transformation is already complete. There is no process or initiation for becoming an atheist (except possibly a "coming out" to others). If you can honestly think, "I don't believe there is a god", you are already an atheist/humanist.
- Understand the difference between belief and truth. Consider the following examples:

A stranger comes to your door and tells you that your child has been killed in a car accident outside their school.

You would feel a pang of emotion, but this is a stranger. Do you believe them? Do they know who your child is? Is this some sort of cruel joke? Do you really believe that your child has been killed? You will be inclined to harbour some strong doubts.

Two police officers come to your door, squad car in the driveway. They tell you your child has been killed. They need you to come with them to identify the body. You will in all likelihood believe them, they are police officers. You will feel the emotion as though you know for a fact that your child is dead. It will be real to you.

The thing to notice is that the difference between these two examples is the authority of the messenger, not the message itself. These examples I have also chosen for their emotional content, because the emotional content is a large part of what makes a situation real to us.

The point is, whether we believe something based on authority, or emotion, or both, we cannot know it is true until we see with our own eyes. The highest authority you can imagine could tell you the simplest thing, and you may believe them, and they may believe themselves, but that does not in any way make it true.

- Be convinced that you are an intelligent human being. Your life is valuable for its own sake. You are not second-class in the universe, deriving meaning and purpose from some other mind. You are not inherently evil, you are inherently human, possessing the positive rational potential to help make this a world of morality, peace and joy. Trust yourself.

- Understand the difference between scientific belief and religious belief. The difference between belief in a scientific theory as opposed to belief in a religious dogma, boils down to the difference between the institution of science and the institutions of various religions. The underlying concept in religious institutions is that the nature of reality is known. Their nature of reality is written in a book or on a tablet. This writing was originally done, or dictated, or inspired, by a god. Religious institutions are primarily concerned with spreading information about the 'known' nature of reality, because in their understanding of reality, that is what they are required to do. Religious 'facts' are not subject to testing, and in most cases cannot be tested. Religious 'facts' are supported by evidence that is open to interpretation, or no evidence at all. Religious 'facts' are not reviewed by all religions to reach a consensus.

The underlying concept in the institution of science is that the nature of reality is unknown. The institution of science is primarily concerned with discovering the nature of reality without making assumptions. Scientific theories must, by definition, be testable (falsifiable). Theories must be published for peer review with the intention of reaching a consensus. Truth does not demand belief. Scientists do not join hands every Sunday, singing, "yes, gravity is real! I will have faith! I will be strong!

Accepted theories are supported by evidence that is not open to interpretation, or is consistently interpreted by qualified scientists. If evidence is found that contradicts a theory, the theory will be abandoned.

One believes in a scientific authority, because they derive their authority from the review process, and because they have an interest in discovering truth. One believes in a religious authority, because they have been given authority by their superiors, who in turn get their authority from their subordinates. Mutually assured re-enforcement. Religion has no interest in discovering truth because the "facts" are already known.

- Remember that you aren't the only person who has found fault with their religion. People throughout history have looked critically at their religious beliefs and found them wanting. If you have issues and problems, then look at them honestly, with the notion that you will not be punished for trying to find what you truly believe. If your beliefs are valid, then they will stand up to scrutiny. Most of the religions that have ever been, have gone extinct. You would be hard pressed to find people worshipping Thor or Quetzalcoatl. Take a hard look at why you don't believe in Thor, or Rah, or Apollo. Would you be Islamic, Christian, or Jewish if you had been brought up in Pakistan, Mississippi, or Israel?

- Consider your ethics and try to understand where they come from. You *don't* need a god/gods to be moral. Atheists/humanists are not unethical. Like many theists, many humanists donate to charity and live lives that are morally similar to those of theists. Humanists just might have different motivations for doing so.

- Understand the difference between atheism and humanism.

   An atheist does not believe that a god/gods exist. Because there is no verifiable evidence that a god/gods exist, they do not incorporate a god/gods into their decision making. Because atheism is merely the opposite of theism, atheists often prefer to be known as humanists because humanism is a complete life-stance and philosophy, independent of theism.

- You do not have to be strongly anti-religion. Most atheists/humanists, however, do disapprove of organised religion as well as the doctrine of faith as a virtue. There are others who still attend religious services (particularly Unitarian) for their own reasons, such as sympathy with some of the moral tenets, membership in a community, or even just a fondness for the music.

- You do not have to write off the *possibility* of unverified or unverifiable phenomena. You can acknowledge that they are possible without insisting or acting as if they are true, or trying to convince others that they are true. Without evidence you just leave them as open questions. Humanists are quite ready to admit that they don't know.

- You do not have to subscribe to any set of beliefs. Atheism/humanism is not a religion. Humanists hold a wide variety of beliefs and outlooks, the most obvious similarity being a lack of belief in a god or gods or other forms of superstition.

- Understand that you do not have to give up your culture. Culture, tradition, and tribal loyalty are important to many people, including humanists. By denying belief in a god/gods, one need not totally dissociate oneself from the culture associated with his or her former religion. Virtually every northern hemispheric culture celebrates a winter solstice holiday. A possible explanation for this is the lack of agrarian work to be performed and the abundance of food stores for the winter months ahead. Such a celebration can be, and is in many cases, still important to a humanist for its intrinsic values, those of sharing and community, among others. Humanists who once were Christians still exchange gifts with their theist friends, put up Christmas trees, and gather with family and friends during Christmas time, without any religious connotation necessary. The same can be said of those formerly of other faiths.

- Learn to see and come to conclusions about the world through a logical lens, rather than through faith. The scientific method is universally accepted as the best way to understand the world.

- Discuss the world in this context with other humanists and with the religious. This will help you understand why people believe what they do and help you understand your humanism/atheism in that context.

- Study various forms of theism. While most humanists argue that theists are making a positive assertion (and thus bear the burden of proof), it is important thoroughly to understand your former faith and its tenets as well as those of other faiths. The more clued up you are on other religions and the more you understand why people believe what they do, the better basis you'll have for your world-view. Also, it will help you fend off those that will try to convert you to their religion, once they learn of your atheism/humanism.

- Communicate your outlook to those who are curious. Do not be shy, but don't be condescending. Try to help them understand your point of view in a non-confrontational manner. However, you may choose to hide your perspective if it is clear you are going to run into trouble. In some countries or regions, the price of atheism/humanism can still be very high.

CULTS

"A cult is a religion with no political power".

Tom Wolfe

A cult can be described as a mainstream religion in its infancy. Many ingredients are the same, the main thing lacking is the large number of followers which afford the main religions legitimacy. Given enough time many of today's cults could become future fully fledged religions. I am including a look at the cult phenomenon because it seems obvious to me that the techniques used by cult leaders and the mind-sets displayed by cult members have a good deal in common with the processes involved in the conduct of normalised religions. Mainstream religions often look upon cults as dangerous aberrations, overlooking the fact that their own history would show a very similar development.

Let me quote the pagan philosopher Celsus, writing in CE 175 about an incipient local cult: '*We see, indeed, in private houses workers in wool and leather, and fullers, and persons of the most uninstructed and rustic character,* (he is talking about Christians here!*) not venturing to utter a word in the presence of their elders and wiser masters; but when they get hold of the* *children privately, and certain women as ignorant as themselves, they pour forth wonderful statements, to the effect that they ought not to give heed to their father and to their teachers, but should obey them; that the former are foolish and stupid, and neither know nor can perform anything that is really good, being preoccupied with empty trifles; that they alone know how men ought to live, and that, if the children obey them, they will both be happy themselves, and will make their home happy also. And while thus speaking, if they see one of the instructors of youth approaching, or one of the more intelligent class, or even the father himself, the more timid among them become afraid, while the more forward incite the children to throw off the yoke, whispering that in the presence of father and teachers they neither will nor can explain to them any good thing, seeing they turn away with aversion from the silliness and stupidity of such persons as being altogether corrupt, and far advanced in wickedness, and such as would inflict punishment upon them; but that if they wish (to avail themselves of their aid,) they must leave their father and their instructors, and go with the women and their playfellows to the women's apartments, or to the leather shop, or to the fuller's shop, that they may attain to perfection;—and by words like these they gain them over."*

The tactics described here of how to indoctrinate children are a clear anticipation of the techniques advocated by the Jesuits in later centuries.

Established religions are keen to label rival systems cults. This enables them to unload the undesirable aspects of bullying and mind control, associated with their own conventional religion onto deviant smaller groups. This fails to take into account that child abuse, sexual abuse, financial extortion and warfare have also been committed by believers of mainstream religions, but the pejorative 'cult' stereotype makes it easier to avoid confronting this uncomfortable fact.

Scholars have estimated that new religious movements, of which some but not all have been labelled as 'cults', number in the thousands world-wide. Most originated in Asia or Africa. The great majority have only a few members, some have thousands, and only very few have more than a million. In Britain the Crown Prosecution Service has ruled that the word 'cult' is not "threatening, abusive or insulting" as defined by the Public Order Act and that there is no objection to its use in public protests.

In the United States religious activities of cults, no matter how weird, are protected under the First Amendment. No other country has as diverse religious groups as the U.S., which has at least 52 major denominations with memberships exceeding 100,000. The Yearbook of American and Canadian Churches lists 223 sects, cults, and denominations, not counting groups such as the First Church of Christ, Scientist, which provide no membership statistics.

The main starting point for all cults and religions is the availability of a charismatic leader. Such a figurehead has the mesmeric ability to get people to follow him unquestioningly. Cult members tend to be devoted to the leader, not necessarily to the leader's ideas. The leader, who invariably is male, has complete control over his followers, there is no questioning his decisions and he is accountable to no one within the group. Most religious cults demand absolute devotion to this single person who is considered to be God or connected to God, the Messiah, a prophet or possessing some other holy status. This is a critical component in maintaining absolute devotion. To the members of a cult, only this person can lead them to salvation. With this exalted status almost invariably come the predictable abuses. In virtually all cults the founder or the leader takes advantage of his position through sexual access to women or minors and if that is not his bag, through financial extortion. How does a person fall into a role like this? One common scenario is the preacher or church member who is expelled from a mainstream church for preaching extreme or unconventional ideas or showing signs of corruption or instability. When he leaves, his followers go with him, or else he joins an already existing cult and eventually gains control. David Koresh, leader of the 'Branch Davidian' cult that was destroyed during a U.S. government siege in 1993, was active in a mainstream Christian church before he was thrown out for "negatively influencing" some of the church's younger members. Reverend Jim Jones, who ordered hundreds of members of 'The People's Temple' to drink poisoned punch in Jonestown, Guyana, in 1978, was an ordained mainstream Christian minister.

But not everybody starts out in mainstream religion. Some cult leaders are simply anti-social, destructive individuals who find out they have a knack for manipulation. Charles Manson fits this description. Manson referred to himself as the re-incarnation of Jesus. He grew his hair accordingly. His followers called him "God" and "Satan" seemingly interchangeably. Manson and the members of his cult brutally slaughtered people, committing what is probably the most famous cult mass murder — the shooting and stabbing of seven people over two days, including actress Sharon Tate (wife of film director Roman Polanski), who was eight months pregnant. Manson, now aged 79 is still in prison, apparently receiving tens of thousands of letters every year from people hoping to become members of The Manson Family.

CULT RECRUITMENT

It is easy to assume that cult recruits must be obviously troubled young persons, maybe mentally ill, readily exploited by unethical cultists. But studies show that people who join cults have only a slightly higher incidence of psychiatric disorders than the general population. Cult members come from all walks of life, all age groups and all personality types. A friend of mine with a doctorate in sociology and a mother of a young daughter, became totally infatuated with Bhagwan Shree Rajneesh (yes, the one of the 90 Rolls Royces!) and ended up in his commune in Oregon. However, one common thread among most cult recruits is heightened stress: Research indicates that a majority of people who end up joining a cult were recruited during a particularly stressful period. This could be the stress associated with adolescence, leaving home for the first time, a bad break-up, losing a job or the death of a loved one. People undergoing significant stress can be more susceptible when a person or group claims to have the answer to all of their problems. Dr. Michael Langone, a psychologist who specialises in cults, has identified some psychological traits that can make a person more likely to be successfully recruited, including:

- dependency - an intense desire to belong, stemming from a lack of self-confidence
- unassertiveness - a reluctance to say no or question authority
- gullibility - a tendency to believe what someone says without really thinking about it
- low tolerance for uncertainty - a need to have any question answered immediately in black-and-white terms
- desire for spiritual meaning - a need to believe that life has a 'higher purpose'

It will readily be noticed that all this agrees perfectly with conditions conducive to the adoption of a religious faith.

Toys for Adults

*"If we expect God to subscribe to one religion at
the exclusion of all others then we should expect
damnation as a matter of chance.
This should give Christians pause when
expounding their religious beliefs".*

Sam Harris

As we all know there are hundreds of religions and
often it is difficult to know precisely what they all
stand for. One method is to portray their tenets
facetiously as toys:

Catholicism: He who assembles the most toys wins
Calvinism: He who denies himself the most toys wins
Hare Krishna: He who plays with the most toys wins
Anglican: They were our toys first
Greek Orthodox: No, they were OURS first
Branch Davidians: He who dies playing with the biggest
   toys, wins
Atheism: There is no toy maker
Polytheism: There are many toy makers
Evolutionism: The toys made themselves
Church of Christ, Scientist: We are the toys

Communism: Everyone gets the same number of toys and don't you try selling yours

Bahai: All toys are just fine with us.

Amish: Toys with batteries are a sin

Taoism: The doll is as important as the dumptruck

Mormonism: Every boy can have as many toys as he wants.

Voodoo: Let me borrow that doll for a second

Quakers: Let's not fight over toys

Hedonism: Let's play mummies and daddies

Hinduism: He who plays with bags of plastic farm animals loses.

Seventh Day Adventist: He who plays with his toys on Saturday loses

Church of Christ: He whose toys make music loses

Baptist: Once played, always played

Jehovah's Witness: He who sells the most toys door-to-door wins

Buddhism: The desire for toys is the cause of all suffering in the world

Pentecostalism: He whose toys can talk, wins

Existentialism: Toys are a figment of your imagination

Confucianism: Once a toy is dipped in the water, it is no longer dry

Pantheism: There are toys within toys

Non-denominationalism: We don't care where the toys came from, let's just play with them

Agnosticism: It is not possible to know whether toys make a bit of difference

Humanism: We don't need toys to enjoy ourselves.

JEHOVAH'S WITNESSES

*"What do you get when you cross a
Jehovah's witness with an Atheist?
Someone who goes from door to door
for no apparent purpose".*

Comedian Julie Barr

Apart from Catholicism which I know about only too well, I have little experience of any of the other religions but as everybody knows there is one sect that makes it difficult for anybody to stay completely clear of. Enter the dreaded door-knock from our friendly Watchtower wannabees:

I well remember my first encounter with Jehovah Witnesses in England. It was in the early seventies when they still made predictions about the world's imminent demise. (It's true they no longer do. They have finally learned a lesson!) I was in my garden pruning trees. The Witnesses made it quite clear that I was wasting my time because the end was nigh. My reply was that they should come back next year, having been proved wrong yet again, to do a spot of weeding as punishment for their scaremongering. The next spring I vainly waited for my green-fingered assistants. On another occasion, in an attempt to ward them off, I spoke Dutch to them. But they had come prepared! In quick succession they held up a set of foreign language leaflets for me to scan, until Bingo! there it was, Gobbledegook in Double-Dutch, a very heady brew. I had to concede defeat and invite them in. That is what I have done ever since. A bit of a masochist you might think. Well, yes, but I can't resist a good argument, even though I know there is no chance of winning. It is difficult to reason people out of what they were never reasoned into. What's more, they are almost invariably polite and modest people. They take their shoes off to protect the carpet. Or do they think an atheist's home is his temple? I offer them a cup of tea. They are surprised. It is the nearest they can come to disbelief. So much kindness; where elsewhere so often foul abuse. A potential convert perhaps?

First some pleasantries; a few kind remarks about the house and unkind ones about the weather. All very human this, we are not so different after all. I ask after G, one of their brethren who used to call but does no longer. Have I turned the tables on them and made a conversion?! Too much to hope for; G. is on another planet. Freudian slip-up there; G. is on another route. Still spreading the good word badly. I once lent him a copy of Carl Lofmark's 'What is the Bible'. It lists many of the yawning contradictions in that book. This prompted him into writing lengthy tracts of tortuous rebuttal. It made me feel quite guilty. I tried to be fair and plough through them but my brain kept jumping out of gear. It takes a special talent to tackle obfuscation. Next time I will call in Rowan Williams, now that he is retired. He could talk their kind of language, but with a posher accent.

The last time G. came he had a deaf friend with him who was being instructed in the faith by wild gesticulation. Well, you try and explain the immaculate conception in sign language. Now down to business with my new-found friends. I always nip the biblical openers in the bud. I have learned that you can cite a hundred references to show that the biblical God is a bloodthirsty tyrant, but if they can dig up two or three verses that say "God is love," they will claim that you are taking things out of context. Debunking the Bible is like taking candy from a baby but there is little point in discussing the intricacies of a raft of fables, allegories and ancient mythology. One might as well dissect Grimm's fairy tales. For me the crunch question is: how do they know it is God's word?

I introduce a cheeky analogy: if I'd come back from a weekend in the Lake District and announced that whilst feeling ecstatic on a mountain top I had heard God's voice and I had noted down outpourings of mystical revelations, which on Monday morning I would regale them with in their Kingdom Hall, would they believe me or call the men in white coats? Alas, it is the men in white coats for me, nice try. David Icke and I, we just haven't got what it takes these days. But why, oh why dismiss me quite so readily! At least I exist in the here and now, not thousands of years ago. And I speak their language. Well sort of, anyhow. And I have some witnesses who saw me in the Lake District. What was it about Moses, Jesus, St. Paul, Mohammed, Joseph Smith and all the other prophets that made them so credible. Better marketing I expect. Perhaps I should enlist the Saatchis.

Or is it that these mystics were successful because they operated in a darker age when science was low and superstition high? So I can't budge the Bible. I dig deep into my Godless arsenal. If everything must have a cause, as they tell me, and this cause is God, who caused God? They don't see my point, they repeat that God has always been. I try again: If God is all good, all powerful and all knowing, how come evil? And if free will is the answer, is man mightier than God? In any case man can't be blamed for earthquakes. The answers are so convoluted I couldn't repeat them here to save my life. I bowl the billions of planets googly. Why this insignificant little speck in preference to any other, or has Christ been crucified all over the universe? His wrists must resemble pin cushions by now. They take such blasphemies with admirable equanimity. No offence taken, at least not shown. Islam could learn a lesson here. Next I am given Paley's watchmaker argument. They think they have got me stumped. I remark that Dawkins has reset that watch to modern time. Alas, Dawkins is not a name they have come across.

The male witness points at the beauty of a flowering plant on our coffee table. Only a creator could have fashioned such a delicate design. This is a fiendish atheist trap. Poor waterers that we are, we switched to silk some while ago. Made in China I expect. I reveal this blow with just a hint of glee. He turns a little crimson and his female companion, who had seen this one coming, manages a wry smile. Otherwise she hardly speaks. Women know their place within religion. It is mostly to please men and rear children. The Witnesses follow this trend. Only men can become elders of the church. In *Let God be True*, their major tract, it says: "woman is merely a lowly creature whom God created for man as a helper".

When all my arguments have fallen on stony ground and have been met by some incongruous biblical quotation, to their entire satisfaction and my entire bafflement, I ask how they have come to their faith.

Almost invariably these people have had a tough time of it. Poverty, bereavement, unemployment, broken relationships and lots of illness. Knocked about they seemed, afloat in a sea of uncertainty. A life raft was sorely needed and their faith provided it. So I shouldn't argue. Mustn't rock their boat. It is just that I feel that their problems could be much better met in human terms. In practice that is what happens anyway. When poor or unemployed they don't await manna from heaven but sign up for social security, provided not by their caring Saviour but by you and me and other fellow humans.

By coincidence there was a Channel 4 TV documentary on the Witnesses the next day. Once again earthly business featured strongly. It is not just Jesus and the Bible who get all the best parts in Kingdom Hall. There was a good deal of very human canoodling and hanky panky going on between the brethren and sisters. Dateline eat your heart out. The elders were keeping a weather eye lest jollity would get out of hand. No old testament begetting before the wedding day. The suitor of a very comely fitness teacher was sleeping in his car outside her flat and was served his breakfast there. The Witness version of meals on wheels. This heroic self denial is not likely to do them much good.

According to an article in the British Journal of Psychiatry, Witnesses are three times more likely to be diagnosed as suffering from schizophrenia and four times more likely to be paranoid schizophrenics. As a writer in the American journal *Free Inquiry* puts it: "Either the Jehovah's Witness sect tends to attract an excess of pre-psychotic individuals who may then break down, or else being a Jehovah's Witness is itself a stress that may precipitate psychosis. Possibly both of these factors operate together". This has got me quite concerned for my Witness friends. I must convert them before it is too late. I 'd better whip round to their houses quickly and put my foot firmly in the door.

Encounters with people of such simple faith make me feel sorry for their wasted lives. It cannot be true that they do enjoy going round knocking on people's doors only to be repelled by indifference and probably some abuse. That's when I am tempted to tell them to stop this arduous task and put up their feet at home. Go for a walk in the lovely countryside. Pursue a favourite hobby. But I must balance my concern for their well-being with theirs for mine. They might concede that I am having a better time of it in the here and now but they will come up trumps in the much longer spell of eternity.

SPIRITUALISM

> *"Seances occur only in darkened rooms,*
> *where the ghostly visitors can be seen dimly at best.*
> *If we turn up the lights a little, so we have a chance to*
> *see what's going on, the spirits vanish."*
>
> Carl Sagan

Nothing baffles and disturbs people more than the thought of death. It bothers me too. Increasingly so as I grow older. It is a disconcerting and unreal thought that in a few years time our house will still be standing here and indifferently look down on my ashes sprinkled on the garden. After a long life the habit of living is so engrained that the thought of one's death becomes almost surreal. So little wonder then that the idea of an afterlife and the possibility of communicating with it is such an attractive notion. Spiritualism feeds on it with relish.

The movement came about almost by accident when in 1848 two girls, Katherine and Margaret Fox in a town called Hydesville, New York State, found that they could terrify their easily frightened mother by creating noises which they did by cracking their knuckles and joints, especially their toes. (I am struggling to resist a pun about a 'crackpot' religion here). Mrs. Fox could not explain the weird sounds and decided they were the works of spirits. She invited neighbours in to witness the manifestations and be in touch with the spiritual world. In her confession forty years later Margaret said that when so many people came we had no option but to keep up the performance. At first they merely rapped when asked to do so. Later they would spell out messages by responding to recited letters from the alphabet.

Their older sister Leah became their agent, organising exhibitions and charging substantial sums per night. Their fame spread rapidly, at first all over America and then to Europe, where Margaret conducted a séance for Queen Victoria and Kate performed in Russia for the Tsar. After that Spiritualism grew with amazing speed. A couple of years later there were hundreds of mediums and by 1858 it was claimed there were eight million believers. The phenomena became more diverse. Table turning sessions were very common, soon followed by levitations of trumpets through which the spirits spoke. Musical instruments played mysteriously and there were full size manifestations of the dead. All these happenings took place in the dark.

In 1888 Margaret Fox made a full confession of her trickery but to no avail. Things carried on as before. As is nearly always the case with the paranormal, once the superstitious genie is out of the bottle, no amount of evidence can put it back. Crop circle devotees continue to believe even though the hoaxers have confessed in public. The Turin shroud was exposed through carbon dating by three different laboratories to be a medieval fake but still the Jesus burial shroud myth continues unabated.

G.K. Chesterton, in 1906, explained how this works: *"No conceivable number of false mediums affects the probability of the existence of real mediums one way or the other. This is surely obvious enough. No conceivable number of forged bank-notes can disprove the existence of the Bank of England."*

During the 1920s, professional magician Harry Houdini, the James Randi of his day, undertook a well-publicised campaign to expose fraudulent mediums. He was adamant that "Up to the present time everything that I have investigated has been the result of deluded brains." In more recent times the movement has adopted a more formal organisation, patterned after Christian denominations, with established liturgies and a set of Seven Principles as well as training requirements for mediums. In the United States the Spiritualist churches are primarily affiliated either with the National Spiritualist Association of Churches or the loosely allied group of denominations known as the spiritual church movement; in the U.K. the predominant organisation is the Spiritualists' National Union, founded in 1890. It is said to be the eighth largest religion in Britain and has a network of groups across the country. The total of SNU-affiliated and associated churches/centres in the UK is 360, broken down into 348 affiliated bodies and 12 associated bodies.

Spiritualists believe in communicating with the spirits of the dead. They believe that spirit mediums are humans gifted to do this, often through seances. Anyone may become a medium through study and practice. They believe that spirits are capable of growth and perfection, progressing through higher spheres or planes. The afterlife is not a static place, but one in which spirits evolve. The two beliefs—that contact with spirits is possible, and that spirits may lie on a higher plane—lead to a third belief, that spirits can provide knowledge about moral and ethical issues, as well as about God and the afterlife. Thus many members speak of spirit guides—specific spirits, often contacted, relied upon for worldly and spiritual guidance. Anyone may receive spirit messages, but formal communication sessions are held by mediums, who can then provide information about the afterlife.

The practice of organised Spiritualism today resembles that of any other religion, having discarded most showmanship, particularly those elements that resemble wizardry. Such activities would only be too readily detectable by present day highly sophisticated technology. There is thus a much greater emphasis on 'mental mediumship' and an almost complete avoidance of the apparently miraculous 'materialising mediumship' that so fascinated early believers such as Arthur Conan Doyle.

THE PARANORMAL

> *"In childhood our credulity serves us well. It helps us to pack with extra-ordinary rapidity our skulls full of wisdom of our parents and our ancestors. But if we don't grow out of it in the fullness of time our nature makes us a sitting target for astrologers, mediums, gurus, evangelists and quacks. We need to replace the automatic credulity of childhood with the constructive scepticism of adult science"'*
> Richard Dawkins

I am not a one-trick Tony. As a thorough-going sceptic I am not just sceptical about religion but pretty well about all other notions and phenomena that are lacking evidence. After all, like religion, these have all come about as a result of thousands of years of misinterpreting natural phenomena, undiluted superstition and story-telling, poured out over this poor confused little planet by its primitive, speculating human contingent. For it does appear that, like hope, superstition springs eternal in the human breast. Although the often poisonous aspects of religion are my first concern I will now pay some attention to other forms of superstition which make humanists shake their heads in disbelief. I will allow that, although they are silly, they tend to be much less harmful than superstition's top dog: religion.

Ever since humans learned to think without understanding there has been room for fanciful notions to flourish. Such notions are fuelled by a desperate need to know the answers. Curiosity and investigation are fine, that is what science is all about, but what religion and superstition are inclined to do is to jump to conclusions before the evidence is in. Occam's razor puts a stop to this. When presented with a baffling phenomenon the first thing to do is to look for a commonplace solution because that would be the most likely one. It's known as the parsimony principle. Don't unnecessarily introduce complications. If that doesn't work keep on searching until the answer is found, if necessary with the aid of others who are better equipped to solve the problem. If no answer can be found don't make up a convoluted one. Don't pick any odd scenario, call it the truth and then go telling everybody else. Before you know you have started a religion. Perhaps you should have been a priest. Mark Twain said: you can never find a believer who has acquired this valuable and saving knowledge by any process but the everlasting and all sufficient "people say".

While working on this book an ant walked delicately across my Kindle text and highlighted the word 'delicate'. Quite a coincidence and a superstitious person might well have attributed some special significance to it. A subliminal message of some kind or other. Possibly 'be more delicate in socking it to the religious'. It would make sense and I am beginning to feel guilty already. But the sensible conclusion to draw in all such cases is that blind chance has been at work.

People's need to believe in something or other can be catered for in many different ways – by mainstream religion, cults, spiritualism, reincarnation, UFO's, crop circles, Loch Ness monsters, ghosts and many other goodies from the superstition larder. The paranormal does seem to be all around us. Hypnotists are given shows on TV. Papers print weekly horoscopes. Many television programmes highlight paranormal events and usually leave out evidence which might suggest an ordinary explanation. There are stories about citizens being abducted by little green men from outer space, oddly for the sole purpose of anal probes. There lurks a Freudian insight there. Articles about hauntings and clairvoyants abound. The Big Ben clock stops, the psychic Uri Geller says that he controlled it by willpower and papers report this as if it were a fact. Experts, including scientists, earnestly discuss whether crop circles might be caused by vortexes or magnetic fields, completely overlooking the obvious man-made mischief, employing a garden roller and a stomping board.

Every bookshop now sports a 'New Age' section, where unscrupulous publishers, out to make a cheap buck, are pandering to the credulous and simple-minded, thus sabotaging the intellectual and educational standards of society and grooming a generation of gullible dupes. The British illusionist Ian Rowland and the famous American magicians James Randi and Penn Jillette have all categorically stated that they have never come across a supposedly paranormal feat that can be repeated under exacting test conditions. Randi has made available a million dollar award for anybody successfully taking up the challenge but so far there have been no takers.

Astrology

*"I don't believe in astrology; I'm a Sagittarius
and we're sceptical".*

Arthur C. Clarke

A hardy perennial among the paranormal and ever popular, is astrology. Human beings have always looked in awe at the magnificent heavens. They have worshipped the sun as the source of all light and life and the moon as the heavenly body of the night. The breathtaking spectacle of the stars and the galaxies has always fascinated human imagination, particularly when humans had to live outside at night time under the starry heavens, wondering what the celestial scene might portend about their origin and destiny. The early religions venerated the heavenly bodies and they were convinced that these extra-terrestrial entities were ultimately related to us on earth, our needs and aspirations, our yearnings and despair and that they offered providential signs and omens as well. These ancient beliefs and sentiments have survived to our present time and have given 'astrologers' scope to exploit them to their advantage. Few people can resist the intrigue of their personal horoscope. You never know there may be something in it. A lot of money for a start, but not necessarily for you.

Horoscope writers are the masters of being all things to all men. In their hands fuzzy abstraction has been perfected to a form of art. They even give theologians a run for their money and easily outscore politicians. The technique is readily exposed by a test. Ask astrologers to draw up personalised horoscopes for two people, secretly swap them round and as like as not, the recipients will still claim an excellent match. This has often been demonstrated and even on a larger scale. A French astrology researcher, Michael Gauquelin, once handed one hundred people a horoscope supposedly their own. In fact they were all given an identical one, written for an infamous mass murderer. The result was that 95 per cent of the sample was quite happy with the description and identified with it. A murderous lot these French!

Why do horoscopes always seem such a good match? They take advantage of the fact that many judgements about our own character are largely subjective. Nobody sees his or her personality in terms of simply black or white. Sometimes we are kind sometimes we are not; one minute we may feel secure the next minute we are lacking confidence. And so on through the whole range of our character make-up. Moreover, horoscopes are careful to avoid specifics and the generalities, if couched in sufficiently vague terms, are bound to have some relevance. For example: "you have a lot of unexpressed creativity." Everyone wants to believe that's true of them and not of everybody else. Or sometimes there are double-headers like, "sometimes you enjoy being the centre of the party and sometimes you like staying at home with a book." Which is another easy hit. Then there is the tendency for people to skip the parts that are less applicable and to focus on what appears the most apposite.

All this makes a mockery of some people's insistence on making important decisions in life, such as a choice of partner, solely based on the compatibility of signs. I don't know whether any studies have been done to measure the incidence of failed marriages that were based on horoscopic harmony, but I promise to eat my hat if any clear trends are found one way or the other. A much better chance of finding a suitable match these days would be to ignore the horoscopes and subscribe to a partner search on the internet. That way it is possible to fine tune the characteristics you are looking for. Compatibility in life choices and philosophy are too important to be left to chance. In this context I have often wondered how people manage to bridge diametrically opposed views on religion. Managing to live in harmony despite this massive chasm must take endless tolerance. A heavy price to pay for believing that positions and motions of stars and planets can affect the lives of people on earth.

Astrology may be seen as harmless fun but the fun soon disappears when powerful people get their hands on it. In his book 'For the Record,' former White House Aide, Donald Regan, disclosed what he insisted was the most closely guarded domestic secret of the Reagan White House years: "Virtually every major move and decision the Reagans made during my time as White House Chief of Staff was cleared in advance with a woman in San Francisco who drew up horoscopes to make certain that the planets were in a favourable alignment for the enterprise". Apparently such enterprises included Reagan's decision whether to stand for a second term and whether or when to bomb Lybia.

It is clear that as long as people remain pre-occupied with their destiny and as long as other people recognise the potential earning power in pretending to supply the answers – this particular farce will run and run.

UFO's and Crop Circles

"I am sure the universe is full of intelligent life; it's just been too intelligent to come here".

Arthur C. Clarke

UFO sightings remain ever popular. People seem capable of believing that somehow space vehicles sent from alien civilisations have come from many light years distant just to appear as some indistinct moving object in the far distance. It doesn't occur to believers that such far off sightings (and this also applies to the Loch Ness monster) must be close to another observer nearer to the source. So some people must get a much clearer view, which unfortunately they keep quiet about. Why should aliens come all this way and never manage a proper witnessed landing.

Don't get me wrong. Amongst the billions of stars and planets in the universe there are likely to be others with intelligent life, similar or more advanced than our own. If life was capable of igniting on this earth it is inconceivable that the process was not replicated elsewhere. One in a trillion uniqueness is very unlikely but for such life to come and find us here is quite another matter. The distances are just too immense. Our nearest star other than the sun is Proxima Centauri, 4.24 light years away. Beyond that space travel becomes even more impossible. The universe is mostly empty space. If you were randomly inserted into the cosmos, the chance of you finding yourself on or near a planet would be less than one in a billion trillion trillion. No, despite my spell-checker's urging I haven't typed trillion twice by mistake. That is the unimaginably large number that the little green men are up against. Nevertheless it would be marvellous if we could detect other forms of life and maybe one day we will succeed. But space ships coming to our shores, sadly must remain a fascinating pipe dream.

Crop circles are a UFO related phenomenon. They were first reported in the late 1970s when circles began appearing throughout the English countryside. These spectacles rapidly multiplied and became widely known in the late 1980s, after the media started to report crop circles in Hampshire and Wiltshire. UFO fans immediately concluded that space aliens were communicating with earth in this fashion and as time went by the patterns evolved from simple circles into Mandelbrot figures and comical shapes, including bicycles and V-signs as if extra-terrestrial schoolboys were competing in an intergalactic graffiti competition.

In 1991, self-professed pranksters Doug Bower and Dave Chorley made headlines claiming it was they who started the phenomenon in 1978 with the use of simple tools consisting of a plank of wood, rope, and a baseball cap fitted with a loop of wire to help them walk in a straight line. To prove their case they made a circle in front of journalists; a crop circle 'expert', Pat Delgado, was called in to examine the circle and declared it authentic before it was revealed that it was a hoax. Inspired by Australian crop circle accounts from 1966, Doug and Dave claimed to be responsible for all circles made prior to 1987. Following their confession circles started appearing all over the world. To date, approximately 10,000 such circles have been reported internationally. Sceptics note a correlation between crop circles, recent media coverage, and the absence of fencing and/ or anti-trespassing legislation.

A researcher found that crop circles in the UK are not spread randomly across the landscape. They tend to appear near roads, areas of medium to dense population, and cultural heritage monuments, such as Stonehenge or Avebury. They always appear in areas that are easy to access. The scientific consensus on crop circles is that all of them are constructed by human beings as a prank. But 'cereologists' (yes, this is the croppies' official title!), the theists' equivalent of the crop circle business, discount on-site evidence of human involvement as attempts to discredit the phenomena. Some cereologists even allege a conspiracy theory, with governments planting evidence of hoaxing to muddle the origins of the circles. Like theists, paranormalists will fight like Kilkenny cats when their pet theories are under scrutiny.

When science writer Matt Ridley wrote sceptical articles in newspapers, he was accused of spreading 'government disinformation' and of working for the UK military intelligence service MI5. It just goes to show that once a superstitious notion is afoot there is no stopping it. My own conclusion is that crop circle enthusiasts are doomed to remain forever clutching at neatly trampled straws.

Extra Sensory Perception

People have always believed that the mind is capable of a number of mysterious abilities for which there is no evidence. The best known one of these is ESP, also known as telepathy. Another one is clairvoyance and there is also PK or psychokinesis, the alleged ability to move or control objects by the power of the mind alone. A friend of mine believes in telepathy because he and his wife regularly hit upon the same topics at the same time. They have known each other for many years and he does concede the point that ESP is only likely to occur between people with a long standing, close acquaintance. What he doesn't realise is that this assertion counts against ESP rather than in its favour. There would be a much stronger case if ESP could be demonstrated to exist between total strangers.

If you think about it there is nothing particularly unusual about frequently overlapping thought patterns between people who live in close proximity, share a lot of interests, read the same newspapers, watch the same TV programmes, know the same people and have a good deal of experiences and memories in common. After many years people do not just grow to look like their dogs they also become an extension to their partners thought processes. The one advantage that ESP has over other unsubstantiated beliefs, such as astrology and re-incarnation, is that it can be tested scientifically in a laboratory. In theory at least. The trouble is that the history of research into ESP is littered with poorly conducted or dubious experiments, carried out by people with an axe to grind, so that even now a clear-cut verdict remains elusive.

We can forget of course about stage magicians, such as Derren Brown, using tricks to guess right every time. For centuries gullible people, often distinguished scientists, have been convinced by charlatans who claim to possess telepathic powers. Strange isn't it, how people readily shrug off magic stunts at a children's party and then acquire a mystical fascination when it is claimed that paranormal powers are involved. When we are shown demonstrations that are not meant to be magician's tricks but the real thing, success hinges simply on somebody's say-so.

For example I once saw a demonstration on TV where Uri Geller in a London studio managed to accurately reproduce a star-shaped figure beamed to him telepathically by a woman assistant standing near the Eiffel tower in Paris. This feat rested solely on her verbal assurance to show host David Frost that she was not in collusion with Geller! As we know people fib all the time; even on oath in court. And probably very readily when their palms are crossed with silver. Of course David Frost was not going to spoil the fun by unexpectedly asking the assistant to transmit something unprepared.

Some para-psychologists have claimed success with what are called 'ganzfeld' experiments which became popular in the mid 1970s. The word is German for 'whole field' and the theory is that by blanking out someone's ability to hear and see, you create conditions conducive to ESP. Wearing headphones and blindfolded the 'recipients' concentrate on receiving one of four pictures which a 'transmitter' in another room is trying to describe telepathically. Afterwards the recipient has to select the picture that has been concentrated on. Quite a few ganzfeld experiments did achieve better than chance results but then Ray Hyman, an American research psychologist of the highest standing, examined the results with great care and found serious flaws. These might not have mattered if the results had been truly impressive - if even one person had been found who could get, say half the pictures right rather than a tiny fraction over the average of twenty five per cent. But the variations from chance were so minute that they could easily be accounted for by error.

Dr. Susan Blackmore, a well-known British psychologist, used to believe in ESP during her time as an undergraduate at Oxford. She then set about ten years of experiments, none of which produced any positive results. Parapsychologists told her that this was because she was not a believer; only believers got results (this is true, but the believers don't draw the obvious lesson, which is that their belief is likely to skew the figures in their favour). When she pointed out that she had been a believer; they replied with splendid circularity that really she could not have been or else she would have avoided getting her negative results. Susan Blackmore describes one of the stages in her transformation to a more sceptical attitude on 'psychic' phenomena:

"A mother and daughter from Scotland claimed that they could pick up images from each other's minds. They chose to use playing cards for the tests because that is what they used at home. I let them choose the room in which they would be tested and insured that there was no normal way for the 'receiver' to see the cards. They failed. They could not get more right than chance predicted and they were terribly disappointed. They had honestly believed that they could do it and I began to see how easy it was to be fooled by your own desire to believe".

It is clear that there is so little evidence that the existence of ESP, even amongst scientists, has become a mere matter of faith. But ESP either exists or it doesn't, there is no halfway house. After all the WiFi signals to my ipad and computer work with 99per cent precision, even without the benefit of a lifelong close relationship with the transmitter! Until telepathic signals are getting through loud and clear we must conclude that ESP along with spiritualism, psychic reading and clairvoyance, belongs to the realm of mythology.

GHOSTS

"If there is a ghost in the machine it won't run on reason".

T.A.

The belief in ghosts, like most things in superstition, is closely linked to a belief in the afterlife and spirituality. For a lot of people it is hard to believe that dead is dead and there is no wriggle room. People, prone to ghost belief, report physical changes in haunted places, especially a feeling of a presence accompanied by temperature drop and hearing unaccountable sounds. They are not necessarily imagining things. Most hauntings occur in old buildings, which tend to be draughty. Scientists who have investigated haunted locations account for both the temperature changes and the sounds by finding physical sources of the draughts, such as empty spaces behind walls or currents set in motion by low frequency sound waves, produced by such mundane objects as extraction fans. Some think that electromagnetic fields are inducing the haunting experience. There are plenty of paranormal investigators that spend their spare time investigating allegedly spooky places. They arrive with torchlights, tape recorders, EMF detectors, video cameras with night vision, metal detectors, and other devices that were not designed to detect ghosts and therefore have no instructions on how to use them for that purpose. The equipment looks scientific, but of course there is nothing to be scientific about. They are as likely to detect a ghost with a Sony camcorder as you are to get the truth out of a house plant by hooking it up to a lie detector.

As a sceptic, all I can say with confidence is that when you look at the requirements for a ghost account to be true, the most reasonable position is that there is a naturalistic explanation for all these stories, but we often do not or cannot have all the details necessary to provide that explanation. We must rely on evidence, which is always incomplete and selective, and which is often passed on by interested, inexperienced, superstitious parties, who are impractical and ignorant of basic physical laws. Thus, there will always be tales like the Bell Witch story that attract much attention, especially when made into movies, that will lead many people to think that maybe there is something to *this one*, even if all the other ghost stories are false. (The 'Bell Witch' is alleged to be a sinister entity that tormented a family on Tennessee's frontier between the years of 1817 and 1821). The likelihood that we don't have all the evidence in this case is proportionate to the number of years that have passed since the events allegedly took place.

During a BBC radio Leeds discussion on the topic, I was asked to comment on a story where a distraught woman had felt compelled to sell the family home because it was haunted by ghosts. She was totally convinced even though her husband had never noticed anything. I predicted three things: she would experience further hauntings in their new house; her husband would remain unaffected and the new occupants of their old house would be ghost free. I also added that perhaps she should consult a doctor. The presenter thought that was a little harsh. But what else is there to say. During the same debate the author of a new book on Poltergeists asked me to prove that the events he had described could not be genuine. That was the same old trick so beloved of God believers, asking atheists to prove his non-existence. The answer to this ploy must be, as always, that atheists or sceptics have got nothing to prove. The onus of proof rests with the people making claims.

FAITH HEALING

> *"Take these evangelists away from their silk suits,*
> *well-coiffed hair and fancy limousines and put them*
> *in animal skins with a few rattles and beads.*
> *You've got a Cro-Magnon shaman, complete*
> *and ready to go to work".*
>
> David Alexander

Claims that prayer, divine intervention, or the ministrations of an individual healer can cure illness have been popular throughout history. 'Miraculous recoveries' have been attributed to many techniques commonly lumped together as 'faith healing'. It can involve prayer, a visit to a religious shrine, or simply a strong belief in a supreme being. Since our good health is our most precious asset, seeking a cure for mental and physical afflictions is the reason why people have always been driven towards those that claim to be possessed of healing powers. Priests of all descriptions and laymen too, have never hesitated to take advantage of this aspiration. It's a fairly simple thing to do. Nature is the greatest healer. Wait long enough and most minor ailments will gradually fade away. A visit to a healer early in that process may speed up the result due to a feeling of elation and a psychosomatic benefit. Then the patient will believe that the healer effected the cure and nature is left to sulk. But subsequently the trouble is apt to reassert itself and nature will get a second chance. Sometimes a doctor is needed.

One thing stands out in all this more than anything else, and this point has cropped up elsewhere in this book when discussing miracles, that there never has been, nor ever will be, a knock-out cure. A real 'put this in your pipe and smoke it sceptics' humdinger of a cure, where there is no further room for quibbling. Case closed. Where a limb grows back there and then on camera, clear for all to see. Or where a lost eye is restored or a bald head instantly regains hair. No trickery, no special effects. And please leave Wayne Rooney out of it. That kind of miracle costs money.

There are of course remarkable examples of natural remission. Cancer tumours may unexpectantly recede. When a faith-healer is nearby this results in banner headlines. Popes will be beatified on the strength of it. When it happens away from the glare of publicity, as it most often does, then only the patient and the family are quietly grateful, crediting any medical treatment they may have been given. But in 90 per cent of all cases it is exactly as it is with all forms of the paranormal, mundane petty stuff, never clear-cut, always tinkering at the edges, leaving room for doubt, deceit and argument. Faith healers usually do not claim magical powers.

Their spiel is that their special prowess comes from God acting through them.

Why a god that can create a universe without corporeal assistance now needs little helpers to trigger his miracles is never explained. Nor is the erratic nature of his interventions. Is it that God is asleep at the wheel until he hears of people's ingrowing toenails or troublesome piles? God may be omnipotent but piles sufferers can redirect the entirety of that infinite power to come to grips with their personal tribulations. If faith healers were as effective as they pretend to be, we would, of course, dispense with our humanly fallible medical profession and leave all healing to them. Every district would have a faith-healer centre where these medical maestros could ply their trade. Where they could cast out malignant germs and viruses, heal open wounds, unblock arteries and splice broken bones quicker than you could say NHS. Even at a pound a head they would soon be wealthy, apart from prayers there are no overheads. Much of the suffering in the world would soon be eliminated. Back in the real world let me give you an example of how faith healing actually works. It comes courtesy of leading sceptic and magician James Randi.

In 1985, Peter Popoff, a German born American, came to national attention when he began campaigning for money to help smuggle Bibles into the Soviet Union. He claimed the Bibles would be tied to helium-filled balloons and sent wafting across the iron curtain. A type of biblical love-bombing. When he had to account for the money being spent, Popoff staged a burglary at his own headquarters. On subsequent broadcasts of his show, he would tearfully beg for more money to help repair the damage. During his appearances at church conventions in the 1980s, Popoff routinely and accurately stated the home addresses and specific illnesses of his audience members, a feat many believed was due to divine revelation and 'God-given ability'. In 1986 when members of Randi's CSICOP team (Committee for the Scientific Investigation of Claims of the Paranormal), reported that Popoff was using a radio to receive messages, Popoff denied it and said the messages came from God. At the time of his popularity, sceptic groups across the United States printed and handed out pamphlets explaining how Popoff's feats could be done. Popoff would tell his audience that the pamphlets were 'tools of the devil'.

His earlier claims were debunked in 1986 when Randi and his assistant Steve Shaw researched Popoff by attending revival meetings across the country for months. Randi asked crime scene analyst and electronics expert Alexander Jason for technical assistance and he was able to use a computerised scanner during a Popoff appearance in San Francisco. Jason intercepted and identified the radio transmissions that were being sent by Popoff's wife Elizabeth, who was backstage reading information which she and her aides had gathered from earlier conversations with members of the audience. Popoff would listen to these promptings with an in-ear receiver and repeat what he heard to the crowd. Randi then went on to plant accomplices in the audience, including a man dressed as a woman pretending to have uterine cancer, of which 'she' was duly 'cured'. Jason produced video segments showing several Popoff 'healings' which included the previously secret audio.

After these were shown on the Johnny Carson show, Popoff's popularity and viewing audiences declined sharply. In September 1987, sixteen months after the Carson airing, Popoff declared bankruptcy, with more than 790 creditors having claims against him.

Randi had initially taken his research to the United States Attorney's office, but never heard back from them. This led Johnny Carson to invite Randi on the show to explain how Popoff operated. Popoff at first denied that he used the tactics Randi alleged, even claiming NBC hired an actress to impersonate Mrs. Popoff on a 'doctored' videotape. However, as the media pressed with more questions, the Reverend Popoff admitted the existence of the radio device, claiming, that 'almost everybody' knew about the 'communicator.' And, he added, "My wife occasionally gives me the name of a person who needs special prayers".

During a 2008 interview, Randi explained that he and Shaw had recorded Liz Popoff using a racial slur to describe an African-American audience member to her husband and laughingly telling him to "...keep your hands off her tits ... I'm watching you." Randi further revealed that when a man dying from testicular cancer came before Popoff during a crusade, Liz Popoff and her aides were hysterically laughing at his visible tumour.

On several occasions, Popoff would tell his revival attendees to "break free of the Devil" by throwing their medications onto the stage. Dozens of his followers would obey and throw away pills and other medication which might have been vital for their continued survival. Popoff's shows also featured audience members who were brought on stage in wheelchairs and then rose dramatically to walk without support. These were some of Popoff's most incredible 'healings', but what trusting audience members and television viewers did not know was that wheelchairs were used by Popoff to seat people who were already able to walk. For this purpose a van full of wheelchairs would be brought to the show. After Randi's sterling work Popoff may have been down but he is not out. Popoff has popped back. Gullibility is an everpresent human trait and thirty years on he is still milking it for all its worth.

In 2008, the UK broadcasting regulator Ofcom issued serious warnings to broadcasters for transmitting Popoff's material, which the regulator felt promoted his products "in such a way as to target potential susceptible and vulnerable viewers". These programs included offers of free 'Miracle Manna' that allegedly provide health and financial miracles. If viewers asked for the so-called manna, they were subsequently sent letters asking for money. In 2009, advertisements appeared in the UK press offering a free cross which contained 'blessed water' and 'holy sand'. The blessed water was supposedly from a source near Chernobyl. Animals drinking from this source were purportedly free from any radiation sickness. The cross also bore the inscription 'Jerusalem'. Requests for donations accompanied the cross and follow-up requests for money from Popoff were also sent out. I took a look at Peter's website. It took a long time to pop up. When it did I was treated to the following priceless message: "*God is no respecter of persons. What He has done in the lives of those you see on this web page...He will do for you*". And of course his trusty helper Popoff will do you for even more. A handy 'donation' button is there to ease things on their way.

Popoff was nominated by the James Randi Educational Foundation, (JREF) to be one of the recipients of the 2011 Pegasus Award, which exposes fraud.

It is truly astounding that the likes of Popoff, despite the numerous exposures of their fraudulent behaviour, should be able to carry on, virtually unhindered. Televangelists in America and increasingly in Britain too, are masters at exploiting religion induced gullibility. They are treated as sacrosanct by governments fearful of offending religion. Not held financially accountable, as are other businessmen and enjoying religious exemptions from various taxes and several government regulations, they easily amass millions of dollars from a gullible public. Only religious faith could persuade dupes to donate money to these charlatans. When I asked an American friend why he thought this was possible he facetiously said 'these programmes have subliminal messages to alter their thinking. Also there are rays from their TVs that suck out their brains.'

PSYCHIC DETECTIVES

"I first realised I was psychic next Monday".

D. Cavanagh

Psychic detectives are the bane of police forces everywhere. Whenever there is a tragic case of a missing person, particularly if it involves a child, self-appointed mystics and psychics rush out of the woodwork and start spreading their theories. They do this because they are encouraged by the media who still don't seem to have cottoned on to the fact that no 'psychic' revelation has ever directly led to a person or a body being found. Yet the police ignore such revelations at their peril because if ever some chance description would prove remotely accurate and they had not acted on it, heads would surely roll.

The very idea that clairvoyance of this kind can work is obviously absurd. If it did work it would be demonstrated regularly and accurately all over the place and the police force would save a great deal of man-hours and resources. The leads would not be vague and confused but precise and to the point. The signals would be loud and clear. There is no fuzzy electricity and wi-fi lets me download books to my Kindle with no spelling mistakes.

Psychic detection goes back a long while. The earliest case on record of a purported psychic hit occurred in France in 1692 when Jacques Aymar-Vernay, a stone-mason, who is credited with inventing the dowser, was called in by the authorities to trace a murder. He claimed to have discovered springs and treasures hidden in the earth using his rod, and even tracked down criminals with it. According to some accounts, when he neared the scene of a murder using a divining rod, he would break into a sweat, shudder, and in some instances, even faint. By swinging a pendulum he identified a 19 year-old boy, a hunchback, as the culprit. The boy was subsequently broken on the wheel. Aymar later became something of a national celebrity for his 'gift'. But when submitting to experiments by Prince de Condé, he failed every single test. More recently, in keeping with an upsurge in the fascination with the paranormal, there has been an upsurge in psychic sleuthing.

This became a veritable deluge in the tragic case of Genette Tate, a Devon schoolgirl who disappeared in August 1978 and has never been found.

The police received nearly 1200 letters from mediums with a variety of suggestions. None of these 'psychics' contributed anything whatsoever to the investigation. And, according to Roger Busby, Public Relations Officer for Devon Police, "One of the first psychics on the scene, a medium from Cornwall, shook like a leaf when he visited the scene and then predicted that Genette's body would be found within two days and the offender arrested the following day". But even if a 'psychic' were to score a direct hit, there is no need to assume a supernatural explanation. It would hardly have been surprising if one of the 1200 supposed psychics had guessed correctly the spot where the girl's body had been dumped, or even vaguely described her murderer. It would be no different from 1200 random people offering their suggestions as to what might have occurred.

The same thing happened a few years later in the Yorkshire Ripper case when again the police were overwhelmed with hundreds of calls, all of which were duly followed up at a huge cost to police time and resources. The fraudulent "I'm Jack" tape wasn't the only thing that muddied the waters of the Ripper investigation.

At the time, Doris Stokes was probably the UK's best-known spiritualist and medium, whose homely demeanour belied her crowd-pulling celebrity as a 'conduit' to the world beyond the grave. On July 1,

1979, she featured on the front page of the Sunday People, giving – through a link with the spirit world – a physical description of the Ripper and saying that he lived on Tyneside or Wearside, in a thoroughfare named either Berwick or Bewick Street. The sorry upshot of this 'tip-off' was the detention of a hapless lorry driver from Berwick Avenue in Sunderland. He was quickly eliminated from the inquiry and with the benefit of hindsight, it illustrates how distracted the investigation had by then become.

Other psychics made their own contributions. Gerard Croiset, the so-called 'wizard of Utrecht,' had the Ripper living in a flat above a block of garages in the centre of Sunderland. There are though, at least two cases in which 'psychics' have accurately aided the police in controversial though less mysterious circumstances. James Randi cites the case of a 'psychic' who provided the police with details about an arson incident. This information turned out not to be psychic but first hand, and he was promptly arrested. Another such case happened in Japan; this involved a businessman who murdered his family.

The Madeleine McCann disappearance in 2007 is also attracting a great deal of psychic interest, initially the police declined to pay attention to that type of lead but when conventional methods failed to come up with anything positive, Scotland Yard decided to look into the more than 100 psychic calls received following a 'Crimestoppers' TV appeal. The information will be examined and entered into the police computer for the first time to ensure no detail has been missed. But it is of course unlikely that any serious development will result unless the leads are corroborated by other evidence. Earlier in the case Portuguese police had already examined 150 paranormal leads without success. A 'psychic' team from the popular U.S. 'Haunting Evidence' show has also visited Praia da Luz. They clearly do not have approval from the New York Police Department, who have stated: "The policy of the Department is that we do not approach psychics in any investigation. Individuals who claim to be psychics have called to volunteer their services, and we do not officially use them".

A Burnley Express feature, dated June 2012, reported that a psychic medium who claimed to have helped the FBI catch a serial killer is on the case. Grandfather John Warne (82) a 'respected' Spiritualist for 57 years, began his own psychic investigation after being annoyed about a claim by television psychic Derek Acorah.

Acorah said that a messenger from the spirit world told him: "She's not on this earth any more", but he has since apologised to Madeleine's parents, saying he was misquoted. John Warne is convinced that the schoolgirl was snatched on behalf of an American, and that she is now living in Minnesota and attending college.

"It doesn't make sense to go to people and say she is dead. It's diabolical. If it was the case that she had died he should have known what happened, who did it and where she is now. It is a terrible thing to say that someone's missing child is dead". Mr Warne's psychic investigation leads him to believe that Maddie was kidnapped to order and that the snatcher was in the Algarve holiday resort the day before.

"The bloke who took her was in his early 30s with brown hair, he was 5ft. 8in. and in a light blue outfit. He checked her out the day before it happened. Once he grabbed her, he put her in a car round the corner and drove to a waiting boat. By the time the alarm was raised they were gone. The guy was an American, but he didn't take her for himself. He was working for someone. I know she is at college in Minnesota. It is a reddish brown building with several storeys. I have never been there, but I can see it."

I feel guilty about quoting this mindless stuff but this is the sort of thing that newspapers love to publish and the police have to be polite about. Gradually however they are learning: Peter Kirkham, a former detective chief inspector with the Metropolitan Police, said he was sceptical about the ability of psychics to help police investigations. "As soon as you have a high-profile case you get a range of people coming forward", he said. "I'm certainly not aware of any case that's been solved by psychics". Once again these examples confirm that the media in particular are only too keen to report psychic involvement as relevant and worthwhile. No amount of failure seems to make the slightest difference.

SCIENTISTS AND THE GOD WORD

*"I have never seen the slightest scientific proof
of the religious ideas of heaven and hell, of future life
for individuals, or of a personal God.
So far as today's religion is concerned it is a damned
fake.....Religion is all bunk"*.

Thomas Edison

The religious are very keen on claiming famous scientists for their cause. Their major scalp is Einstein who unfortunately was in the habit of using the 'G' word when referring to cosmic laws e.g. in the infamous "God does not play dice" statement. There is no doubt that Einstein was an atheist as the following quote makes clear: *"it was of course a lie what you read about my religious convictions, a lie which is being systematically repeated. I do not believe in a personal god and I have never denied this but have expressed it clearly"*. A similar problem occurred when the mathematician Stephen Hawking ended his book *'A Brief History of Time'* with the phrase "and then we shall know the mind of God". There seems little doubt that this line was put in at the behest of his publisher with sales to the American market in mind. It certainly appears to have done the trick, the book having achieved more than 10 million sales so far. Not bad going for a science book barely understood by many.

The following Hawking quote will set the record straight: "*I believe the simplest explanation is, there is no God. No one created the universe and no one directs our fate. This leads me to a profound realisation that there probably is no heaven and no afterlife either. We have this one life to appreciate the grand design of the universe and for that, I am extremely grateful.*"

Even Darwin has been fingered by the pious. There was the usual deathbed conversion rumour. The claim was firmly denied by members of Darwin's family. Darwin's son Francis wrote to Thomas Huxley on 8 February 1887, that a report that Charles had renounced evolution on his deathbed was "false and without any kind of foundation" and in 1917 Francis affirmed that he had "no reason whatever to believe that he [his father] ever altered his agnostic point of view". Charles's daughter Henrietta (Litchfield) wrote in the London evangelical weekly, *The Christian,* on 23 February 1922, "I was present at his deathbed. Lady Hope was not present during his last illness, or any illness. I believe he never even saw her, but in any case she had no influence over him in any department of thought or belief. He never recanted any of his scientific views, either then or earlier. The whole story has no foundation whatever".

Darwin always was a very private man. Because his wife was a Christian he never publicly expressed his own beliefs. But in an autobiographical passage, not published until after his death he made it clear what they were:

"*Disbelief crept over me at a very slow rate, but was at last complete. The rate was so slow that I felt no distress and I have never since doubted even for a single second that my conclusion was correct. I can indeed hardly see how anyone ought to wish Christianity to be true; for if so, the plain language of the text seems to show that the men who do not believe, and this would include my father, brother and almost all my best friends, will be everlastingly punished. And this is a damnable doctrine".*

NATURE PROGRAMMES AVOIDING GOD

Not only are some scientists inclined to use the 'God' word as a metaphor for a gap in their knowledge, there remains an almost universal reluctance for scientists to point out in their books and documentaries on TV that the world and the universe they are talking about bears not the slightest resemblance to the biblical version to which a substantial proportion of their readers and viewers still subscribe. Sir David Attenborough is the star of ubiquitous natural history programmes, discussing the origin of life on earth, dating back millions of years. There is the geologist Prof. Iain Stewart, presenting documentaries such as: *Earth: The Power of the planet*, broadcast in America as *Earth the biography*, again going back in time to the beginning of the planet, some 4.5 billion years ago. Another one is the physicist and cosmologist Prof. Brian Cox, the natural successor to the late Patrick Moore and the American Carl Sagan, presenting the programmes *Wonders of the Solar System* and *Wonders of life,* once more discussing the origins of the solar system and planet earth. All of them to audiences in Britain where God belief still hovers around 40 per cent and where, according to a 2006 Mori poll, 22 per cent believed the creationism view that God created humankind pretty much in its present form at some time within the last ten thousand years. And to American viewers where God belief is 80 per cent, with 45 per cent still believing that the earth's age is just six thousand years.

And not once, dear readers, not once do any of them refer to the One who is meant to have set it all in motion and is still in full control. This you will agree is very strange. It is like talking about a Henry Moore sculpture at length and in detail. How it was made; what materials were used; what was in the maker's mind and so on without once mentioning the sculptor's name. Or discussing the running of a country, its economics and social policies without ever mentioning the government. You could say that since these scientists no doubt believe that there is no such maker or government, they have no reason to mention them. That would be fine of course if nobody watching didn't either. But if you were lecturing to an audience, say at the Hay Literary Festival, about a steady state universe and you knew that half your listeners believed in an expanding one, wouldn't it be a good idea to address this theory head on with convincing argument? Not doing so would be remiss and unprofessional. However when religious notions are involved, people, including scientists, must suddenly develop blindness and amnesia and give the troublesome alternatives a very wide berth. So when Attenborough talks about life evolving over millions of years he must steadfastly ignore the elephant in the room, the rival theory believed in by a sizeable number of his audience.

Worse it is for a physicist like Brian Cox, who is addressing himself to an even larger percentage of dissenters and as for cosmologist Carl Sagan in America, he must have been insulting half his audience. And strangely enough the religious never protest. Their precious religions and beliefs are made to look irrelevant if not downright stupid, but not a murmur. This is very uncharacteristic. Taking offence is what the religious normally do so well. Perhaps it is all sown up behind the scenes. The ultimate act of political correctness. A cosy arrangement to maintain the status quo: If you don't protest about all this evolutionary stuff and the 4.5 billion years instead of 6000, the countless galaxies and the blatant ignoring of the Great Architect in the sky, then we in turn will refrain from pointing out that your religion is at best a semi-amusing fairy tale. But, alas, a more likely explanation is that creationists, with their heads deeper in the sand than long-necked ostriches, don't watch that type of programme, they are probably pre-occupied with 'Songs of Praise', football pitches, or pitches for money by televangelists.

TIMELINE OF THE UNIVERSE AND PLANET EARTH

"Two things are infinite: the universe and human stupidity and I am not sure about the universe"

Albert Einstein

But whereas scientists on TV are forced to pussyfoot around religious sensibilities, failing to address the yawning gap between the true evolutionary development of our planet and the Biblical version, readers of my book are entitled to a clear picture of the fascinating time-scales involved. These will demonstrate that Homo Sapiens had to wait some quarter of a million years before God saw fit to send his only son to lend a helping hand and to introduce some morality to human proceedings. It is of course somewhat of a mystery how humanity managed to survive and run its affairs all those thousands of years without the benefit of Divine guidance. As for the significance of human history, measured in terms of our earthly time-scale, consider this: if you span its age with your open arms, the complete epoch of human culture would drop from the end of your fingernails at a single stroke of a nail file.

Years Before Present	Timeline of the Universe, Planet Earth – The emergence of life on earth – Evolution of Mankind
14–15 billion	The 'Big Bang' – Start of the Universe
5 billion	Origin of the Sun
4.6 billion	Planet earth forms from the accretion disc, revolving around the young sun
4.5 billion	According to the giant impact hypothesis the moon is formed when planet earth and planet Theia collide, sending a large shower of moonlets into orbit which coalesce to form the moon.
4 billion	Formation of bio-molecules. Formation of Greenstone belt in Canada, the oldest rock belt in the world.
3–4 billion	Cells resembling prokaryotes appear; organisms with no nucleus. Bacteria develop primitive forms of photosynthesis
3 billion	Photosynthesising cyanobacteria evolve, using water as a reducing agent, producing oxygen as a waste product.
2.7–1.6 billion	Appearance of eukaryotes; cellular organisms with nuclei. Bacterial viruses emerge.
1–0.6 billion	Simple multi-cellular plants and animals begin appearing in the oceans. Sexual reproduction first appears in the fossil records, increasing the rate of evolution

Years Before Present	Timeline of the Universe, Planet Earth – The emergence of life on earth – Evolution of Mankind
600 million	Cambrian explosion or radiation. Relatively rapid appearance of diverse plants and animals. The accumulation of atmospheric oxygen allows the formation of an ozone layer.
550 million	First fossil evidence for comb jellies, sponges, corals and anemones. Major diversification of living things in the oceans.
500 million	Plants and fungi colonise the land, soon followed by arthropods and other animals. Fish and proto-amphibians appear.
485 million	First vertebrates with true bones
435 million	First primitive plants move onto land
400 million	Insects and seeds emerge. The first known tetrapod tracks on land
360 million	By the start of the carboniferous period the earth began to be recognisable. Insects roamed the land and would soon take to the skies. Sharks swam the oceans, vegetation covered the land with seed bearing plants and forests soon to flourish
320–300 million	Emergence of reptiles and amphibians
280 million	Earliest beetles; seed plants and conifers diversify
225 million	Earliest dinosaur species appear

Years Before Present	Timeline of the Universe, Planet Earth – The emergence of life on earth – Evolution of Mankind
200 million	Emergence of mammals and premoral sentiments and behaviours. First accepted evidence for viruses that infect eukaryotic cells
150–100 million	Emergence of birds and first blood-sucking insects
130 million	Emergence of flowers
100–80 million	Earliest bees and ants
65 million	Emergence of primates and elaboration of premoral sentiments and behaviours.(Extinction of dinosaurs)
50–30 million	Emergence of bats, butterflies and moths,
20 million	Emergence of Hominidae (family of great apes) along with giraffes, hyenas, zebras, lions
7–6 million	Emergence of hominids (human ancestors) from common ancestors, shared with modern bonobos, chimpanzees, gorillas and orang-utans
3 million	The great American Interchange, where various land and freshwater faunas migrated between North and South America. Armadillos, opossums, humming birds and vampire bats travelled to North America, while horses, tapirs, sabre-toothed cats and deer entered South America
2 million	Emergence of genus Homo erectus, stone tool use

Years Before Present	Timeline of the Universe, Planet Earth – The emergence of life on earth – Evolution of Mankind
1 million	Controlled use of fire by Homo erectus
600,000– 100,000	Emergence of various hominid species, including Homo Heidelbergensis followed by Neanderthalensis. Improved tool making. Emergence of human social organisation in bands of 10s–100s individuals
250,000– 200,000	Anatomically modern humans (Homo sapiens) appeared in Africa. Around 50,000 years ago they started colonising the other continents
100,000	Development of human moral thoughts and behaviours
35,000	Emergence of language and sophisticated symbolic communication. Improved tool making. Socio-cultural factors increasingly control and shape Homo sapiens' moral behaviour and ethical systems
13,000	Homo Sapiens have spread to nearly every region on earth and lived on hunting, fishing and gathering. Emergence of tribes numbering 100s –1,000s of individuals
11,000	First domestication of animals (dogs, goats and sheep)
10,000	Starting point of incipient organised religion
9,000	First domestication of cereal crops

Years Before Present	Timeline of the Universe, Planet Earth – The emergence of life on earth – Evolution of Mankind
7,500	Emergence of human chiefdom in the Fertile Crescent of Western Asia. Groupings of 1,000s–10,000s individuals
7,000	Development of settlements into cities. Beginning of Buddhism. Domestication of horses
5,500	Human chiefdoms begin to merge into states – numbering 10,000s–100,000s of individuals
4,000	Foundation of Hindu and Egyptian religions
3,400–3,200	Invention of writing in Sumer and Egypt
2,500	Foundation of Confucianism in China
2,000–700	Human conurbations. 10,000s–100,000s individuals. Beginning and spread of the Abrahamic religions

This then is the fascinating story of the development of the known universe. It is a truly extraordinary realisation that for creationists, i.e. a large wedge of humanity, only the last 5 entries of the total of 45 have any relevance.

HEAVENS ABOVE

*"It's an incredible con job when you think about it;
to believe something now in exchange for
something after death.
Even corporations with their reward systems
don't try to make it posthumous".*

Gloria Steinem

Religion's most powerful tool is the promise of eternal life. It is just too hard for people to accept that death is the final frontier. That dearly departed will never be seen again. Much better to hold out for re-unification in an afterlife. A notion too attractive to dismiss. So it is argued that when humans die they are somehow able to carry on just as they were, even though all their atoms have been scattered to the winds. The question must be asked: is this fanciful, self serving, afterlife scenario a credible, scientific proposition or does it sound like another example of wishful thinking? Is belief in an afterlife not taking self-preservation a step too far? A humanist must answer yes, but for others these paradise fictions provide much comfort and support. It takes tremendous realism to dismiss such consolation. When my brother stood at the grave side of his 19 year old daughter, killed in a road accident, he said "Connie, desperate as we are to believe that we may meet again in a better world, we will have to accept that this is not going to be and that today we must say goodbye for eternity". A reality so harsh that he had to confront it publicly.

Other people, understandably, prefer to go along with the more palatable belief of a back-up life in heaven. But do they ever consider how this would work in practice? The ergonomics are very daunting. There is the difficulty of differential in time. Will I meet my mother at age 90 when she died or will she be older still. And will she recognise me if I too live to 90? And will the souls of all the young soldiers who died in wars still fancy their geriatric wives or would they wish to swap them for younger models? Such sobering, baffling questions are either not given further thought or countered with the explanation that earthly conditions no longer apply in paradise and that somehow a satisfactory solution will be made available. No details can be given but once again believers must have faith. Another burning question (any questions about the afterlife from an atheist would involve some burning I suppose) is how God re-assembles all the bits. Even his most devoted followers on earth are rather worried about his ability to perform this trick; that's why they prefer not to be cremated. What about missionaries eaten by the natives garnished with a sprig or two of parsley? The chemistry gets very nasty there.

And what about the daily routine in this celestial scenario. Eternity is a very long time. Extreme boredom is a distinct possibility. Would it not be a wrench to still be praising God after, say, 50 or 60 billion years? Will there be sporting activities; will there be computer games? Is sex still looked upon askance? How does one interact with others who have made the heavenly grade but who were not one's favourites on earth. Will old grievances be forgotten or will battle re-commence? Will the catering be to taste? So many questions so few answers. The one answer I suspect the theologians will proffer is that I have got the physics wrong. I am being anthropomorphic. (An interesting role reversal here!). People will no longer be corporeal. They are floating about as souls. This mysterious entity that manages to keep us going just as well without a body; all functions and faculties intact. One might ask why bother with a body in the first place? Much simpler to be born, live and die as souls. Easier for women to give birth and easier to explain what is to become of suicide bombers blown to smithereens. Souls, we are told, have different concerns. What these concerns entail is yet another source for deep conjecture.

For thinking people the idea of a disembodied psyche or soul is as meaningless a concept as that of the grin on the Cheshire cat, without the cat. The soul is really the consciousness of human personality conceived naively as substance. Unfortunately the soul word is so commonly established that it is easy to believe that lurking somewhere in a small corner of the universe is a soul that will someday come forward and proudly announce itself. But here my speculative powers dry up and I must once more pass the baton to the theologians. They are the masters of Father Christmas down the chimney explanations.

I can't resist quoting here a hard worked woman's take on heaven, found on a grave stone in Bushey churchyard ca. 1860. For one thing it answers my question about the catering up there:

"Here lies a poor woman who always was tired
For she lived in a place where help wasn't hired.
Her last words on earth were, dear friends, I am going
Where washing ain't done, nor sweeping nor sewing.
And everything there is exact to my wishes
For they don't eat and there's no washing of dishes.
Don't mourn for me now, don't mourn for me never
For I'm going to do nothing for ever and ever!"

Humans have been very selfish in reserving for themselves all the rewards that heaven brings. Animals, our fellow creatures are left out in the cold. Some people are hoping that their dogs may also make it to the pearly gates in case guard dogs are needed. But even for our nearest cousins, the chimpanzees, oblivion is ensured. It all seems very unfair. Fish have started to rebel against this selfish human zoo-phobia and thanks to Rupert Brooke's delightful poem **'Fish Heaven'** we know exactly what they are thinking. It deserves to be quoted in full:

"Fish (fly-replete in depth of June,
dawdling away their wat'ry noon)
ponder deep wisdom, dark or clear,
each secret fishy hope or fear.
Fish say, they have their stream and pond;
but is there anything beyond?
This life cannot be all, they swear,
for how unpleasant, if it were!
One may not doubt that, somehow, good

shall come of water and of mud;
and sure, the reverent eye must see
a purpose in liquidity.
We darkley know by faith we cry,
the future is not wholly dry.
Mud unto mud! - death eddies near-
not here the appointed end, not here!
But somewhere, beyond space and time,
is wetter water, slimier slime!
And there (they trust) there swimmeth One,
who swam ere rivers were begun,
immense of fishy form and mind,
squamous, omnipotent and kind;
And under that almighty fin,
the littlest fish may enter in.
Oh! never fly conceals a hook,
fish say, in the eternal brook.
But more than mundane weeds are there,
and mud, celestially fair;
fat caterpillars drift around,
and paradisal grubs are found;
unfading moths, immortal flies,
and the worm that never dies.
And in that heaven of all their wish,
there shall be no more land, say fish".

There could be somewhere on a far away planet a
sophisticated life form who, if they could witness the
religious merrymaking here on earth, would look upon
the human notion of an afterlife very much as we now
chuckle at the touching, doomed ambition these fish
display in their hope for "*an eternal brook, where fat
caterpillars drift around and paradisal grubs are found*".

For Christians these grubs might represent everlasting worship of the Almighty. For Muslims they could more pleasingly come in the guise of 72 virgins. Evolution tells us that people have developed from fish and clearly this is still reflected in the intelligence of some. Aldous Huxley put it this way: "You never see animals going through the absurd and often horrible fooleries of magic and religion. Only man behaves with such gratuitous folly. It is the price he has to pay for being intelligent but not, as yet, quite intelligent enough".

I think a lot of mischief could have been avoided had people followed my daughter's Billy the rabbit's philosophy. Apparently he doesn't know and he doesn't care. Just acknowledge that we are not (yet) smart enough to understand everything. Do not come up with Heath Robinson solutions that are not capable of explaining anything. Keep slashing away with Occam's razor. Meanwhile be kind to your fellow creatures (Billy is very kind) and keep on taking the carrots.

Prayer

"The most preposterous notion that Homo sapiens has ever dreamed up is that the Lord God of Creation, Shaper and Ruler of all the Universes, wants the saccharine adoration of His creatures, can be swayed by their prayers, and becomes petulant if He does not receive this flattery. Yet this absurd fantasy, without a shred of evidence to bolster it, pays all the expenses of the oldest, largest, and least productive industry in all history".

Robert A. Heinlein

"If you pray for rain long enough, it eventually does fall. If you pray for floodwaters to abate, they eventually do. The same happens in the absence of prayers."

T.A.

Prayer, according to the Shorter Oxford dictionary, is: "a solemn request to God or an object of worship; a supplication, thanksgiving, or other verbal or mental act, addressed to God". A less flattering definition is found in Ambrose Bierce's *The Devil's Dictionary*: "Prayer: To ask that the laws of the universe be annulled on behalf of a single petitioner, confessedly unworthy".

People have prayed to God or gods since time immemorial and in view of the precarious condition that mankind has endured for most of its existence that is hardly surprising. Exposed to the harshness of nature and ignorant of most of the phenomena confronting him, man had little option but to cry out for help in coping with his predicament. It is only in recent times that science has managed to come up with explanations for most of the mysteries surrounding human existence and as a result the role of prayer has diminished and has changed character. Instead of a basic, universal tool wielded to stave off the forces of nature, hunger and disease, prayer now has become much more person- alised. In the hands of ego-centric people it has become a means of asking for special favours of an increasingly frivolous nature.

People pray for a win on the lottery, athletes cross themselves before the start of a race. In asking for personal gain no allowance appears to be made for the fact that one person's gain is often balanced by somebody else's loss. But what happens if two or more athletes cross themselves? We have all come across cases where the selfish nature of prayer is only too obvious. This first struck me years ago when an item in the news opened my eyes to the blatant disregard that religious survivors often show for those who have not been so lucky. A reservoir dam in America had given way during the night and in the resulting flood some 20 people, including a number of children, all part of a bible study group camping nearby, had drowned. One of the adult survivors claimed that far from his faith in God having been weakened, it had been strengthened. Because whilst praying he had heard God's voice urging him to get up and save himself. The Lord be praised; I at least live to pray another day!

Everybody will have seen interviews on TV with survivors of plane crashes or other disasters who claim that they were miraculously saved by God. They didn't get on to the plane because they were stuck in a traffic jam laid on by God above. They dare say this out loud whilst corpses of other passengers are on the way to the morgue. Amazingly these selfish, egotistical simpletons are never challenged about these offensive statements. It concerns religion so it is deserving of tacit respect. Reporters, having to listen to these 'I am alright Jack, tough on the rest of them' tales, are reduced to polite silence. For such people their faith in God is only (usually temporarily) shaken when tragedy strikes at home. After John Kennedy's assassination Jackie Kennedy complained: "I am so bitter against God". She should have been bitter against God long before about the forty a day murders in America.

Following the catastrophic flooding in the Indian Ocean on Boxing Day 2004 there was an interview with an evangelical pastor on ITV. He was asked has this disaster shaken your faith in God? "On the contrary it has strengthened it. There was this old man and he had lost all his family except his little grandson and it had brought them closer together." In that pastor's scales of justice there was on the one hand an improved relationship between grandfather and grandson and on the other 200.000 people dead and an estimated 2 million having lost a close relative. God always a winner.

To a sensible observer it is so crystal clear that illness, accidents and disasters are totally random events, affecting the good and the bad equally, that no further proof of the uselessness of prayer is required. But because the childish notion that a heavenly father is on the other end of the line will not go away, American scientists have gone to the trouble of conducting further research. The STEP project (Study of the Therapeutic Effects of intercessionary Prayer), carried out in 2006 by Harvard professor Herbert Benson, was a large study involving 1802 patients across six hospitals covering a period of nearly ten years. Using double blind protocols patients were randomly selected into three groups and were prayed for by Catholics and Protestants over a two-week period, starting the night before bypass surgery. The first group of 604 patients received prayers after being told that they may or may not receive them. The second group of 597 patients did not receive prayers after being told that they might or might not receive them. None of the doctors knew who was being prayed for in the first two groups. The final group of 601 patients which tested for possible psychosomatic effects, received prayers and were told that they would definitely receive prayers. Major complications and thirty-day mortality occurred in 52 percent of those who received prayer (group 1), 51 percent of those who did not receive it (group 2) and 59 percent of patients who knew they would receive prayers (group 3). So in this study prayed for patients fared marginally worse than those who did not receive prayers. A 2007 systematic review of 17 intercessory prayer studies noted that the most methodologically rigorous studies failed to produce significant findings. No great surprise there. I doubt that any countries other than the US would have bothered with such a frivolous exercise. They would spend their research money in more deserving fields.

I have personal experience of the heartbreaking effect of failed prayer. My mother's favourite brother Jan was cruelly struck down with a severe form of polio at the age of seventeen. He was a well-trained craftsman, looking forward to joining his father in the family business. In a wheelchair for the rest of his 78 years and hardly able to speak he was a model of quiet courage and forbearance, who never complained and always had a smile for everybody. But when you caught him off guard you could see him staring out of the window in despair. There hardly was a more deserving case for a miraculous cure. He was taken to Lourdes twice. How the family prayed and prayed. But of course his condition was beyond the powers of the Blessed Virgin. There is an unspoken rule in the miracle business that serious conditions do not qualify for cure. Miracles are reserved for lesser problems, headaches, backaches, the sort of symptoms normally taken care of by the natural healing process and occasionally an unusual remission of something more serious like cancer which also occurs in cases where prayer is nowhere to be heard. Crutches jettisoned in Lourdes in a moment of religiously induced ecstasy are often quietly retrieved the next day. But still the stream of prayer flows on. It takes a long while for naturally trusting people to reconcile themselves to the conclusion that after all God is not going to help them.

The efficacy of prayer survives solely on the hearsay evidence of the gullible, selectively quoting their successes and conveniently forgetting their failures. However this masking of God's unresponsiveness cannot be so readily achieved in cases where parties pray for opposite results. In case of war, for example, where both warring factions expect to have God on their side. During the great wars of this century daily services were held in both camps, all seeking to enlist the Lord's fire power on their side, as expressed in Sir John Squire's quatrain:

"God heard the embattled nations sing and shout
"Gott strafe England! And God save the King!"
God this, God that and God the other thing.
"Good God" said God." I've got my work cut out".

It is enough to make you pity the great schizophrenic beyond the clouds.

In 1938, when Prime Minister Neville Chamberlain returned from his meeting with Hitler in Munich with "peace in our time", the Archbishop of Canterbury described their agreement as *an answer to the great volume of prayer which has been rising to God"* and he called upon Christians throughout the land to hold services of thanksgiving because 'the Good Lord had saved us at the last moment from the scourges of war'. (The fact that the Czechs had not been saved clearly did not seem to bother him). But a year later, when war broke out after all, the Archbishop did not call upon Christians throughout the land to gather in their churches and curse the Lord for changing his mind.

It never seems to occur to supplicants that their omniscient God might consider it a touch impertinent to be told where to direct his ministrations when some lowly minion is seeking to acquire a share in his omnipotence. Would he really interrupt his own great scheme of running the universe to attend to athletes' races, lost pets and lottery tickets. What kind of gargantuan ego is required to imagine that the same God who is so patently failing to prevent massive suffering elsewhere in the world will attend to your boxing match (Bruno's crosses were no match for Tyson's) or make your Premium Bond come up. The God that allowed Auschwitz and Dunblane will help you pass your driving test! When in a debate Christopher Hitchens' fundamentalist opponent remarked that "God almighty doesn't hear the prayers of a Jew", Hitchens replied: "this is the only instance known to me of an anti-Semitic remark making sense".

I knew a family who were in the habit of saying a prayer for a safe journey at the start of every trip by car. On at least three occasions this did not stop them from suffering an accident. The man wasn't the best of drivers. But then they gave praise that at least nobody had been killed. God off the hook again. A logical person would ask why allow the accident in the first place.

These days the main religions band together; strength in numbers and all that. Why don't they organise a world-wide prayerthon in all churches, synagogues and mosques. Dear God, Jaweh, Allah eradicate the scourge of cancer from this world once and for all. We know what would happen: absolutely nothing. It would be back to scientists and doctors, chipping away at cures, making gradual progress, just as mankind has always had to do in tackling all other problems of existence.

It's time I introduced to you the most effective and reliable debunkers of any claims for the effectiveness of prayer: *insurance companies*! Actuaries in insurance companies are wizards in determining odds and probability. On their ability to calculate probability rest the fortunes of their companies. Now you would have thought that over the thousands of years that mankind has been beseeching its god(s) for favours, at least a minuscule trend of success would have become apparent. After all if only one prayer in twenty would be heard that would still amount to a five per cent success rate and over time this would have shown up in all kinds of beneficial ways.

Fewer road accidents, better health, better crops, increased business success etc. Such a trend, you can be sure, would not have been lost on the eagle eyed boffins of insurance companies who are quite happy, for example, to offer substantial premium discounts to people who undertake not to smoke or not to drink. Conversely, they penalise younger drivers who, the records show, are more likely to be involved in accidents.

If there was any evidence for effective prayer Christians would be in line for discounts and Muslims, duly pointing east on their prayer mats five times a day, would also benefit. As for atheists with their dented cars, burned down houses and ruined healths, bump up their premiums sky-high or don't touch them with a bargepole.

And how strongly do these masters of chance rate the power of prayer? You guessed; there isn't even an entry on the form! To test the appreciation of your prayerful lifestyle by insurance companies next time try asking Churchill for a prayer discount and don't be surprised if he says you must be barking mad. Either the insurance companies don't know their business or Omnigod is imaginary.

Similar complete disregard is shown to religious manifestations by athletes in sporting events. Sportsmen and women clearly believe that crossing themselves or praying will benefit their performances. Yet obviously no event administrators do. If they thought prayer would have even the slightest effect, a split second in time or an inch in distance, it would be penalised with disqualification. But all officials, even religious ones, and all commentators, totally ignore such acts of advantage seeking. And why? Because they all know full well that none of it makes a jot of difference.

Ironically, people who pray don't really believe in it either. They use it as an optional extra on the basis of "you never know" and "It can't do any harm". If they did believe they wouldn't wear crash helmets or fasten safety belts. They have their possessions insured like everybody else. When ill they pray, but soon run to their doctors. The state colludes in this. It is a criminal offence for parents to pray for their sick children without seeking medical care.

The sentiment is expressed in many well established observations such as Cromwell's: "Praise the Lord but keep your powder dry". Or as Cervantes put it: "A leap over the hedge is better than good men's prayers". There is an Indian proverb: "Call on God, but row away from the rocks". Escaped slave Frederic Douglass said "I prayed for twenty years for freedom but received no answer until I prayed with my legs". The philosopher George Santayana agreed: "prayer among sane people has never superseded practical efforts to secure the desired end". The last word goes to Arthur Koestler: "God seems to have left the receiver off the hook and time is running out".

WOMEN AND RELIGION

"A woman's road to paradise is the three p's route:
prayer, pregnancy and penance"

T.A.

Ido like women. Women make the world go round.
Most of my friends are women. They are peaceful,
gentle, caring. They are much less troublesome than
men. No wars are started by them. There are very
few women in prison and the ones that are, are rarely
there because of violent behaviour. But because of
superior physical strength men have bullied women
since the dawn of Homo Sapiens. And religion is the
worst offender. Every major world religion – without
exception – is intensely patriarchal. Every one of them
engages in the systematic devaluation of women, in
the systematic exclusion of women from positions
of authority, and in the systematic oppression and
even enslavement of women. There is not a single
major religion that bucks this trend. Considering
how little many of these religions have in common
otherwise, this is a truly remarkable pattern. A few
denominations, influenced by the feminist movement
and other moral advances, are only now beginning
to redress this glaring inequity, but for the most part

progress has been extremely slow and the vast majority of religions still treat women as second class citizens.

Despite its having been house-trained by the Enlightenment, Christianity is one of the worst offenders. Although some Christian denominations have taken faltering steps towards women's equality, all those denominations still believe in and endorse the Bible, which is without a doubt one of the most misogynistic books in existence.

In the book of Genesis, for example, the very *existence* of women is depicted as a divine afterthought, and the fall of the human race out of original Paradise into a world of toil and death is unambiguously depicted as woman's fault. The text makes it clear from the very first that women are expected to be obedient and submissive to men:

> Unto the woman he said, I will greatly multiply thy sorrow and thy conception; in sorrow thou shalt bring forth children; and thy desire shall be to thy husband, and he shall rule over thee.

—Genesis 3:16

The Ten Commandments proclaim wives to be their husband's property, listing them together with livestock and servants as "thing[s] that [are] thy neighbour's" (Exodus 20:17). The Torah states that women who give birth to daughters are "unclean" for twice as long as women who give birth to sons (Leviticus 12) and values women's lives at half the value of men's lives (Leviticus 27:3-7). It rules that women who are raped in cities and do not cry out are to be stoned to death (Deuteronomy 22:22-24), while those are raped in the countryside are merely required to marry their rapists (Deuteronomy 22:28-29).

The New Testament joins in the denigration of women as well. It endorses the Old Testament's subjugation of them to men, saying that "the head of the woman is the man" (1 Corinthians 11:3). It also commands women to remain silent in church, saying that it is "a shame" for women to speak in church (1 Corinthians 14:34-35), and adds that women must "learn in silence with all subjection" and must never be allowed to teach or hold authority over men (1 Timothy 2:11-15).

And then there is one of the most subtly and pervasively sexist ideas in Christian thinking: the Trinity. The early Christians had three gods to choose from and made every one of them a male. One might have thought that instead of the set of three made up of Father, Son and Holy Ghost, it would have made more sense to go for Father, Son and Mother. That seems like a more logical arrangement but it overlooks the fact that this peculiar doctrine was invented by an exclusively male and misogynist church hierarchy that sought to deny the female gender any role in creation or in the divine. (A recent Harris poll found that over one-third of Jews and Christians believe God is male, while only 1per cent believe God is female. It makes you shudder to contemplate exactly where godliness is centred).

Many modern denominations have followed these anti-woman verses to the letter. The Catholic church, one of the worst offenders in this regard, still denies women the ability to join the priesthood, even despite a crippling lack of trained clergy to fill many available posts. The Southern Baptists have likewise declared that women should be submissive and obedient to their husbands, as though it was exclusively the man's job to command and a woman's job to follow. The Russian Orthodox church has stepped into the act as well, with a prominent bishop's recent claim that the idea of equality between the sexes is "destructive" to families. It is astonishing to think that Christians who claim to be "pro-family" go out of their way to disparage the gender that makes the existence of families possible.

The offshoots of Christianity have followed a similar path. Most notably the Mormon church, which from its beginning endorsed polygamous marriage – for men only, of course; it was considered an unspeakable sin for a woman to attempt to take multiple husbands. The institution of polygamy in Mormonism reduced women to little more than property, intimidating them into being obedient and submissive lest their husband decide to take additional wives as punishment, or worse, lest they be damned, for Mormon doctrine originally held that women who opposed the doctrine of polygamy would be condemned to Hell. Mormon belief also holds that a woman cannot access Heaven alone, and that only through marriage can a woman be saved – by her husband, who will "pull her through" to the other side upon her death. (One wonders what happens to women who die before their husbands.) Though the Mormons were forced by external pressure to disavow polygamy, many of their other sexist beliefs and practices remain intact.

Religious sexism occurs in Judaism as well, especially the conservative sects. Orthodox (male) Jews are taught to pray to God in thankfulness every day that they were not born as women, and some ultra-Orthodox sects refuse to send their children to school when the school buses are driven by women. In accordance with biblical law, Orthodox women having their menstrual periods, or who have recently given birth, are considered unclean and forbidden to have any physical contact with a man. Orthodox women are often strongly discouraged from taking any public role in a position of leadership, or from acquiring an education beyond the most basic aspects of religious observance and homemaking.

Islam, too, is one of the worst offenders when it comes to women's rights. Consider the following verses from the Koran, which, like the Bible, considers women as less valuable than and inferior to men. It states that men are to control women, while good women are obedient to men, and it explicitly gives men permission to beat disobedient women:

> "Men are in charge of women, because Allah hath made the one of them to excel the other... So good women are the obedient, guarding in secret that which Allah hath guarded. As for those from whom ye fear rebellion, admonish them and banish them to beds apart, and scourge them."

—4:34

The Koran also states that a woman's testimony is worth only half as much as a man's, and her inheritance likewise is only half that of a man:

> "And call two witness from among your men, two witnesses. And if two men be not at hand, then a man and two women..."

—2:282

"Allah chargeth you concerning (the provision for) your children: to the male the equivalent of the portion of two females..."

—4:11

And when fundamentalist Muslims gain political power, the repercussions are far too obvious. Despite the overthrow of the Taliban, there are still many Islamic countries that implement the law code known as *sharia*, which has many cruel effects on men as well but degrades women by far the most, reducing them to slaves and non-persons. The *sharia* code denies women their right to an education, to medical care, or to go out in public unaccompanied by a male relative, in addition to many other inhumanities, and punishes transgressions with barbaric acts such as flogging and stoning. In many Muslim countries, the practice of "honour killing" – murdering female relatives who have been raped, as a way to cleanse the shame they have brought on their family by being the victim of such a crime – still takes place. And then there is the best-known manifestation of Islam's inhumanity to women: the suffocating shrouds of black cloth designed to strip them of their individuality and to make them faceless, invisible and less than human.

Even the supposedly more enlightened Eastern religions are not much better when it comes to treating women as equals and as human beings. In Hinduism, the most infamous example is probably the practice of sati, (suttee) in which widowed women were expected to burn themselves to death on their husband's funeral pyre. Although this was allegedly a voluntary act, in practice it was often enforced, with women drugged, bound or otherwise restrained before being committed alive to the flames. As recently as 2002, incidents of this nature have been reported in India. Other Hindu traditions, less violent but still terrible, enforce seclusion and isolation on widows in the belief that some sin of the woman caused her husband's death, and expect her to atone by spending the rest of her life in silence and destitution. This rule, dramatised by the film maker Deepa Mehta in her 2005 film *Water*, was applied even if the widow was a young child in an arranged marriage who had not even met her husband prior to his death.

Buddhism, as well, despite its reputation as a socially progressive faith, has its share of discriminatory teachings about the role of women. In one passage from the Theravada Buddhist tradition, the Buddha's own aunt, Prajapati, shaves her hair and walks barefoot for many miles to meet the Buddha and entreat him to permit women to join the *sangha*, the Buddhist monastic community. The Buddha at first refuses her plea outright, and only relents when his disciple Ananda persuades him to change his mind; however, he imposes a set of eight rules upon nuns that are stricter than those demanded of monks, and in some variants, warns that the *sangha* will only last for five hundred years due to the presence of women, when it would otherwise have lasted for a thousand. In modern Buddhism, Thailand in particular has shown strong patriarchal tendencies, refusing to allow women to be ordained.

It is tragic, but understandable, why so many men throughout history have supported these sexist and patriarchal belief systems. It is hard to escape the conclusion that men who love God tend to hate women.

What's more incredible is how many women have willingly taken part in their own subjugation by joining and participating in religions that have done their utmost to deny them the full equality and equal rights which they deserve. Many, perhaps, have fallen prey to the ancient and transparently obvious deceit that by doing so, they will gain access to an eternity in Heaven. The mega carrot that has sustained religion through the ages. Although, given that most religions straightforwardly extend their earthly conceptions of hierarchy to the afterlife and picture Heaven as an eternity of male dominance and female submission, one wonders just how appealing that promise could be.

Not all women have been taken in by this con, however, and there have been and are many women who work for reform and equality within their own religious tradition while continuing to believe in it. This is a noble effort, but ultimately misguided. Religion in general, especially the large, institutional, male-run churches like Catholicism, is too dogmatic and too oligarchical for any progress to be made soon enough to help the millions of women who are still suffering under sexist yokes. And as long as people continue to believe in books and traditions that contain these sexist injunctions, the seed of bigotry will always lie dormant, waiting to be rediscovered and reborn. There is only one realistic way to end religion's harm to women and that is to cut it off at the source: every feminist should be an atheist. Sadly that is not a likely outcome. Religion not only makes women servile, it possesses the supreme art of teaching them to love their chains.

I have personal experience of the lowly status occupied by women in the church. My priestly uncle

Heeroom, mentioned earlier, once hit my younger sister in the face because she had the nerve to challenge him on abortion. He would not have done that to a man. He was lucky I was not on the spot. I dread to think what I would have done to him. Tighten his dog collar a notch or two I imagine. When I was an altar boy I was sometimes shunted to a side altar to help out with a ritual which I have since learnt is known as 'churching'. From the back of the empty church a woman, soberly dressed and veiled, would furtively approach the altar and kneel in front of the priest. I still vividly remember the palpable sense of condescension and disdain pouring out of the priest whilst he attended to his business of murmuring Latin and sprinkling holy water. The woman having given birth had to be purified. Presumably because she had sinned at some point in the process.

ABORTION

> *"No woman can call herself free who does not control her own body".*
>
> Margaret Sanger

Because the numbers game is vital to the church, women have always been under pressure to breed to the maximum effect. A role similar to livestock or a garden plot, ready to receive the male seed. Great care is taken that there is no possible escape. No sex education, no contraceptive, no abortion. The fundamentalists fear that if women gain control over their bodies they will go on to fight for full control over their minds and lives and shed the superstitions, fears and prejudices pumped into them over centuries of patriarchal rule to keep them in subjection, mere receptacles for producing babies. A woman's body in the church is not her own, it serves the greater good of boosting the numbers of the faithful to such an extent that if there is a choice between the life of the mother and the embryo the latter must come first. A woman's duty is starkly stated by St. Augustine: "Any woman who does not give birth to as many children as she is capable, is guilty of murder."

But an embryo is not a baby, just as the fish-like progenitors of the human race, crawling ashore from the oceans, were not people. It is illogical to value the life of a human foetus with the faculties of a worm, over the life of a thinking and feeling chimpanzee. It is only when the foetus develops a functional central nervous system with the ability to feel pain that it acquires incipient human rights. The abortion argument in a nutshell is this: if a researcher in a laboratory isolated an ovum and a spermatozoon and disposed of them, there would be no protest. However if before disposing of them he permitted them to fuse into a single cell he would be called a child murderer by anti-abortionists. But if we are dealing in absolutes, why stop at ova/sperm interaction? Why not say, because we are advocating the unbounded right to life, all male and female reproductive cells are entitled to fulfil their life-creating functions? Aren't we otherwise denying potential life on the vastest scale?

Following this line of thought all females of reproductive age should be kept constantly pregnant and the collective sperm/ova production of the world's adult population should be preserved in freezers for future use. Not only that, but efforts should be made to rescue all spontaneous abortions, which by the way, nail

God as the greatest abortionist of them all. Even right to lifers will agree that some potential life is impossible to safeguard. Choices must be made and it should be the woman to decide. Nature has allotted her the monumental task of ensuring the continuation of the human race. But this must not make her the prisoner of her own body or her future destiny. If the pregnancy is wrong then she should have the right to end it. No ifs, no buts, *her* choice. That's how it would be if men were in her position.

The point must not be made here that abortion is a good solution. It is not. It is a tragic failure that in most cases could have been prevented. But a failure that is facilitated by precisely those who are most opposed to it. Anti-abortionists tend to be moralists. Conventional, religion driven, morality dictates that young people be kept ignorant of the facts of life as long as possible. If people were genuinely concerned about abortion you would expect them to leave no stone unturned to promote sex education and all methods of birth control.

The fact that anti-abortionists are at best lukewarm about such measures is clear evidence of ulterior motives. The sanctity of life dissolves into the sanctimony of life. Their crocodile tears are not for the unborn. I suspect there is a hidden desire to punish women who have sinned and must not get away with it. Elsewhere such people don't live up to the role of sentimental protectors of innocent life either. They tend to support the death penalty, ironically turning pro-life for embryos into pro-death for adults. They ignore the millions in shanty towns, where abortion is not an option and advocate violence against abortion clinics and doctors. Nor are they capable of compassion towards women who face the agonising choice between an abortion and a much unwanted child. Until birth control is adopted on a much wider scale there will be no alternative to abortions on the just premise that the welfare of those already here constitutes the greater good.

THE EMERALD ISLE (THAT CAN BE VILE)

Ireland, until the priestly abuse scandals broke some years ago, used to be a near theocracy and a hellhole for any woman finding herself with an unwanted pregnancy. At independence from the UK in 1922, the Offences against the Person Act 1861 remained in force, deeming all abortions to be illegal and subject to punishment. One of Ireland's best-known abortionists, Marnie Cadden, was infamously sentenced to death by hanging in 1957, when one of her patients died. – this was later commuted to life imprisonment. In 1983 the Irish constitution was amended to add the Eighth Amendment, which asserted that the unborn had an explicit right to life.

In 1992, a suicidal 14 year old girl, who was pregnant from statutory rape, was prevented from leaving Ireland for an abortion in another country. This outrage made me so mad that I fired off a letter to Prime Minister Albert Reynolds: "Dear Sir, What is the matter with your country that at the end of the twentieth century you should allow a fourteen year old child to be treated as nothing more than a plantpot for passing rapists with no way of escape. No wonder your nation is often looked upon as an international joke. I suggest that you try to climb out of the dark ages as soon as possible, cease acting as a satellite to the Vatican and join the rest of civilisation. With best wishes for a speedy return to sanity." This may conceivably have done some good because another referendum followed later in the year which opened the way to foreign travel and the right to information.

A further abomination occurred, as recently as 2012, when a 31 year old dentist was refused an abortion while miscarrying in hospital, dying of septicaemia as a result. This then led to a further loosening of the stranglehold on the bodies of Irish women but abortion in most circumstances still remains illegal. Some 4000 Irish women a year travel to the UK to seek an abortion under British law. Not only has Ireland's Catholic legacy given it this appalling record on compulsory childbearing it has also been the international front-runner on priestly sexual abuse.

The Catholic sexual abuse scandal in Ireland forms a major chapter in the world-wide epidemic. Unlike the Catholic sexual abuse scandal in the United States, the scandal in Ireland included cases of high-profile Catholic clerics involved in illicit heterosexual relations as well as widespread physical abuse of children in the Catholic-run childcare network. Prior to 1980 the accepted norm in the Irish Church was that its priest-hood was celibate and chaste, and homosexuality was a sin as well as a crime. The Church forbade its members to use artificial contraception, campaigned strongly against laws allowing abortion and divorce, and publicly disapproved of unmarried co-habiting couples and illegitimacy. Therefore it came as a consid-erable surprise when the Irish media started to report allegations that the priesthood itself had been ignoring these moral strictures and had been committing wide-ranging abuse.

Starting in the 1990s, a series of criminal cases and Irish government enquiries established that hundreds of priests had abused thousands of children in previous decades. In many cases, the abusing priests were moved to other parishes to avoid embarrassment or a scandal, assisted by senior clergy. In response to the furore aroused by the media reports, the Irish government commissioned a study which took nine years to complete. On 20 May 2009, the commission released its 2600-page report, which drew on testimony from thousands of former inmates and officials from more than 250 church-run institutions. The commission found that Catholic priests and nuns had terrorised thousands of boys and girls for decades and that government inspectors had failed to stop the chronic beatings, rapes and humiliation. The report characterised rape and molestation as 'endemic' in Irish Catholic church-run industrial schools and orphanages. Investigations continue in cases where Irish abusers were sent abroad by the church to other countries, where they abused other children.

In June 2014 another scandal came to light. A mass grave containing the remains of 796 babies and children, was discovered at the Tuam 'Mothers and Babies' Home in County Galway. The children had been buried in a disused septic tank. The Tuam home was run by the Bon Secours Sisters, as one of their ten institutions to which about 35000 unmarried pregnant women, so called 'fallen women' are thought to have been sent in the years between 1925 and 1961.

One is entitled to wonder if the constant stream of horrors emerging from the priest and nun dominated episode in Irish history will finally persuade the Irish people that they would be much better of waving their fond goodbyes to the Catholic church for good.

To escape unwanted pregnancies, women in many other countries and American states, are forced to travel long distances at great inconvenience and expense to obtain deliverance elsewhere. Even then hazards remain. Abortion clinics are often targets for abuse. Since the mid seventies in America there have been over two hundred arson and bombing attacks. Other methods of disruption are Butyric acid attacks and Anthrax threats. There have been 7 murders of clinic staff. Some pro-life campaigners want doctors dead. Let me quote Randall Terry, founder of Operation Rescue, an organisation for intimidating abortion providers: "When I, or people like me, are running the country, you'd better flee, because we will find you, we will try you and we will execute you. I mean every word of it. I will make it part of my mission to see to it that they are tried and executed".

This man was talking about doctors who provide abortions. In another statement he makes it clear what 24 carat Taliban Christians like him would like to see America become: "I want you to just let a wave of intolerance wash over you. I want you to let a wave of hatred wash over you. Yes, hatred is good. Our goal is a Christian nation. We have a Biblical duty, we are called by God, to conquer this country. We don't want equal time. We don't want pluralism. Our goal must be simple. We must have a Christian nation built on God's law, or the Ten Commandments. No apologies". The worrying thing is this fascist has lots of company. On abortion at least, Islam fares a little better. Muslims regard abortion as wrong and haram (forbidden) but concede that it is permitted if continuing the pregnancy would put the mother's life at risk.

FEMALE GENITAL MUTILATION – FORCED MARRIAGE

"...a noble practice which does honour to women."
(Sheikh Gad Al Haq, commenting on FGM)

However Muslims do less well when it comes to the barbaric practice of FGM, female genital mutilation. This ritual is carried out mostly on girls before the age of five. A staggering 125 million girls and women in 30 countries in Africa and the Middle East have undergone this appalling procedure. There are no health benefits. The main purpose is to enforce virginity and fidelity. In other words it is strictly for the benefit of men. Although its origins are pre-islamic, it became associated with Islam because of that religion's focus on female modesty and chastity and is found only within Muslim communities.

In the UK the true extent of FGM is hidden. It is estimated that some 70 thousand women have been cut. The practice has been illegal since 1985 but no doubt because of cultural and religious sensitivity, no cases have yet come to court. This is further proof that there is little concern in Britain for the welfare of ethnic minority girls. The authorities would rather condone this ghastly ritual than run the risk of offending those who promote it. Under the multicultural umbrella even vile torture is sacrosanct. Can you imagine the outcry if just a single case of FMG was perpetrated on a white British child! The brutal thugs who cut away at young girls genitals remain at liberty whilst sad old men who had wandering hands when young forty, fifty years ago, are now languishing in prison. Why do you think that is? It is because we are dealing with untouchable culture and religion, doubly protected by the ever present slur of racial discrimination. An October 2007 study revealed that over 20,000 girls could be at risk of Female Genital Mutilation in the UK. 16,000 girls under the age of 15 at high risk of WHO (World Health Organisation) Type 3 and over 5,000 at high risk of WHO Type 1 or 2. I will spare you the unpleasant details of what these types signify.

Another example of cultural iniquity is forced marriage of which the annual number in Britain is estimated at 8000. Some charities say the actual number is far higher because many victims are afraid to come forward. The practice has been condoned for years but now a new law has come into effect in England and Wales that makes it a crime to force people into an unwanted marriage. Advocates of the law say it represents a benchmark shift in thinking because—after decades of kow-towing to multicultural sensitivities—British policymakers now view forced marriage as a gross violation of human rights rather than a socially acceptable cultural difference. They also say the law will create a deterrent effect because many perpetrators will fear criminal prosecution.

The new law, which came into effect in June 2014, makes forced marriage a self-standing criminal offence in England and Wales (the law does not extend to

Northern Ireland and will be introduced in Scotland at a later date) and is punishable by up to seven years in prison. The law also makes it a crime to breach a so-called Forced Marriage Protection Order (issued by courts to prevent people from being married against their will) in England and Wales, in line with Scotland where this is already the case. This crime now carries a penalty of up to five years in prison. In addition, the law makes it a crime to take a British national overseas with the intention of forcing them to marry, even if the forced marriage does not ultimately take place. It is estimated that every year, hundreds of British girls are being taken out of school and flown abroad to be married, sometimes to men who may be two or three times their age.

In 2013, one thousand three hundred victims of forced marriage sought help from the Forced Marriage Unit, a special agency established by the British government. Some 82 per cent of victims were female and 18 per cent male, while 15 per cent were under the age of 15. The forced marriage cases in 2013 involved 74 different countries, with 43 per cent relating to Pakistan, 11 per cent to India and 10 per cent to Bangladesh. Most of the other cases stemmed from Afghanistan, Egypt, Iran, Iraq, Morocco, Nigeria, Saudi Arabia, Somalia, Tunisia and Yemen. As is the case with FGM there will be reluctance to vigorously implement the new law. There may be some evidence in support of this scepticism. In Scotland, for example, where Forced Marriage Protection Orders were introduced into law in 2011, there have been no prosecutions for breaches of the orders since then.

Not surprisingly, nearly everyone involved in the debate seems to agree that ending the epidemic of forced marriage in Britain will require much more than a change in legislation. The new law is a "huge step forward," said NSPCC director Ash Chand. "However, there is still much work to be done. Choosing a life partner is a basic human right ... yet, despite this, many children and young people are being coerced or even forced to do so without their consent."

Britain is not the only European country coming to grips with forced marriage. Austria, Belgium, Cyprus, Denmark, Germany, Malta and Norway have already outlawed the practice. In addition, 23 European countries have signed, and 11 have ratified, the Council of Europe's Istanbul Convention, which commits state parties to introduce new laws at the national level to outlaw forced marriage and other forms of violence against women.

In recent years women have finally been gaining some recognition. Not out of remorse for past misogyny, you understand. It is more expedient than that. There is a growing manpower crisis. The Church of England is setting the pace. First after much agony and prayerful debate: women vicars. They have been a great success. Much better in the job than pompous men. Next stop women bishops and who knows, eventually a female archbishopess. The Church of Rome is struggling too. Vocation is not what it used to be. Which budding paedophile would want to join that club, now that this tempting perk has been suppressed. They cling to doctrine a little better at the Vatican but in due course a way will be found to tweak the scriptures and the dogma so that they too can get the priesthood back up to strength. Because survival of the business trumps doctrine every time. No doubt first married priests and if that is not enough a nose holding operation to get the dreaded women into cassocks. But until that comes about the question remains how self-respecting women can possibly feel comfortable within this woman hostile religion.

HOMOSEXUALITY

> *"Just last week I saw two homosexual men at the supermarket. The supermarket! In broad daylight! That's what you get when you worship the creation instead of the creator".*
> [Rev. Terry Glidden, Washington Post].

Another category of humanity unloved by religion are homosexuals. Theists seem never to have discovered the fact that sexuality is on a continuum, ranging from strongly heterosexual to strongly homosexual with many transgendered stages in between. Nor have they learned, even though it's obvious, that these conditions are innate and not somebody's choice. In forming their attitude towards it they take their instruction from the bible. Lev. 18:22: "you shall not lie with a male as one lies with a female; it is an abomination" There are at least three further quotes making clear that homosexuality is a sin, an abomination unto the Lord. Leviticus 20:13 demands that homosexuals be put to death. And this is exactly what the Christian churches did for over 1,800 years. They followed literally and precisely the murderous incitements of Leviticus 20:13, sponsoring the mass murder of gays. They were stoned to death in antiquity, burned alive during the medieval era and, in Britain, hanged from gallows until the mid-nineteenth century. This persecution took place with the official blessing of successive Popes and Archbishops of Canterbury.

The murder of gays in the name of God is comparable to the Nazi extermination of Jews. Both Christianity and Nazism demonised, scapegoated and murdered minorities. Nazi anti-Semitism parallels Christian homophobia. The Bible is to gays what Mein Kampf is to Jews. It is the theory and practice of Homo Holocaust.

While the church no longer advocates the death penalty for gay lovers, it still preaches a gospel of sexual apartheid, arguing that homosexuality should not be accorded the same moral or legal status as heterosexuality. The unctuous phrase 'love the sinner, hate the sin' sums up their attitude.

This claim for the moral superiority of heterosexuality is analogous to the way the leaders of the Dutch Reformed Church defended white superiority during the apartheid era in South Africa. It echoes their theological justification of racial discrimination against black people. If church leaders advocated similar discrimination against black or Jewish people, there would be a nation- wide outcry and near-universal calls for their resignation. They would be shunned and disgraced. Islam too is homophobic. All major Islamic sects forbid homosexuality which is a crime under Sharia law and treated as such in most Muslim countries. The GPA (Gay Police Association) was reprimanded for an ad which implied Christians were responsible for a huge rise in violent attacks on homosexuals. The advert, placed in the Independent newspaper under the banner "in the name of the father" showed a Bible and a pool of blood. It was a one-off, used to back the GPA's claim that the association had recorded a 75 per cent increase in homophobic incidents, where the sole or primary motivating factor was the religious belief of the perpetrator. The association said Christians were not the only group accused, in fact a quarter of the alleged incidents were provoked by Muslims.

For the Catholic church the issue calls for massive hypocrisy. I know from my own boarding school experience that homosexuality is rife amongst Roman Catholic clergy. This was confirmed when Journalist Mark Dowd, a former Dominican friar, approached Channel 4 with a proposal for a documentary on homosexuality and the Catholic Church with a simple pitch: "I want to show why my church is so anti-gay". "Why is your church so anti-gay", came back the obvious question. "Because it is so gay", he replied. He then spelt out the logic. Having interviewed clerics and ex-seminarians in the UK, US and Rome, he had uncovered a huge irony: the very institution that teaches that homosexuality is 'intrinsically disordered' attracts gay candidates for the priesthood in numbers way in excess of what one would expect, based on the numbers in society at large. One seminary rector based on his own experience told him the number was at least 50 per cent.

A further irony was the recent resignation of Cardinal Keith O'Brien, the very man whose trenchant rhetoric on the subjects of gay adoption and marriage has been brought down by accusations of improper same-sex behaviour from no less than four men who crossed his path in the 1980's, either as a seminary rector or as archbishop of Edinburgh. This blatant two-facedness applies not only to the church of Rome. Colorado evangelical preacher Ted Haggard, married and father of five children spent years assuring that LGBT individuals would be getting their fair share of hellfire and brimstone, before his 20 year old male lover, Grant Haas, spilled the beans on the *'Larry King Live'* show. He said Haggard had told him: "You know what Grant, you can become a man of God and you can have a little bit of fun on the side". Then there was George Rekers, Baptist minister and leading light of the Family Research Council who had sloped off on a not-so-secret European holiday with a younger man.

In future any gay person hearing a senior cleric describing his orientation in hostile and uncompromising language is entitled to ask the question: 'is this really about me, or is it more about you'?

The humanist view of course is that all sexual orientation and conduct is up to the person(s) concerned and if no harm is done, is nobody else's business.

Religious Prudery

Puritanism – the haunting fear that someone,
somewhere, may be happy.

H.L. Mencken

Although theists are formidable breeders they have
never been relaxed about the means of procreation.
Sex and religion are very uncomfortable bedfellows. In
fact they much prefer separate rooms. Their prudery
knows no bounds. Sex to the religious is a dirty shame-
ful business. It is like a gardener feeling guilty about
planting seeds. They have a whole lexicon of disgust to
show their deep distaste: smut, dirt, filth, obscenity,
indecency, wantonness, depravity, pornography. This
strange aversion can only be explained by the dire
warnings from their holy books where sin is liberally
basted onto matters sexual when not in full pursuit of
procreation. It used to be said that Mary Whitehouse's
Festival of Light did it in the dark. Because there could
be no openness about matters sexual, the levels of
hypocrisy were staggering. Philip Larkin expressed it in
a poem: 'Sexual intercourse began in nineteen sixty
three, between the end of the Chatterley ban and the
Beatles' first LP'. Sex was the taboo to end all taboos.
This meant no sex education or birth control advice.

In the ensuing Vatican roulette, families of up to fifteen were not exceptional. Good for the churches' power game but calamitous for the poor woman on the receiving end. As a means of birth control Catholic women may employ arithmetic but they are still forbidden to resort to physics and chemistry.

Mary Whitehouse is long dead but her legacy lives on. The sin and guilt attached to sex in the religious mind surfaces in many different ways. Such people have hang-ups about what is permitted and what is not and suffer grievously if their personal proclivities clash with what they think the Lord demands. Hence the large number of US preacher types and in England naughty vicars who fulminate against homosexuality from the pulpit only to be caught with rent boys in the bushes. Prof. Robert Trivers has conducted research on men who do not like homosexuals, using complicated technology and gay porn. The results suggest that the more antagonistic you are, the greater the extent of your latent homo-sexuality. Thus it might be said 'the ladyboy protests too much'. As for Roman Catholics priests we all know what has been bothering them. Lord Longford, a porn again Christian, went all the way to Denmark to be scandalised by Scandinavian pornography. Afterwards he became Myra Hindley's most sympathetic prison visitor. Lay religious adults too are troubled about sex. They have their knickers firmly in a holy twist. Why has sex acquired this unsavoury reputation? Is it because God is watching them? It has been reported that some religious couples turn pictures of Jesus and Mary to face the bedroom wall.

Strangely enough they are in the habit of conflating it with violence. Sex and violence, a phrase as familiar as 'bacon and eggs', and 'stocks and shares'. Why this linkage is always made is hard to fathom. Possibly because to get such people anywhere near a bedstead violence was unavoidable. In reality censorship is almost entirely restricted to sex, and violence has free reign. When most of the sex scenes were cut from the TV version of the 'Fatal Attraction' film the ghastly rabbit boiling incident, desperately upsetting for children (and animal loving adults too) was left in. Similarly in a documentary about undesirable computer games everything of a sexual nature was excised but there were no reservations about showing sickening scenes of people being decapitated and having their limbs cut off.

There are countless nature programmes aimed at children shown before the watershed, often depicting ghastly hunting scenes were animals are torn apart by predators. All without the slightest warning. Without our speedy remote controls to edit out the violence I could no longer watch these programmes. I am not calling for censorship but do they really have to focus so much on the unpleasant aspects of nature so that the ghouls amongst us can have their fill. In justification we are told that nature behaves like that and they are show-ing how it is. However to spare the children's blushes scenes of animal matings are carefully edited out.

The message is quite clear: violence gets the thumbs up but for nudity the alarm bells ring. Predictably there is little call for censorship of violence on the internet but there are plenty 'net nanny' programmes, intercepting anything of a remotely sexual nature. This has led to such ludicrous examples as the shortening of Scun-thorpe into Shorpe. I am pretty sure there is no clean-up software that is designed for blocking pictures of people being beaten, shot or otherwise assaulted. Bloodied bodies are preferred to denuded bodies. No masking function for words like shoot, pow, biff or kill. Communications regulator Ofcom has examined the amount of violence in soaps, Eastenders, Hollyoaks, Coronation Street and Emmerdale at different times in the past twelve years. Taken together the amount of violence has increased; 62 per cent of episodes had violent scenes in 2001, rising to 77 per cent in 2013. Films too are censored for explicit sex scenes but rarely for violence. If pornography is expected to corrupt why are the censors not corrupted and why are they queuing up to do the job?

Puritanism also has an aggravating effect within the judiciary. In September 2013 and June 2014 there were two almost identical court cases involving lorry drivers in Birmingham and Telford, driving at 55 miles an hour, both causing fatal accidents due to inattention. One was sending texts, the other downloading pornography. The texter was given 6 months; the pornographer got 5 years. The naked rambler spends his life in jail. The logic in all this is hard to find.

Children are not meant to become violent so we are showing them in detail how it is done. Children are meant to become sexually active later in life, so we are keeping them as unaware as possible. It is like training up an electrician without telling him/her about voltage. Like those ignorant about sex, they would be in for quite a shock! Children are not born with sexual guilt, it is inculcated by adult carers who are puritanical. Sexual images tend to pass children by until they understand and are interested. Prudish adults calling for censorship use children as an excuse. They daren't admit that they themselves have a problem for fear of ridicule. But we suspect what bothers them. They become moral busybodies because their bodies are not busy. Moral indignation permits envy or hate to be acted out under the guise of virtue. Plagued by censors famous Italian film producer Vittorio de Sica said: "moral indignation is in most cases 2 per cent moral, 48 per cent indignation and 50 per cent envy".

Child protection has grown to ridiculous proportions. Some schools are instructing male teachers not to pick up girl pupils fallen over in the playground. When I visited a school for a conference about religious education I was followed around the corridors by a female supervisor all the way to the male toilets! Typically enough ministers of the cloth at the same conference were exempted from this embarrassing surveillance. Will people never learn?

Currently Britain is consumed by a massive witch hunt, looking for alleged sexual abuse dating back some forty to fifty years. Octogenarian celebrities are in court accused of various touchings, gropings and fumbles in the distant past. A 93 year old man in court, leaning on his Zimmer frame, has been sent to prison. I am not talking rape or violence here. The reason anonymous accusers give for not complaining earlier is invariably that they would not have been believed. Not by parents, teachers, neighbours, friends, social workers, the police!? Even if a child doesn't talk, severe distress would readily be apparent and adults would ask searching questions.

I have heard grown men weeping on radio, explaining that their lives have been ruined because many decades earlier someone had touched their private parts. I must be sceptical here. I have seen too many cases at boarding school where boys willingly traded sexual fondlings from priestly tutors for a variety of favours without undue repercussions. If grown men are now in tears I suspect either a guilt-laden, religion induced hang-up about sex or an Oscar worthy acting performance in pursuit of financial compensation.

Like some social workers I feel that there is too much emphasis on physical abuse of this kind and not enough on sometimes horrific emotional abuse. This is also the view of the charity Action for Children whose director Helen Donohoe has said: "I've met children who have been scapegoated, bullied, left alone in dark rooms in beds full of maggots, they are vilified and victimised by their parents, the very people who are supposed to love them best of all". Personally I would happily swap any physical 'touchings' in the wrong places for the years of emotional abuse suffered at the (in my case non-physical) hands of the Catholic church.

Whilst humanists may not agree with all of my opinion here, they certainly would not look upon sex as an ominous dark force to be reviled as sinful and kept away as far as possible, only to be engaged in when all other options have run out. They see consensual sex as one of the most pleasurable activities that nature has provided. And like the bonobos they attach no guilt. As for all the gratuitous violence let's expose it for what it is: sensationalist trash to be put to ridicule at every opportunity. Humanists don't like censorship because where films and books are burned people will be next. But if we got to have it at all let's turn our bullet free guns on to mindless violence and leave sex safely alone.

POPULATION GROWTH

*"Which is the greater danger - nuclear warfare or
the population explosion? The latter absolutely! To bring
about nuclear war, someone has to DO something; someone
has to press a button. To bring about destruction by
overcrowding, mass starvation, anarchy, the destruction
of our most cherished values, there is no need to do anything.
We need only do nothing except what comes naturally -
and breed. And how easy it is to do nothing".*

Dr. Isaac Asimov, biochemist and science writer.
(In this 1966 interview he predicted that world population
(then at 3.3 billion) would reach 6 billion around 2000.
Most leaders dismissed his prediction as outrageous.
The population passed 6 billion in 1999.)

Looking at it selfishly, being part of a large family has
its advantages, but from a wider societal perspective
unchecked procreation is of course calamitous.

As an adolescent I came across the writings of
Malthus and I soon realised that exponential population
growth had to be one of the major threats to the long
term well-being of mankind. I remember writing to an
uncle of mine who had managed the considerable feat
of producing no fewer than sixteen offspring, pointing
out that if everybody else behaved in such reckless
fashion the Dutch population, in the space of just one

generation, would balloon from around 8 million to more than 30 million.

When I met him again, some 40 years later, at my father's funeral, he still had not forgiven me. By that time the population had doubled to 16 million so other people had been at it as well but in a more restrained fashion. Looking back I am surprised at the depth of my outrage at that early age, risking my parents' displeasure if found out. But ever since unbridled breeding has remained my number one concern about the human condition.

Most pernicious of all is unplanned, unrestricted, mindless propagation at the behest of religious dogma. The go forth and multiply command, issued in some ancient obscure script, is still pointlessly and sheepishly obeyed today. At one point in history optimising fertility will have been necessary to sustain the human race but there is no case for excessive growth in our time. The resources and space on earth are finite and cannot accommodate a doubling of population every fifty years. The advocates of "go forth and be fruitful" seem to me to be either amazingly ignorant or very wicked. People with large families have been known to say that they can afford to have their brood and that therefore it is *their* choice and nobody else's business. Would that we could live in isolation from such people. They overlook that their ten offspring will require five times more housing, food, water, clothing, transport, than everybody else's statutory two. Do they really believe that their freedom to breed like rabbits has no effect on everybody else's circumstances? John Donne once said "every man's death diminishes me" but would it not be truer to say that "every man's birth diminishes me"?

As millions must live in desperate poverty in ghastly overcrowded shanty towns as a direct result of preachings against birth control and abortion, all the religious leaders choose to do is stand aside, utter pious platitudes and exhort their flock to further prayer. Then these tearstained crocodiles slink back to their palaces and are short of nothing. For the faithful the whole perilous exercise is underwritten by the catch-all "God or Allah will provide". The trouble is these gods won't provide as future generations will learn to their cost.

GROWTH TRENDS AND STATISTICS

Whereas in Europe population growth has virtually come to a standstill, globally the picture is much more alarming and the chief driving force is religion. Population projections for the year 2050 confirm the disproportionate growth numbers for the major religions. The world Christian population (Catholics and Protestants combined) in the year 2000 numbered 2000 million. Projected growth for the year 2050 is 1050 million, an increase of 52 per cent. For Islam growth is higher still: From a year 2000 base of 1200 million, growth is expected to amount to 1040 million, a frightening rate of 87 percent. Overall it is predicted that the world's Muslim population will grow twice as fast as that of non Muslims. At this rate Muslims will make up more than a quarter of the global population by 2030. Across all religions the rule is, the more orthodox the religion, the higher the growth rates. Orthodox Jews in Israel have three times more children than other Israelis. At least a quarter of Israel's population of under 17s is expected to be ultra-ortho-dox by 2025.

Mormons in America have grown from six people in a log cabin in upstate New York in 1830 to some 15 million today. If their growth pattern continues the Mormon religion will emerge as one of the major world religions in the next century. In the past 20 years the Amish population in the US has doubled from 123,000 in 1991 to 250,000 in 2010. The average number of children per family is six. Conservative American Protestants have increased from a 40 per cent minority of white Protestants born in 1900, to a two-thirds majority among those born in 1975. The slight fertility advantage of conservative over liberal Protes-tants accounts for three-quarters of the rise. The number of Latinos in the States has soared due to immigration and a high birth-rate. A tiny number in 1960, they now number 15 per cent of the population. The US census bureau projects they will make up a quarter of the total by 2050.

Rodney Stark, a sociologist of religion, has shown how a slight demographic advantage for early Christians – a function of superior care of their sick, a family-centred ethos and a high percentage of female converts – explains much of the increase in their ranks between 30 and 300 CE (Common Era). He calculates that 40 per cent growth per decade is sufficient to account for the expansion of the 'Jesus movement' from just 40 to 6 million converts in the period prior to Christianity becoming Rome's official religion.

German researcher Dr Michael Blume, has shown quite vividly that non-religious people everywhere are being dramatically out-produced by religious people of any faith. Across a broad swath of demographic data relating to religiosity, the godly are gaining traction in offspring produced. For example, there is a global-wide positive correlation between frequency of parental worship attendance and their number of children. Those who 'never' attend religious services bear, on a world-wide average, 1.67 children per lifetime; 'once per month' and the average goes up to 2.01 children; 'more than once a week' equates to 2.5 children. A Swiss Statistic Office poll, conducted in the year 2000, revealed that the score for non-religious Swiss mothers was a measly 1.11 children. Austria is the only country that records religious beliefs of parents. Their figure of 0.85 children per atheist couple is far below the replacement level of 2.1.

In his study *'Breeding for God'* Dr. Eric Kaufman of Birbeck College, says that "in an analysis of European data from ten W-European countries in the period 1981-2004, I found that next to age and marital status a woman's religiosity was the strongest predictor of her number of offspring".

The religious population holds two demographic advantages over its non-believing counterpart. First it maintains a 15 to 20 per cent fertility lead over the non-religious. Second, religious people in the childbearing 18-45 age range are disproportionally female.

It is difficult to predict what proportion of Europe's population will be of non-European descent in the future because few European countries collect census data on ethnicity and religion. The sometimes cited figure of 30 per cent ethnic minorities in Western Europe by 2050 is little more than an educated guess. One of the few countries to collect ethno-religious census information is Austria where a recent projection, based on a conservative estimate of 20,000 immigrants a year and various assumptions about religious abandonment and fertility, predicted that Muslims would make up between 14 and 26 per cent of the population by 2050 up from just 4 per cent today.

In Britain 4.7 per cent of those under 16 are Muslim, compared to just 0.6 per cent of those over 65. Muslim families are larger than others- the total fertility rate of Muslim women is about 65 per cent higher than that of the average British woman. 27 per cent of Muslim families have three or more dependent children, compared to 14 per cent of Sikh, 8 per cent of Hindu and 7 per cent of Christian families. If immigration stopped tomorrow, Muslims' higher fertility and young age structure would still ensure a rise in the share of the total, which would be most in evidence in the maternity hospitals and primary schools. Though Muslims are younger and more fertile than Sikhs, Buddhists and Hindus, this is not a solely Islamic phenomenon. In Britain in 2001, 8.5 per cent of the population was born abroad, but one in five births were to foreign-born mothers, rising to one in two in London. This compares to one in three for Paris.

Drastic reductions in immigration are not likely to happen. Europe's native population is ageing and declining. This will stimulate a demand for further economic migration by employers' groups, as well as the NHS and other public services. Asylum seeking, boat people landings, sham marriage and illegal immigration are difficult to control in liberal societies, so the flow of roughly 250.000 Muslims into the European Community each year will probably continue.

So what does the future hold? Dr. Kaufman's projections for many west European countries find that Muslims will make up between 4 and 14 per cent of the population by 2030, a large increase from the 2-6 per cent range today. Sweden will be the most Islamic country in Europe. Britain's Muslim population will be close to 7 per cent, or 5 million, compared to 2.8 per cent in 2001.

One may well ask why are the religious so inclined to procreate. Apart from the old testament commandment, there is the strength in numbers objective. Both major religions are vying for supremacy. Head-counts give them vast advantages. It is quantity that counts, quality is a secondary issue. In a democracy the majority vote determines policy. People not egged on by religious leaders are unlikely to choose large families. To humanists unbridled breeding is complete anathema. They know rapid population growth and harmonious society cannot co-exist. It is the single gravest threat to a benign future for both the human race and non-human animals. They are fully aware that the price of personal freedom in making childbearing decisions may be the destruction of the world in which children and grandchildren will have to live. But as long as humanists are not strongly represented in national governments and world bodies such as the UN it is unlikely that their concerns will receive much attention.

Theists who have handed responsibility to a Deity can afford to be more sanguine. There is now incontrovertible evidence for man-made climate change and since we are adding two cities the size of Bath to world population every single day, it does not take rocket science to understand that in the not too distant future the world faces disaster. Lets look at the growth statistics in an historical perspective. It took two million years to reach a two billion population. Then 45 years to arrive at the second two billion and a mere 30 years to achieve the third two billion. Economic growth trends are published everywhere and we are given updates each month, but unsustainable population growth is largely ignored.

The world began without man and unless there is drastic change, it will complete itself without us. People are blissfully unaware of the dangers of exponential growth. It creeps up on you and then suddenly grabs you by the throat. Let me illustrate: if a pond fills up with frogs in 30 days, doubling in numbers each day, it will still only be half occupied on day twenty nine. On day thirty a ghastly blow befalls the frogs, suddenly they find themselves in Oxford Street on the last shopping day before Christmas. In cricketing terms it could be said that the globe is in the last over, batting for survival and mankind is about to be hit for six.

The key point to remember about exponential growth is that a long history of exponential growth in no way implies a long future of exponential growth. What begins in slow motion will eventually overwhelm us in a flash. Countries with frightening birth rates might one day find themselves in this position. Bangladesh is almost there. The indifference to this menace can be likened to falling off a skyscraper and whispering "so far so good" whilst sailing past the final floor. It is easy for the oldies amongst us to take the 'it will last my time' view but this is a harder thing to do when children and grandchildren are involved. I know that the human race is mightily resourceful and the dire predictions made in

'The Population Bomb' by Paul Ehrlich in 1968 have not (yet) been born out. But postponement may not mean cancellation and many dangers do remain. A few rats in a cage may peaceably co-exist but increase the numbers and fights will become the norm.

Neither of the main religions is inclined to help stem the numbers. Both are vehemently opposed to abortion and birth control is erratic or non-existent. Everywhere there are calls for less destruction to rain forests, less pollution, fewer roads, railways, fewer housing developments on green land, nothing in my backyard, but people ought to realise that without turning off the population tap, no amount of mopping up, no amount of protest about the repercussions, will hold back the tide. Every additional human will feel entitled to food, clothing, shelter and an increasing range of extras, including schooling, transport, entertainment and hospital care. All these take their toll on the environment. There is a stark choice here: either switch to a carefully planned, sustainable human life support policy or be brutally forced into that switch by nature through the untimely deaths of large numbers of human beings.

What will eventually put paid to the numbers is difficult to predict. The main dangers are starvation, disease and warfare. Food shortage is probably of the least concern. So far agriculture has more than kept up with population increase. Technology is playing an increasingly important part in food production. Progress in the output and efficiency of farm machinery, better quality of seeds, chemicals, irrigation methods, fertilisers, pesticides and genetic engineering are playing major parts in improving yields, without further land clearance. This will mean that for a long time to come increasing yields per hectare will keep up with the demands of a growing population. But a time must come that even agricultural elasticity will be stretched beyond breaking point.

More worrying is the ever lurking danger of disease. Development of antibiotics is struggling to keep up with constantly mutating bacteria. Pandemics such as Ebola, Influenza, Cholera and HIV/Aids and even Bubonic plague, are always lurking in the shadows.

My own worst fear is nuclear warfare. Now that nuclear arsenals are in the hands of volatile regimes such as North Korea, Pakistan and possibly Iran, there is the constant danger that one day this devastating balloon will go up. Strife in the world will continue and probably worsen as population numbers increase. Currently United Nations peacekeepers have no teeth. The blue berets in Bosnia were reduced to helpless spectators.

My proposal for an attempt at lasting world peace goes like this: all nations must simultaneously surrender their nuclear arsenals and armies (yes, you too, America and Russia!). Local police forces may remain. All nations contribute arms and soldiers to build a UN army more powerful by far than any individual country's internal forces. If then some upstart dictator anywhere is misbehaving he (and doubtless it will always be a he) will be given a single warning. If this is not heeded the UN special forces will step in and lock him up. Regretfully such a scheme is unlikely to get off the ground. Countries are just too nationalistic. But the status quo will guarantee further mayhem, increasing in severity as populations grow and are forced to compete for dwindling resources.

MULTICULTURALISM

*"Happily integrated immigrants adjust to the host
country's civilisational norms. Those who carry a bed
of native earth with them, like Dracula's 'undead'
are doomed to the pain of perpetual exile"*

Sunanda Datta-Ray, Indian Journalist

Multiculturalism is one of the most emotive and
sensitive subjects in British politics. When it
comes to a definition it seems that a distinction can be
made between three types: first there is the 'live and
let live' multiculturalism of the 1950s which assumed
that if people could keep significant aspects of their
culture they would choose to integrate in their own
way; second the 1980s 'soft' multiculturalism of tolerance and equal rights and third: the more recent 'hard'
multiculturalism of positive promotion of religious
and ethnic identities, promulgated under the Labour
government of Tony Blair. This version of multiculturalism is a notion that cultures, no matter how anti-thetical
to the norm of the host nation, should be allowed to
develop unhindered, without criticism. Not only has
there been this relaxed attitude to diverse cultural
customs, it has gone hand in hand with virtually unrestricted immigration. This unfortunate strategy has

meant that immigration from non-EU countries has increased enormously in the last 30 years. It has been running at more than 100,000 a year for a decade. But by no means all of the new arrivals, many of whom come from what are categorised as ethnic minorities, have found it easy to adopt British values.

Labour ministers, as they dismantled almost all immigration controls, imagined that there would be no problem about integration. They thought the only issue would be racism from the local population. That was a complete misreading. Some of the arriving groups have deep commitments to religious views that place women in a subordinate position, and which lead them to think that practices such as homosexuality are an abomination that should be severely punished.

Values that most of us would think of as essential elements of being British – tolerance, recognising the importance of equality before the law, or even the primacy of democratic elections as the way of deciding who should govern – have not been accepted by a significant minority of immigrants. Some even wish to cut themselves off from liberal and tolerant Britain completely. They hope to perpetuate their own religious values by having their own education system. The doctrine of 'multiculturalism' does not see a problem with that. In the 1980s, multiculturalism's high noon, Bradford city council adopted a policy that declared that every section of the 'multicultural, multiracial city' had "an equal right to maintain its own identity, culture, language, religion and customs".

Everyone else in the country in a position of power held the same opinion. Diversity was a good in itself, so making Britain truly diverse would enrich it and bring 'significant cultural contributions', reflecting a widespread belief among the ruling classes that multi-culturalism and cultural, racial and religious diversity were morally positive objectives whatever the conse-quences. This was the unthinking assumption held by almost the entire political, media and education establishment.

Dr. Rowan Williams, when still Archbishop of Canterbury, said that adopting Sharia Law is inevitable and would help maintain social cohesion. He stated that "An approach to law which simply said — there's one law for everybody — I think that's a bit of a danger". Muslims should be able to choose to have marital disputes or financial matters dealt with in a Sharia court, for example. This would, he claimed, remove the need for Muslims to choose between "the stark alternatives of cultural loyalty or state loyalty". What he was doing (and using Islam as a sort of Trojan horse) was to advance the demands of the religious for separate, religiously-inspired laws which trump the common civil law.

Many of us, particularly humanists, see all this as a highly alarming development. It opens the door to the creation of a divided Britain, where different communi-ties do not interact with each other and all sense of a common identity is lost, replaced by a Babel of languages and conflicting cultures and religions.

Its principal effect has been to harden dividing lines between ethnic groups. This is not just a matter of whites living in different areas from non-whites, but also of (for example) Pakistanis living in one neighbourhood, Bangladeshis in another, Sikhs in a third, and so on. The highest levels of segregation recorded anywhere in the UK are those between Indians and Pakistanis in towns in the north of England. Those towns also exhibit a markedly higher degree of segregation between blacks and Asians than between whites and blacks. This suggests that the explanation for the division is not white racism, but rather the lack of a common culture that would allow different groups to share anything significant. The isolation of communities helps to perpetuate beliefs and practices that are opposed to indigenous values. Whereas the offspring of Caribbean Christian immigrants have to an extent secularised and intermarried, African Pentacostalists are determined to keep separate. Second-generation Muslims, Sikhs and Hindus are also as religious as their parents, in part because their religion serves as a marker of identity.

We are paying a heavy price for the creed of Left-wing politicians. They pose as champions of progress yet their fixation with multiculturalism is turning back the clock. In many of our cities, social solidarity is being replaced by divisive tribalism, democracy by identity politics. Real integration is impossible when ethnic groups are encouraged to cling to customs, practices, even languages from their homeland.

Legal philosopher Paul Cliteur attacked multiculturalism in his book *'The Philosophy of Human Rights'*. Cliteur rejects all political correctness on the issue. He says Western culture, the rule of law, and human rights are superior to non-western culture and values. They are the product of the Enlightenment. Cliteur sees non-western cultures not as merely different but as anachronistic. He considers multiculturalism primarily as an unacceptable ideology of cultural relativism, which would lead to acceptance of barbaric practices, including those brought to the Western World by immigrants. Examples he gives are: oppression of women, homophobia, ritual slaughter, racism, anti-Semitism, female genital mutilation, discrimination *by* immigrants, suttee, and the death penalty.

Such contrasting values are most in evidence amongst Britain's Muslim population which now numbers 2.7 million or 4.8 per cent of the population. Migrants to the US know it's necessary to submerge their inherited identity in the American Dream, but some immigrants to Britain believe they can carve out a cultural ghetto that blends the political activism of the Muslim Brotherhood with Saudi-based Salafist fundamentalism. While Tony Blair's slavish participation in George W Bush's wars against Afghanistan and Iraq alienated many young British Muslims, the London bombings and other incidents showed how easily some of them fall victim to Al-Qaeda's propaganda.

There have been a number of recent surveys and polls, measuring Muslim sentiment towards British society. Poll findings must always be treated with some caution because phraseology of questions can produce different results. With that in mind some of the findings are as follows:

- 46 per cent disagreed with the statement that "Muslim clerics who preach violence against the West are out of touch with mainstream Muslim opinion"
- 46 per cent think of themselves as Muslim first and British second. Another 42 per cent do not differentiate between the identities. A mere

12 per cent see themselves as British first and Muslim second.

- 40 per cent would prefer to live under Sharia (Islamic religious) law than under British law and hope for the U.K. one day to become a fundamentalist Islamic state.

  Half of those who express a preference for living under Sharia law say that, given the choice, they would move to a country governed by those laws.

- When asked, "Is Britain my country or their country?" only one in four say it is my country.

- Just 56 per cent agree with the statement that "Western society may not be perfect but Muslims should live with it and not seek to bring it to an end."

- Nearly half of those polled believe the 9/11 attacks on New York were a conspiracy between the United States and Israel.

- (NOP research broadcast by Channel 4): 78 per cent support punishment for the people who published cartoons, featuring the prophet Mohammed. 68 per cent support the arrest and prosecution of those British people who 'insult' Islam. When asked if free speech should be protected, even if it offends religious groups, 62 per cent say no, it should not. The NOP survey furthermore reports that "hardcore Islamists" constitute 9 per cent of the British Muslim population. A slightly more moderate group, polled at 29 per cent, is composed of "staunch defenders of Islam". Individuals in this group aggressively defend their religion from internal and external threats, real or imagined. The worrying finding was that only 3 per cent of

British Muslims "took a consistently pro-freedom of speech line on these questions".

- Nearly a third of 16 to 24 year olds believed that those converting to another religion should be executed, while less than a fifth of those over 55 believed the same.

I am listing these extensive findings to highlight the widespread disaffection from British society, particularly amongst younger Muslims. Instead of condoning this dangerous trend politicians of all parties should do their utmost to turn it around. The obvious starting method would be fully integrated schooling. If they don't then one day they will be held to account for the inevitable dire consequences.

Surveys in the Netherlands also confirm the low level of Muslim integration. A poll taken days after the twin tower outrage in 2001 revealed that 73 per cent of Dutch Muslims could understand it and 6 per cent expressed outright approval. A 2003 NIPO poll found that 85 per cent of Muslims don't feel welcome in Dutch society, 69 per cent said they will always feel outsiders and 24 per cent felt that Western culture was a bad influence. 40 per cent of Moroccan youth in the Netherlands reject western values and democracy.

Muslim secularisation would certainly improve this picture but a look at surveys of ethnic minorities in Europe reveals little evidence for this happening. Europe-wide surveys show that Muslims under 25 are as devout as those over 55, a big contrast with Catholics or Anglicans. Afro-Caribbeans and eastern European

Christians tend to be less religious than their elders but more so than the wider population. A consequence may well be that as these groupings increase in size, there will begin a long term drift back towards more conservative social values leading to demands for more religious education, opposition to abortion and gay marriage. Interfaith co-operation on these issues is likely since ecumenical structures are already in place in most countries to facilitate it. The diversity of religious groups in Europe will guard against a separation of religion and state but this cannot protect secular public policies from being eroded by a coalition of religious forces who have agreed to submerge their differences.

Religious lobbyists, couching their claims in the rhetoric of relativism and diversity, will question why the secular point of view on issues like abortion, blasphemy, pornography and evolution is entitled to be the default position. So there may be a danger of an emerging 'culture war' between fundamentalists of all faiths and those who back the secular status quo. Muslim-origin secularists will make common course with white secularists against Islamists and other funda-mentalists. Sadly this is a clash that fundamentalists are poised to win because fertility differences based on theology do not fade like those based on ethnicity.

In America fundamentalists are reaching out across faith lines to combat secularism. In 1960 eighty six per cent of practising Catholics under 40 backed the Catholic President Kennedy. By 2004 seventy four per cent of young conservative Catholics opted for evangelical George W Bush in preference to their co-religionist John Kerry. So too did two-thirds of Orthodox Jews, despite the overall Jewish record of voting Democrat. These days religious intensity is more important than denomination in predicting how people vote. Conservative Protestants, Catholics, Mormons and Jews tend to vote Republican while their more liberal co-religionists and secularists back the Democrats. Prior to 9/11 Muslims participated in this alignment.

As a result politicians will need to stay on the right side of religious sentiment to ensure that they are not outflanked by their opponents. Growth of religious culture and influence can only mean one thing: increases in population numbers.

It's only fair to acknowledge that the majority of British Muslims do want to succeed in non-sectarian terms. But the community is torn between two poles like women who cover their fashionable Western-style designer outfits with the top-to-toe burqa. Almost every serious politician now recognises that multiculturalism is a recipe for the segregation of communities and that it would work against the development of a single set of basic values that could bind members of British society together. But while multiculturalism may have been abandoned as government policy, its legacy is everywhere. Ministers, judges, and officials are reluctant to insist that the first condition of British citizenship for any immigrant should be to adopt British values – such as speaking English, accepting all citizens' equal rights and recognising that the only procedure for deciding on legitimate political authority is free elections to Parliament.

As we dither on this, multiculturalism continues its divisive work and it will soon be too late to do anything about it: Britain will have permanently fractured into factions united by nothing except mutual incomprehension and antipathy.

I have included the multicultural issue in the book not only because it is of interest to humanists in terms of how a society can cope with a plethora of religious belief, but also because as an immigrant myself I feel I have a front seat in the debate. Although humanists are staunch believers in individuality they also feel responsibility for a smooth running of society. For this it is necessary for individuals to fit in with the environment in which they have chosen to live. When I lived in Canada I wore chequered trousers, played ice hockey and adopted a Canadian accent. Now in England I once again attempt to seamlessly assimilate. My sense of humour has improved, I queue with great forbearance, my upper lip is getting stiffer, I drink tea with milk, talk a great deal about the weather and I own three umbrellas. It makes for much better harmony. My only failure is that unlike the British I am not overly polite, as this book does testify.

Separating people along religious lines militates against social fellowship. It creates divisive societies with all its inherent dangers. So worried am I, personally, about the prospect of an alien religion spreading its oppressive tentacles across my green and pleasant adopted land, that I am willing to swallow hard and vote for any party that promotes a vigorous policy to stem this trend. Many people, normally liberal and tolerant, are now forced to take this view. Once the danger has been averted (if it isn't already too late) normal service can be resumed.

FAITH SCHOOLS

*"Scientific education and religious education are
incompatible. The clergy have ceased to interfere with
education at the advanced level, but they have still got
control of that of children. This means that the children
have to learn about Adam and Noah instead of Evolution;
about David who killed Goliath, instead of Koch who killed
cholera; about Christ's ascent into heaven instead of the
Wright brothers. Worse than that, they are taught that it is a
virtue to accept statements without adequate evidence, which
leaves them a prey to quacks of every kind in later life and
makes it very difficult for them to accept the methods of
thought which are successful in science".*

Biologist JBS Haldane

Education, education, education is a mantra oft
repeated by politicians but the slogan more fittingly
belongs to Humanism. How else can humanity overcome its legacy of ignorance and superstition? More
reason therefore why Humanists should be especially
concerned about our government's disastrous conviction that the best education is religious education or at
the very least education in a religious ambience.

If you think of it dispassionately there really is
something odd about the idea of schools segregated

according to different strands of religious dogma. If we hadn't got used to it over the centuries we would consider it very weird indeed. Of all the harmful influences in British society faith schools probably top the list.

There is no such separation when it comes to teaching any other discipline. No schools for pupils whose parents are climate change believers or deniers. No schools for genetic engineering opponents or Keynesians versus 'supply side' economists. But when it comes to religion, parents views are paramount and may be reinforced in schools. This splitting of hairs about whether Mary was the mother of God or whether wine turns into the blood of Christ would be funny if it wasn't also lethal. People haven't gone to war over mathematical disputes but religious wars are commonplace.

To groom children ready for further conflict is not only absurd but also very dangerous. For the state to act as chief architect for this lethal enterprise, at tax payers' expense, is bordering on the criminal. And yet this is exactly what is going on in Britain. It's worst example is Northern Ireland where 90 per cent of schools are segregated along Protestant and Catholic lines, in the iron grip of sectarian indoctrination. This only serves to perpetuate the deep seated 'them and us' mentality that has bedevilled that benighted province. It may be argued that the divide is not strictly religious, that political factors play a role. Well, true of course, but how do you pinpoint the opposition? Do they attend republican classes or loyalist ones? Do they drink in communist or capitalists pubs? No, they are saddled with Catholic and Protestant labels because they were originally acquired in schools. If everybody en bloc in Ulster were to withdraw their religious allegiance tomorrow, it would soon become impossible to identify targets for violence. Then children could readily be transferred from denominational schooling to a non-sectarian environment where they could unlearn the factional mentality.

Armed with the shining Ulster example of how not to do it, the government is nevertheless ploughing on with plans for more faith schools, religious free schools and academies in the rest of Britain. A third of all primary schools are run by CofE, Catholic, Jewish and increasingly Islamic religious interests and now there are plans for rapidly extending religious influence in the secondary sector as well. In doing so they ought to be disconcerted by the thought that Adolf Hitler would have approved. I quote from his speech leading to the Nazi-Vatican Concordat of 1933: *"Secular schools can never be tolerated because such schools offer no religious instruction. And general moral education without a religious foundation is built on air"*.

There is little doubt that faith schools academically are outperforming integrated schools. David Blunkett, when secretary for education, once exclaimed "if only I could bottle the secret of faith schools' superior performance". I think I can bottle it for him. The government likes to give the impression that it is the religious ethic and discipline that is responsible, whereas a much more obvious determinant is the unpalatable fact that in their heart of hearts most people are not ready for a racially integrated society and Christian schools are simply functioning as white British middle classes' last stand against multiculturalism. The same motives that drive white Britons from inner cities make them enrol their children in Christian schools. Apartheid by another name. I am not suggesting here that people are racist, merely that they feel uncomfortable to be confronted with an alien culture that they perceive as threatening their traditional way of life. (This, by the way, is the foremost reason why the Ukip party has suddenly made such giant strides in British politics.) If in consequence people are having to affect religious belief then that is a price worth paying. Pew hypocrisy for the children's sake.

This trend explains that the superior results achieved in such schools have more to do with professional middle class selection and less with religious ethos. Children of the white middle classes come equipped with all the benefits that this background brings: intelligent, educated parents, books in the home and a stimulating environment. It is of course highly politically incorrect to point this out and thus it is possible to perpetuate the myth that it is the religion that makes the difference. There are other factors boosting faith school performance: pupils in faith schools are much less likely to be on a low income that entitles them to free school meals and much more likely to have English as their first language. The schools also admit fewer children with special needs. Pupils arrive at faith primary schools about a term ahead of children at other schools which makes for better results in end-of-school exams.

The rising level of segregation is not only a phenomenon of 'white flight' but also the flight of those from other religious-ethnic minorities. Polite society may not notice but the stark reality is that Hindu and

Sikh parents do not wish to send their children to schools where there is a preponderance of Muslim children and vice versa. So what have arisen are 'mono-faith' neighbourhoods and schools.

A recently surfaced consequence of the inclination towards Islamic values in Britain has been the so called 'Trojan Horse' attempt by Islamic extremists to impose a 'narrow, faith-based ideology' at some schools in Birmingham. According to Ofsted, (Britain's Office for Standards in Education), dedicated Islamists have taken a leaf out of the Jesuits' 'catch them young' book and are trying to subvert school education to indoctrinate school children. Examining 21 schools in Birmingham, Ofsted inspectors noted that Islamists threatened headmasters and created a 'culture of fear'. Some Muslim-dominated schools are accused of axing national curricula, so that instruction is anything but broad and balanced. They are poorly administered, teach homophobia and avoid sex education. Ofsted has demanded that curricula stress 'fundamental British values' and recommended spot inspections. Apparently, when schools had notice of inspections, they quickly laid on all-faiths programmes and Christian-oriented shows.

Given the enormous importance of the formative years in life, this insulation can have a highly significant and lasting effect on how children from different backgrounds relate to each other. There is likely to be a deleterious impact on integration and cohesion from heightened levels of segregation of children and this surely does not augur well for the goal of a socially cohesive society. If a Muslim child is educated in a school where the vast majority of other children are also

Muslim, how can we expect him or her to work, live and interact with people from other cultures when he or she leaves school? If segregation of communities is not a desirable outcome and is an obstacle to improving social cohesion then it is certainly also true for children in schools.

But none of the Birmingham development should be surprising; it is entirely foreseeable that leaders of 'faith communities' should wish to impose values and practices in schools in their neighbourhoods that are in accordance with their religion. The damaging emphasis on a multifaith society makes it easier for minorities to see their primary status in terms of faith. Community leaders and parents with strong religious identities seek to protect their children – especially girls – from Western secular influences which, quite frankly, they deem immoral. Such protection is likely to be employed when faith-based schools, as well as state schools, in segregated communities vigorously police the behaviour of pupils strictly in line with their religious doctrines and cultural mores. An inescapable outcome is the accentuation of divisions along religious lines. This is not only profoundly harmful to schoolchildren who are seen as no more than properties of their parents, but flies in the face of the government's stated goal of increasing integration and social cohesion.

Given that both the previous and present governments are in the habit of describing Britain as a multifaith society, it is entirely to be expected that leaders of those groups for whom their faith trumps all other indicators of identity, will seek robustly to instil the values and practices of their religion. In this context it has been unhelpful for Prime Minister David Cameron and his

Communities Secretary Eric Pickles to stress that Britain is essentially a Christian country. In doing so they provoke many within the faith minorities to emphatically say "no, we are not" and to assert their own non-Christian faith identity with even greater vigour.

Anybody with a capacity to learn from history will be aware that sectarian and racial pigeon holing of this kind is the policy of the madhouse. Even the strongly religious United States had the foresight to keep state and religion apart. The longer this situation is allowed to persist the greater the danger. In the long term it will be impossible to sustain two parallel societies in close proximity without serious repercussions. Why are no special efforts made to tackle the problem at the roots? Why do children still continue to grow up within the carefully erected stockades of racial divide, sectarianism and bigotry, without ever getting to know what things are like inside the other camp? Surely the one thing that should receive all possible priority and encouragement is integrated education. But having established the principle of faith based education by creating large numbers of Christian denominational schools, equity dictates that other religions too should get their fair share of apartheid.

With fast growing Muslim, Hindu and Sikh population numbers there will come increasing pressure for more schools to cater to these faiths. Putting this into practice would not only mean segregation of children of Asian origin from the host population, they would also be divided from one another, importing into Britain the religious conflicts and resentments that are wide-spread on the Indian sub-continent. What's more they would inevitably exacerbate the already existing prejudices and reservations against Asians.

Already established ethnic minority schools are having the effect that Ofsted inspectors are departing from their standard inspection procedures so as not to tread on any religious toes. In recently updated guidance on inspecting publicly funded faith schools, inspectors are advised that in Muslim faith schools: "boys and girls may well be taught or seated separately according to the specific context, particularly during collective acts of worship. This should not be taken as a sign of inequality between different genders". The guidance also cautions inspectors to be mindful to not misinterpret the wearing of the 'hijab' or headscarf as a sign of repression but instead to "understand that Muslim females see this as a part of their identity and a commitment to their beliefs within Islam". The guidance says most schools have a uniform for boys and girls which represents the "Islamic principle of modesty". Inspectors are advised that art and music lessons in Muslim schools can be "restricted", that health and sex education will be taught within Islamic studies and that daily prayers will often "dictate the shape of the school day". In a section on 'etiquette', female inspectors are advised to "wear a trouser suit or longer skirt and jacket to cover their arms". Female inspectors are also recommended to "carry a scarf in case they enter the prayer room".

According to the recommendations "Muslim men do not usually shake hands with women, and Muslim women do not shake hands with men". Ofsted advise the "best policy is not to offer to shake hands unless someone offers their hand to you". It says inspectors also need to be aware that they may find themselves providing feedback from a lesson to a teacher that may be wearing a full 'niqaab' (face and head cover). In some schools male inspectors are told they will need another female present in order to give feedback to a female teacher. The guidelines lay down that when inspecting single-sex religious schools, the inspection team should "reflect the gender of the school". In mixed sex Jewish schools, inspectors are told that boys and girls are "in reality" taught separately – sometimes on two different sites some distance from one another. When inspecting Jewish schools female inspectors are advised to wear a skirt rather than trousers and a blouse, but that any blouse worn should cover the collar bone. When inspecting strictly ultra-orthodox schools, inspectors are warned to "avoid wearing bright colours, and red in particular".

The National Secular Society has called on Ofsted to review its guidance. Keith Porteous Wood, NSS executive director, said: "These guidelines reveal a disturbing capitulation to oppressive religious demands in publicly funded schools. It also highlights the extent to which religious identities are being foisted on young people whilst at school. The guidance serves to normalise practices inconsistent with values such as personal liberty and gender equality, which should be promoted in schools, not eroded. The apparent willingness to sacrifice the National Curriculum and sex and relationships education in order to accommodate religious dogma betrays children's rights and poorly equips pupils for life outside the school gates."

With a host of religious proselytisers out there desperate to get access to those awkward children who stubbornly will not attend their churches and mosques, the free schools and academies, which the government are enthusiastically promoting, are as far as the religious are concerned a true 'God-send'.

SACRE DIEU!

The Education Reform Act 1988 required that all agreed syllabuses for religious education *"reflect the fact that religious traditions in Britain are in the main Christian, whilst taking account of the teaching and practices of other principal religions represented in the country"*. The government further required that all existing agreed syllabuses be reviewed and revised with the result that many of them had to be rewritten. This led to the establishment of SACREs (Standing Advisory Council on Religious Education). These committees, tasked with putting together the syllabus are made up of a selection of religious spokespersons representing a wide range of denominations, C of E, Methodism, Baptism, Catholics, Islam, Judaism, Sikhism, Bahai and further odds and ends, depending on where you are in the country. All these folk enjoy full voting rights except for humanists, who have observer status only.

This despite the fact that recent polls are showing that at least 40 per cent of pupils consider themselves non-religious, making it by far the largest grouping, easily outscoring even the CofE. As a member of a local humanist group in Leeds some years ago, I somehow got myself involved with this enterprise. I had been given to understand that these gatherings were friendly low key affairs where kindly vicars, imams, rabbis and the like, exchanged pleasantries and bent over backwards to be ecumenical with the truth.

And by and large that is how it was. They felt little need for competition, after all there was a religious trough for every snout. Until it came to the task of revising the syllabus and they got wind of a secular runt amongst the litter. When religions collide with atheism they show remarkable unity of purpose. The demon unbelief outweighs doctrinal friction. Ranks are closed with lightning speed. They had been intent on steamrollering the new version through with minor alterations, in keeping with new Department of Education guidelines. When I had the audacity to make a strong case for humanism, on behalf of the large percentage of pupils from a non-religious background, who according to these same guidelines must be catered for, all Christian charity and ecumenical spirit soon went out the window.

When it was published the updated Leeds RE syllabus, in the country of Darwin's birth, had no place for evolution. All my hard fought for additions of 'philosophies', 'secular views' and 'life stances' to the incessant usage of 'faiths' had mysteriously disappeared. 'Humanism' did manage a single appearance, on page 44, to be precise, where it mentioned Humanist funeral services. Pupils will probably conclude that we are a firm of undertakers. Separate programmes of study were included for CHRISTIANITY which was in bolder print to show who was the skydaddy of them all, and for Buddhism, Hinduism, Islam, Judaism and Sikhism. If David Koresh, of Waco fame, had pitched his tent in Leeds, he too, no doubt, would have been accorded recognition.

I must explain that humanists are not against religious education as such. Like it or not religion is here to stay (at least for a little longer). But what should be taught in school is *comparative* religion with emphasis on ethics and morality, explaining to pupils the history and main tenets of all major religions, including the history and meaning of humanism and freethought, allowing no room whatever for partisan indoctrination.

COMPULSORY WORSHIP

"The happiest man is he who learns from nature the lesson to worship"

Ralph Waldo Emerson.

As if faith schools were not quite enough there also is in Britain, believe it or not, a legal requirement for an act of compulsory worship in state schools. How this timeworn remnant of medieval ritual managed to sneak into the legislation of an advanced country in the 21st century, remains a mystery but there it is, licking its chops, saddling heads of school all over the country with major headaches. The audacity of this imposition is astounding. By contrast just imagine humanists being awarded a daily school assembly in praise of Charles Darwin. There were pathetic attempts to skirt around the problem by seeking refuge in the etymology of the word 'worship' as 'worth-ship' and to focus on beliefs and attitudes held to be of worth. This desperate exercise in semantics was soon nipped in the bud by the government which issued a circular specifying that *"worship in its 'natural and ordinary meaning' meant something special or separate from ordinary school activities, concerned with reverence or veneration of a divine being or power"*. Not much wriggle room there then.

At that point I wrote to the Secretary of State asking her if she was trying to outmoral the Archbishop of

Canterbury and suggested a suitable assembly prayer along these lines: *"Oh Lord, omnipotent and all good, thank you for earthquakes, droughts and floods. Thank you for disease, pain and hunger. Thank you for free will that caused the death of 6 million Jews and another million in Rwanda. Thank you for all the wars conducted in your name these last 2000 years. Thank you for a Tory government that has enabled us to worship you daily in gratitude"*. This could then be followed by a brief lesson in elementary logic.

Kids unfortunate enough to have been landed with religious parents and hence with religion in the home and church, are now suffering the triple whammy of religion in school too. Non-religious parents are also caught up. True, they have magnanimously been given the option of withdrawing, but which caring parent is prepared to make a spectacle of her/his child? Moreover the law does not compel head teachers to make extra provision for withdrawn pupils and in practice most parents are reluctant to subject their child to such exemption. Children like to conform and not draw attention to themselves. After more than twenty five years of this abomination lots of schools are finding their way around it but the obligation remains intact.

Although the idea of a compulsory act of worship of a Deity in a state school in a predominantly secular society is of course outrageous, my objection to it is tempered by the thought that for a lot of children this act of religious bullying may well mean that it turns them off for keeps. I speak from experience here. For sixteen long years I was exposed to ubiquitous religion in home church and school. It never made an impact. All it did was strengthen my resolve to drop it all as soon as I was able. The only regret I have is that instead of countless hours being exposed to liturgy, make-believe and prayer, I could have been taught something useful, more science for example.

There is indeed evidence of religion acting as a turn off. In countries such as the Netherlands, Scandinavia and Britain where religion used to play and is still playing a very important role in education, the drift away from religion has been precipitous, whilst in America where religion is kept out of schools, religious adherence in the population is still remarkably high. For this reason parents ought perhaps not to worry unduly about their children being exposed to RE and worship in school. If nothing else the relatively minor dose of nonsense and boredom will stand a good chance of immunising them against religion for the rest of their lives.

FREE TRANSPORT

Not only are faith schools being created in increasing numbers, the government is bending over backwards to facilitate their use. If no conveniently located faith school is available, religious parents are offered free public transport to have their children bussed to schools of their choice. No such option is available to the non-religious. Locally I came across a case where Herefordshire Council told a fifteen year old pupil that she could not travel free on the school bus to the Catholic school she attended, because she was a non-Catholic. Catholic pupils at the school could travel free. The council said that it was not practising discrimination on the grounds of religion, simultaneously admitting that the girl concerned could not travel free because she was a non-Catholic.

There was a time, in America, when black passengers on buses were forced to give up their seats in favour of whites. Half a century later, in Herefordshire, a similar outrage is being played out, except for blacks read non-religious and for whites substitute Roman Catholics. Can you imagine the uproar that would ensue if a Catholic child were to be denied some benefit that other children enjoyed. The annual cost nation-wide of such discretionary transport to the public purse amounts to some £70 million pounds.

Although humanists, like religious parents are quite convinced that their life stance is the correct one, they are reluctant to foist it upon their children. They are willing to expose their children to contrasting world-views, even religious ones, confident that their children will reach rational conclusions of their own. After all the common sense cards are stacked strongly in their favour. Naturally they would regret it if the humanist outlook was rejected but still accept that in the end it must be the child's own choice. There are no humanist faith schools nor would we want them. We would prefer a mixed team in the playground. Footballs are dogma free. It's the religious who seem to have so little confidence in the persuasive powers of their doctrines that they feel compelled to keep their offspring well away from challenging beliefs.

BIBLICAL LIGHT RELIEF

Pushing the bible, God and worship into schools may irk Humanists, but think of the payback in laughter alone. Here are some examples of what pupils actually remembered:

- Adam and Eve were created from an apple tree
- Adam blamed Eve, Eve blamed the serpent and the serpent didn't have a leg to stand on
- Noah's wife was called Joan of Ark. Noah built an ark, which the animals came on in pears.
- Lot's wife was a pillar of salt by day, but a ball of fire by night.
- The Jews were a proud people and throughout history they had trouble with the unsympathetic Genitals.
- Samson was a strongman, who let himself be led astray by a Jezebel like Delilah.
- The Egyptians were all drowned in the dessert. Afterwards, Moses went up on Mount Cyanide to get the ten amendments.
- Moses died before he ever reached Canada.
- The greatest miracle in the bible is when Joshua told his son to stand still and he obeyed him.
- David was a Hebrew king, skilled at playing the liar. He fought with the Finkelsteins, a race of people who lived in Biblical times.
- Solomon, one of David's sons had 300 wives and 700 porcupines.
- When Mary heard that she was the mother of Jesus, she sang the Magna Carta.
- Jesus was born because Mary had an immaculate contraption.
- God is a doctor because the Bible says the Lord gave the tablets to Moses.

- Jesus enunciated the Golden Rule, which says to do one to others before they do one to you.
- It was a miracle Jesus rose from the dead and managed to get the tombstone off the entrance.
- A Christian should have only one spouse. This is called monotony.

BBC (Baffling Belief Crusaders)

For centuries the smothering duvet of religion has kept most of the world panting for air. Only fairly recently has the oxygen of freethought managed to lift a corner and bring relief. But in Britain the bulwark of church and state, loyally aided by the BBC, is gamely fighting to yank the duvet back. Being publicly funded the BBC has a duty to be neutral but ignoring the rapidly declining number of believers, the BBC continues to cater to them disproportionately. There are a considerable number of religious programmes and programmes with a religious bias but the two that are the most blatant and inappropriate are the infamous 'Thought for the Day' (TftD) inserted into Radio 4's flagship 'Today' current affairs programme and the lesser known, but equally biased 'Pause for Thought' on Radio 2.

The BBC radio 4 'Thought For The Day' slot, ever since it saw the dark of day in the sixties, has been a major irritant to rationalists. Not so much because it is important in itself but because it represents the blatantly privileged position that religion still holds in society, even at the supposedly balanced BBC. Its format follows a predictable pattern. For a minute or two the speaker burbles on about some issue in the news in a neutral sort of way, lulling the listener into a false sense of security. Then just as you start thinking this isn't too bad they suddenly hit you with the Bible or with Jesus. I call this the 'pulling the rabbit' moment.

Over the years I have had many a go at this religious Trojan horse, shoe-horned into the heart of a serious current affairs programme and it would be nice to think that eventually I shall have played a small part in its reform or preferably its demise. Here is a sample letter:

"Why is it that the BBC with its enviable international reputation for fair and balanced reporting blatantly abandons this position when it comes to dealing with religion? The 'Thought for the Day' slot normally offers anodyne religious homilies which rationalists tend to suffer quietly but it is a different matter when religious spokespeople are given platforms to give one-sided views on serious and topical issues without opportunity for rebuttal. A case in point was Bishop Tom Butler's polemic against assisted dying. It is outrageous that his statements about palliative care and the slippery slope of euthanasia should go unchallenged. Would you allow a Humanist to attack a Church of England doctrine without rejoinder? And please don't side-step the argument by claiming that TftD is part of religious broadcasting and not a current affairs item. In that case have the honesty to call it 'Religious Thought for the Day'. That would also make it easier to eject the slot from the excellent 'Today' programme where it has no place".

Such missives are invariably replied to with an explanation that TftD is a religious programme; that Britain is a predominantly Christian country and that freethought gets a look in everywhere else. There are several things wrong with that. For one thing this certainly is no longer a wholly Christian country. Multiculturalism and growing irreligion have put paid to that. Many polls are showing that practising theists are massively outnumbered by the non-religious. According to a Home Office survey church attendance has been in decline in each of the last six decades and religion is only regarded as ninth in importance to self-identity, although this is higher among those from minority backgrounds. The point about freethought elsewhere in the programming is a specious one. It may sound reasonable enough until you turn the argument on its head: How would the religious feel if Humanism were allocated a dedicated spot bang in the middle of a current affairs programme and religion would have to take its chances amongst the rest of BBC output, where again humanism would often be given the last word?

Yes, there are programmes with input by the non-religious, for example the 'Moral Maze', but in all such debates the BBC ensures that any non-religious viewpoints are fiercely contested, often with the religious spokesperson being allowed to wrap up. There are no programmes where this is not the case. That's why on the BBC you will never see programmes like the riveting, two hour long, discussion between the 'four horsemen of the Apocalypse': Richard Dawkins; Dan Dennett, Sam Harris and Christopher Hitchens. A rare collection of erudition and eloquence unmatched by a googolplex of theologians. Such delights are restricted to Youtube. The horsemen must not frighten the BBC's horses. Nor are philosophers and scientists much in evidence on the Dimbleby discussion panels 'Question

Time' and 'Any Questions'. They are mostly given over to party line pushing politicians and a sprinkling of clerics and celebs.

The unanswerable fault with TFTD is that it treats the non-religious like lepers; offering the religious an unopposed platform at the heart of a popular current affairs programme, something the BBC would (rightly) never extend to the non-religious. Even Sinn Fein at the height of the troubles got a better deal than humanists. They at least were allowed to speak through actors. Over time the TftD slot has been reduced from five to three minutes so progress is being made. But BBC governors and the BBC Trust, stocked, top down as they are, with religious placemen, have stubbornly refused to open the broadcast to humanists. They seem to think that it is their duty to hold the fort for the establishment and they are determined to keep religion in its privileged position.

BBC staff members at the coalface are taking a different view as can be gathered from these extracts from their house magazine *Ariel* : responding to a colleague who had said: "I am left wondering exactly what kind of thought for the day atheism has to offer. I can't see despair or defeatism or self-pity going down too well at that hour in the morning".

"TftD should not be a religious item. In practice it is a daily piece about ethics and morality. Restricting it to the religious maintains the fiction that one must have religion to have morality. Where is the despair in knowing you have just one life and living it to the full? Where's the defeatism in working to improve your world for those around you and those who follow

you? Where's the self-pity in realising that, without someone to wipe your slate clean, you alone can take responsibility for your actions? Recently there has been much talk about making TftD less trite. May I humbly suggest that this could be achieved by inviting contributors who have to think hard about their morals, rather than those who have them dictated by a very old book".

- *"May I reassure X that I suffer no anguish whatever in finding no need for a supernatural explanation of the world. Nature is just as astonishing, beautiful and fascinating whether we believe that it's part of an unfathomable plan, or that it just blunders along on its own. Tragedy and suffering are neither explained nor lessened by the proposition that they serve a greater being's hidden purpose."*
- *"Atheism is an empowering philosophy which values reason over ignorance, enquiry over acceptance. That's why theists have always striven to devalue and censor it. How sad that people like X and the producers of 'Thought for the Day' are still fighting the battles of the Middle Ages."*

Powerful well argued stuff, but as long as the powers that be are in cahoots with church and state nothing much will change. It is curious, isn't it, that religious people, who after all are said to have God on their side, are being bolstered by any number of supporting programmes, whereas humanists, who also have to cope with life's vicissitudes, are left to fend for themselves. It should be recognised that there is now a substantial proportion of the population who are not religious and who are entitled to have their life's philosophy reflected in BBC output, in a recognisable and supportive manner.

It is not that humanists are desperate to take part in these mostly anodyne homilies. It would be better if they were abolished altogether but as long as they go on, there ought to be a place for a non-religious voice. Otherwise the unavoidable impression will be left that good thoughts are the exclusive domain of the religious. If the content were restricted to exhortations for moral living, that would apply to people of all faiths and none, it would still look out of place within Today, but it might be more acceptable. Surely the purpose of TftD is to spread reflection and goodwill, not to annoy consistently a large proportion of listeners.

Whilst the religious get their brows soothed on 'Thought for the Day' and several other slots, specifically catering to their needs, there is nothing equivalent aimed at the growing size of the non-religious audience. I would argue that general discussion slots such as the 'Moral Maze' do not go far enough in supplying specific guidance to those listeners who do not subscribe to a religious creed. Whereas there are plenty of opportunities for the religious to receive pastoral care in the home, at school, in church and on radio and TV, there is no equivalent support available for the non religious. The point I am getting at is that the religious do not have a monopoly on the knocks dished out by life and secularists too may be in need of moral support from like-minded people.

As things stand, the attitude seems to be that if people want solace of this kind they should turn to religion or sort things out for themselves. As a result young people frequently can go through their entire education without ever hearing about the humanist alternative. At the other end of the spectrum picture the older person, often living alone, unable to believe the traditional answers and having to face death and eternity without the benefit of hearing from others in a similar position. In any other field such neglect would be considered cruel. So what I, and many others, would like to see is not only philosophical discussion programmes involving ethical and moral values, with the secular viewpoint fairly represented, but also agony aunt type counselling programmes aimed specifically at those who are not religious. Unlike religious people, freethinkers tend not to be organised, they have no churches or chaplains to turn to and if there is nothing for them in broadcasting either, they could rightly claim to be the forgotten people.

I do feel that freethought, in some respects, is still in a predicament not dissimilar to that of the Suffragettes, one hundred years ago and I have not forgotten the anguished years of my youth, when I thought I was the only unbeliever shipwrecked in a sea of faith. A determination not to let this happen to others is what fuels my motivation.

But if the BBC cannot bring itself to face reality and broaden their coverage to embrace freethought then no doubt the task will fall to the internet where already there is huge rebellion against the status quo. Check any lists of commentary following broadcasts and newspaper articles, discussing matters of faith and you will notice overwhelming support for secular views. Educated people, as most internet users are, make it very clear that the received wisdom pushed by Church and government in the religious sphere is hopelessly out of date.

CHURCH BUILDINGS

*"Churches are the only places where
sound moves faster than light".
"A church steeple equipped with a lightning
rod shows a lack of confidence".*

T.A.

Whether it is Remembrance Day or another national occasion, for example the Falklands victory service held in St. Paul's Cathedral, the public events attended by the great and the good on behalf of all of us, almost invariably take the form of a Christian service with Bible readings, hymn singing and praising God, thus automatically taking away from non-Christians and humanists the ability to contribute to the occasion in a manner reflecting their world-view.

When some years ago I saw the gay rights campaigner Peter Tatchell unceremoniously dragged down from the pulpit in Canterbury Cathedral by Christian wardens I was reminded of scenes of Fascist rallies in the thirties when protesters interrupting Oswald Mosley's rants were jumped upon by brown-shirts and roughly dealt with. I pointed out in a letter to the Times "that it would have been more Christian for the then archbishop Dr. Carey to have bidden Peter welcome in his house, to have invited him to take a pew and to have heard him out". But church services and discussion are mutually exclusive. One may wonder why churches put 'All are welcome' signs outside their buildings when clearly the welcome runs out very quickly once you start disagreeing with anything you are being told. Their signs should be re-phrased to read: 'All are welcome provided you bring your nodding donkey accreditation'.

I remember, when still forced to attend church as an adolescent, how frustrating it was not to be able to challenge the frequently fatuous statements emanating from the pulpit. By invoking a sense of unreality, the presence of God, the Holy Spirit and other mystification, religious services have put a stop to normal human interaction, thus creating fertile ground for unopposed indoctrination. With help from the state they have even managed to reinforce this cosy monopoly with belt and braces legal protection. The origin of the ecclesiastical law which is so far-reaching in its remit that if taken to the letter, a bad bout of hiccuping in church could land you in court, is unclear but you can bet your bottom dollar that it has a great deal to do with providing a vehicle for keeping the peasantry in its place, the vicar in his sumptuous vicarage and the local squire and the king in their respective castles. So used have ordinary people become to centuries of this manipulation that they now feel genuine unease when anything untoward happens in church. The aura of sanctity based on nothing but indoctrination has done its job and open discourse has gone out of the stained glass window. It is little wonder that religion has to rely so heavily on stifling debate. Its message of put up here on earth and reap your reward in heaven is increasingly more difficult to sell.

In a follow-up interview, jointly with Keith Porteous-Wood of the National Secular Society, on the Jimmy Young show, I was asked the much recurring question: "would there not be anarchy if everybody took to disrupting other people's meetings to air their views. How, for instance, would we like it if Christians came to interrupt our Humanist meetings?" The reply; that we don't shun debate and certainly would not drag anybody into court provided they didn't break any heads or furniture, must have come as a surprise to most religious people who seem to have great difficulty in having any of their sacred cows milked in public. In any case it is not an exact comparison. Humanist meetings do not subscribe to rules and ethics that are highly discriminatory to certain minorities in the population. If we did, we should rightly be challenged at every opportunity and in all our gatherings, private or not.

Churches, on the other hand, have a long history of advocating illiberal and discriminatory doctrines. Statements, for example, that slavery and servitude were God ordained conditions; that abortion was wrong in all circumstances; that contraception was immoral; that divorce should not be allowed; that women could not qualify for the priesthood; that there should be no shopping on Sundays. Due to outside pressure the churches have had to give way on all these points. One of their remaining bastions of prejudice is homophobia and Peter Tatchell is doing what Martin Luther King, and the Suffragettes before him, had to do in order to bring about progress.

One of the more outrageous analogies received in reply to my related letter published in 'The Times' came from a Scottish brain surgeon who asked me how

I would like it if I were on the operating table and Peter Tatchell came to interrupt the proceedings. To him I could not resist the riposte that his analogy was perhaps a little far-fetched, unless of course he felt that what came down from pulpits on most Sundays was frontal lobotomy surgery of the spiritual kind.

REMEMBRANCE DAY

During various trips to France and Belgium I have had occasion to visit a number of war graves from both world wars. It is hard to put into words what goes through one's mind when confronted with acres of gravestones as far as the eye can see. All belonging to young lives who have cruelly missed out on the extra fifty plus years I have been lucky to have had. 'They shall not grow old..... We will remember them...' I always end up in tears. It is one of the most sobering experiences available in life, perhaps second only to a visit to Auschwitz. And we must remember them even though they will never know that after all these years the world is still haunted by their loss.

That is why I wanted as chairman of our local humanist group to take part in the 11th November wreath laying ceremony at the Ludlow Market Place Memorial. Our participation was arranged through the British Legion Ludlow branch chairman, who much appreciated our interest. Our initiative was mentioned in the local paper which, acting on our prompt, reported: *"Remembrance Day ceremonies tend to have a religious influence but this year, for the first time and with the agreement of the British Legion, the Welsh Marches Humanist Group are laying a wreath at the*

Ludlow War memorial. This is to emphasise that the non-religious too are aware and appreciative of the sacrifice made by the brave men and women, religious and non-religious, who laid down their lives so that others may live in freedom".

But it turned out that prior to the wreath laying we had to sit through a lengthy religious service at St. Laurence Church. I had anticipated a reasonable amount of prayer and hymn singing, after all we were in a church, but little had prepared me for over an hour of full on, wall to wall god and religion, with no opportunity for a non-religious tribute. Clearly we were there, not to remember the fallen, but to worship almighty God. It said so in the first sentence introducing the service. It was downhill all the way from there. I gave up on the god count once it had soared above one hundred.

In my view it is nothing short of scandalous that on remembrance day the Church of England should take advantage of its captive audience this way. The fact that it owns the largest building in town (although its upkeep is funded by public grants and local fund-raising) should not give it licence to treat the general public, who have come for the sole purpose of remembering the fallen, as if they were all devout members of a CofE congregation. On remembrance day the British Legion should be centre stage, not the Church of England.

The church's self-appointed role as the nation's focal point on national occasions is becoming increasingly inappropriate in view of the finding, in a recent survey, that church attendance on Sundays now stands at less than 2 per cent of the population. Their blatant hi-jacking of the event got me so cross that during the service I resolved to write to the local paper to air my grievances:

"The wreath laying ceremony at the Market Place memorial, Ludlow, was a very moving occasion, paying respect to the brave men and women who gave their lives so that others may live in freedom. Contrast that with the preceding service in St. Laurence church, where the first sentence in the introduction read: "We are here to worship Almighty God, whose purposes are good, whose power sustains the world he made;" No!, we were **NOT** *there to worship God, we were there to remember the fallen. As for God's good purposes, what is good about 6 million murdered Jews, 20 million dead service men and women, world-wide, and an equal number of innocent civilians? God's apologists mention free will. But if God allows Hitler free will to start a global war and commit genocide then God has abandoned all responsibility and has handed over control to a murderous dictator. That leaves God either complicit or helpless and point-less. But enough of God. These days intelligent people, in their heart of hearts, know that God doesn't really exist and that mankind's only hope of avoiding further major conflict is through diplomacy, understanding and co-operation"*

I also wrote to the bishop of Ludlow, suggesting a brief dedication from a non-religious perspective in recognition of the fact that many of the fallen will have been without religion. This request was turned down as expected and I could not bring myself to repeat the hurtful process the following year. I could not again be part of a service praising somebody else's god for not preventing the slaughter of tens of millions of people in the two great wars. It was with regret because remembering the war dead is something that I feel very strongly about. It would be splendid if the Church could move with the times and make the memorial service more inclusive, to allow for the fact that increasing numbers of people do not feel that God should take centre stage when it comes to remembering our dead.

Would it not be much more appropriate if instead of the usual hymns a remembrance service could include the deeply touching lyrics of the beautiful Chris de Burgh song 'Snow is falling':

Snow is falling, snow is falling on the ground,
In the forest, in the forest there's no sound;
A shallow grave is where we lie,
The boys and men who died,
And snow is falling on the ground,
And we are calling to be found;

And the seasons, and the seasons come and go,
In the springtime, birds will sing and flowers grow,
At summer's end, the autumn breeze,
Will whisper through the trees,
And leaves are falling on the ground,
And we are calling to be found;

And in our homes, so many tears,
They don't know where we have gone,
And snow is falling on the ground,
And we are calling to be found,
We are calling to be found......

CHAPLAINCY

State-funded Chaplaincy services are another example of a church privilege, not available to humanists. The NHS has employed chaplains to give spiritual care and support to patients and staff since it was formed in 1948. The argument goes: "If a patient's illness is providing them with a religious crisis, or if the patient is dying and the family is very anxious that someone should come and say prayers in line with that person's faith, then it is part of the care offered by the hospital to ensure that that happens. One can't rely on volunteers to come in, in the middle of the night to provide those prayers. They need to be members of staff who are trained and equipped and who understand hospitals". Humanists have no quarrel with the principle of Chaplaincy but they do object to funding it from the public purse.

Research by the National Secular Society has revealed that apart from the estimated cost of £40 million to the NHS (at an average cost of £49,000 per chaplain), there is a further cost of approx. £10.3 million to the prison service to fund the 358 directly employed chaplains in public sector prison service establishments in England and Wales. There are also "sessional chaplains" who come into public sector prison service establishments on an ad hoc basis to conduct pastoral duties. But there is no central recording of sessional chaplains, so no indication of how much is spent on them. There was no central costing for the value of "places of worship" and no separate costings for their upkeep and repair. The law requires there to be a chaplain in each prison, but there is no equivalent statutory requirement for hospitals.

Bearing in mind the precarious financial situation overall in the health service, with the large number of redundancies among front line staff, it does make it hard to justify the health service paying for chaplains' salaries. Since the number of people wanting the services of chaplains in hospital must be small, one would have thought that ministers of religion could provide their spiritual services free of charge. But if they have to be paid why not pay them on an hourly basis and only send for them when patients specifically ask for them? One would think that if the churches and other religious bodies feel chaplains are so important they ought to make some better arrangement at their own expense. If humanism were to grow in numbers no doubt we would have plenty of volunteer hospital and prison visitors at no cost to these services.

ANIMAL WELFARE

"The question is not, "Can they reason?" nor,
"Can they talk?" but "Can they suffer?"

Jeremy Bentham.

In the primitive past most people believed that non-human animals didn't have feelings or intelligence. It was thought that animals weren't important and that they existed simply for people to use for food, clothing, transport, labour and entertainment. As human society has advanced, most people have come to realise that animals do matter. We are aware that animals are capable of feeling physical pain just as we are. We also know that they experience emotions such as fear, sadness, loneliness and depression. No-one suggests that animals should have the same rights as people. The right to vote, or to freedom of speech would make no sense to a dog. But the right not to be tortured or hurt unnecessarily is as important to an animal as it is to a person and the right not to be imprisoned is important too. We know that social animals such as monkeys and mice suffer emotional distress when they are kept on their own in captivity.

Some people argue that animals can't have rights because they don't understand or know what it means to have rights. Humanists would point out that young babies and people with severe mental disabilities don't understand either, yet this does not prevent us from giving them rights. Furthermore, animals such as chimpanzees are more aware of what's going on around them than are human babies. It is also said that animals cannot be granted rights because they are not as intelligent as human beings. In some cases that is debatable, but if you think about it your rights don't depend on how intelligent you are, a professor of physics has no more basic rights than a person with learning difficulties. It is sometimes argued that animals are cruel to each other so people should not feel bad about abusing animals. It is true that some animals kill other animals for food. The difference is that these animals are not knowingly cruel – they are simply behaving naturally in accordance with the vagaries of evolution and are not aware of the suffering they can cause. A lion doesn't know that he is hurting a wildebeest, but he knows instinctively that he has to kill to survive. Humans on the other hand are aware that other animals can suffer and they can decide to change their actions accordingly.

Theists and humanists take different views as to the difference between humans and animals. Theists believe that humans are a uniquely different species, made in the image of God and animals are mere commodities for their convenience. Whereas humanists feel that humans are merely sophisticated naked apes, forming an integral part of the animal world, be it the most highly developed one and that animals deserve humane consideration.

Because it is claimed in the Bible that God has given humans dominion over animals the religious boot is still going remorselessly into the animal world. And not just the boot, sharp knives too. Muslims and orthodox Jews have got it into their heads that when it comes to killing animals for food this can only be done by cutting their throats without pre-stunning. Because this barbaric, pointless practice comes under the heading 'religious freedom', EU and UK laws have cravenly allowed exemptions from EU regulation 1099 that requires pre-stunning in abattoirs. The UK government has sought to justify its stance by claiming that banning this form of slaughter in the UK would result in people importing meat from other countries where this practice is permitted, thus providing no improvement for animal welfare. This lame excuse could of course be used just as easily to justify not imposing warranted restrictions to almost any product obtainable from abroad. The argument is simply a cynical ruse, motivated by a reluctance to take on strident religious interests.

This type of slaughter is now becoming commonplace in Britain. Industry estimates suggest strong Muslim demand for chicken and lamb has resulted in about 40 per cent of poultry and 30 per cent of lamb, consumed in the UK, meeting halal specifications. Kosher and halal slaughter is banned in Latvia, Switzerland and the Scandinavian countries Norway, Sweden and most recently Denmark. A bill to ban the practice in the Netherlands was rejected by the Dutch upper house in June 2012, following fierce opposition by Jewish and Muslim groups. A sorry sign of the backward slide now taking place in that once enlightened country, fuelled by mass immigration.

In Britain Prime Minister Cameron is strongly opposed to a ban. Talking to the Jewish press in March 2011 he said: "*We have no plans to outlaw in any way that practice. There is no stronger supporter of shechita* (Jewish method of slaughter) *in the cabinet than me. The Jewish community has been an absolute exemplar in integrating into British life in every way but integration doesn't mean that you have to give up things that you hold very dear in your religion and it seems to me the issue of shechita is a very good example of that. I fought as a back-bench MP at the last attempt by the Farm Animal Welfare Council to do something to change this and I will always stand up for it*". A remarkable and chilling statement. "*doesn't mean that you have to give up things that you hold very dear in your religion*". Is he talking 'carte blanche' for any savage religious notion that some people may carry in their heads, regardless of consequences to people or animals? Female genital mutilation? Death to apostates, perhaps?

I wonder what a Muslim or Jew would choose if he found his head poking through a hole and given the option of a bolt to the head or a blade through the throat. Not quite so sanguine, I imagine. By all means read your old books and believe your archaic dogma. By all means waste your precious life preparing for an eternity beyond, but please do not inflict your heartless ideas on innocent suffering animals.

If religious groups are given privileged exemption from UK law, it seems reasonable to expect consumers to have the right to avoid meat from animals killed under that exemption. In fact, this kind of meat is only supposed to be for the consumption of Muslims and Jews, but for economic reasons this targeting of supply is not enforced and because there is no requirement under EU or UK law for the meat from non-stun slaughter to be labelled, it is routinely sold on to the open market – which leads to unsuspecting members of the public being duped into buying meat which is the product of religious slaughter methods, whilst at the same time artificially subsidising the religious slaughter industry.

Many food outlets, private and public bodies, including schools and hospitals regularly serve halal meat to all customers, often for reasons of convenience.

Some Christians have argued that their rights under article 9 of the European Convention on Human Rights are infringed by not being able to avoid meat which has been dedicated to another god. Many Sikhs also consider it against their religion to eat ritually slaughtered meat. This further strengthens the case for labelling.

Here we have another example of religious ideas causing a great deal of havoc but the main concern to humanists in all this remains the suffering of animals. And there is no doubt that they suffer. The president of the British Veterinary Association John Blackwell, a man who knows more about animal behaviour than all theologians put together, said British abattoirs should follow Denmark's example. *"Our view has always been that animals should be stunned. They should be imperceptible to pain as death supervenes. We are looking for a meeting of minds to review the evidence base which clearly shows that slaughtering animals without stunning compromises welfare. If that can't happen then I would like labelling at the point of sale that gives the consumer informed choice. If that is not possible we would be looking for a ban on killing without stunning".*

He acknowledged that there were likely to be sensitivities surrounding the issue but that the debate was preferable to relying on beliefs handed down hundreds of years ago, that may have made sense at the time. Research in New Zealand has also confirmed that animals being slaughtered without pre-stunning do feel pain. The investigation was carried out by Dr Craig Johnson and his colleagues at Massey University, New Zealand. They were awarded a prize for their work by the Humane Slaughter Association. The research shows that calves do appear to feel pain when slaughtered by *dhabiha* (Muslim) and *shechita* (Jewish) ritual methods, which involve hanging the animal upside down and slitting its throat, allowing it to bleed to death. "I think our work is the best evidence yet that it's painful," says Dr. Johnson. "It wasn't a surprise to me, but in terms of the religious community, they are adamant animals don't experience any pain, so the results might be a surprise to them."

What is most ironic in all this, is that Muslims and Jews, normally at daggers drawn, are showing a cosy united front when it comes to ignoring animal welfare. Due to the similarity between both methods of slaughtering, Kosher meats, which are consumed by Jews, are also acceptable to Muslims. Humans have enslaved the rest of the animal world and have treated our distant cousins in fur and feathers so badly that beyond doubt, if they were able to formulate a religion, they would depict the Devil in human form.

ANIMAL TESTING

Less clear-cut are the ethics surrounding animal experimentation which involves a highly contentious balancing act between animal welfare and human welfare. The difference between animal rights and animal welfare has been summed up like this: animal rights advocates are campaigning for no cages, while animal welfarists are campaigning for bigger cages. Animal rights supporters believe that it is morally wrong to use or exploit animals in any way. Animal welfare supporters believe that it can be morally acceptable for human beings to use or exploit animals as long as the suffering of the animals is either eliminated or reduced to the minimum and there is no practicable way of achieving the same end without using animals.

There is no question that anyone today would defend the sight of rows of strapped in rabbits forced to smoke cigarettes. But Colin Blakemore, a professor of neuroscience, who happens to be a humanist, argues that, provided suffering is reduced to the very minimum and testing is restricted to medical research only, a case can be made. Antibiotics, insulin, vaccines for polio and cervical cancer, organ transplantation, HIV treatments, heart-bypass surgery: all these were developed and tested using animals. He says that if there are reliable alternatives they are used. Magnetic resonance imaging, computer models and work on isolated tissues and cell cultures can be useful, but they cannot provide the answers that animal research can.

Animal research has contributed to 70 per cent of Nobel prizes for physiology or medicine. Without it we would, medically speaking, be stuck in the dark ages.

He contends that far from being ashamed of this kind of research we should be proud of our scientists, whose work offers hope to those suffering from incurable disorders. Those who object are entitled to refuse treatments that have been developed through animal tests – even if that means rejecting virtually every medical treatment that exists. But they don't have the right to force that opinion on the majority who expect and long for new and better treatments.

Blakemore stresses that medical researchers are not a bunch of scalpel wielding sadists. His colleagues are compassionate, humane people who carry out their work with great caution and consideration and with every effort to minimise suffering. Other humanists would argue that regardless of advantages to the human race, there is no right for us to exploit our superior intelligence to the detriment of our fellow creatures.

NATURE VERSUS NURTURE

*"Nature seems at each man's birth to have marked
out the bounds of his virtues and vices and to have
determined how good or how wicked that man
shall be capable of being"*

Francois de La Rochefoucauld

The influence of genetics on personality, aptitude and behaviour is a fascinating topic surrounded by much controversy and because of its special importance to Humanists I will discuss it here at length. The relevance to humanism stems from the objection that humanists have to the theistic notion that people are created equally, yet have a choice in what they intend to do with their own blueprint.

A friend of mine, who is a good swimmer, believes that he could have become an Olympic champion had he been given the opportunity of intensive training at an earlier age. He is a subscriber to the 'at birth every human being is a blank sheet of paper' school of thought. Human beings can become anything they choose, provided they are trained properly and show sufficient dedication. A believer in this doctrine is the father of the famous Hungarian chess prodigies, the Polgar sisters. He claims that given early access and complete control he could turn any child, picked at random off the street, into a world-beater at chess. Before embarking on this project he did however seek out a wife who possessed the right credentials for this experiment.

To treat such claims seriously it is first necessary to differentiate between humans and the rest of the animal world. For Darwinists like myself this is a particularly unbefitting thing to have to do, but necessary, lest we are seriously expected to be able to train up cart horses to triumph majestically in the Grand National. So it is on humans that our 'the sky is the limit' hopes must rest. No need to worry about pedigree, disregard the shapes and sizes. Billy Bunter or Daley Thompson; the odds are even.

I suspect that underlying this quaint idea is not just political correctness but also the religious 'we are all created equal in the image of God' assertion, for nothing in the field of genetics and heredity would appear to bear it out. People's ultimate body shape, size and bone structure, their cardio-vascular constitution, the circuitry in their brains are largely determined at birth. No amount of training could have turned Mike Tyson into a successful marathon runner, nor I daresay, a grandmaster at chess. Equally, I have a problem envisaging Nigel Short as a champion heavy-weight boxer.

And yet all this and many more astounding feats are possible if the 'blank slate' theory is to be believed. An expression of this are the advertisements frequently seen in the press, offering books and courses on memory improvement. We are told we need never forget another name, or telephone number. It is all done, they say, by special techniques, by association, by translating numbers into words, words into pictures, anyone can do it. What they don't point out is that people with poor memories have difficulty even remembering the codes on which such systems are based or retaining the pictures necessary for the associations. Some people are able to play multiple games of chess, blindfolded. Others can barely remember the last two moves.

Although some progress can always be made no amount of training can bridge that size of gap. You might as well try to teach a colour-blind person all the shades of an autumn forest.

Or take the plethora of books on personality improvement. Dale Carnegie's "*How to win friends and Influence People*". Or Peale's "*The Power of Positive Thinking*". We must all have read some in our time and how many introverts have become raging extroverts as a result? The Leopard does not change its spots is a lesson closer to the truth. I think 'the blank tablet' notion is an invidious proposition which, if followed, can lead to much disappointment and heartache. Of course it is true that with effort and determination people can better themselves in many fields and such efforts are to be commended, but to hold out unlimited potential and success, provided the commitment is strong enough, condemns many young people to ambitions beyond their capability and ultimately to disillusion. For every Becker, winning Wimbledon at seventeen, there are thousands of youngsters, training equally hard, who are never going to make the grade. It is only fair to point this out to them in time so that they are given the opportunity to pursue their talents more profitably elsewhere.

Couples in a long term relationship will have learned that no amount of preaching or nagging will achieve a major change in character or behaviour in their partners. If such drastic change were possible people would lose their personality and become somebody else entirely. Yet some persist till death do them part because they have been taught to believe that such changes are achievable. When no such change is forthcoming the nagging partner is frustrated and the recipient bears grudges.

When the political correctness is taken a step further still and is extended to the men v. women controversy, then the madness really starts. There are those who preach that apart from the obvious difference of gender there are no inherent differences of aptitude or inclination between the sexes. Any noticeable dissimilarities are believed to be the result of upbringing and the environment.

Before I say anything else about the relative merits of men and women I want to emphasise that the matter of gender is not as straight-forward as is generally believed. Gender is not always a case of either/or. Sexual physiology is on a broad continuum, ranging from overt masculinity to overt femininity, with in between a complex overlapping stratum of hybrid sexuality and homosexuality. Although, as far as I am concerned all these conditions are of equal value, in order to avoid the red herrings of Tamara Press and Liberace, I shall disregard the relatively small group in the centre and address my remarks to hetero-sexuality alone.

Looked at this way, one has to be particularly blind or obdurate not to be able or willing to recognise the differences between the sexes. Overtly male: assertive, aggressive, confident, adventurous. Overtly female: caring, conscientious, cautious. It is there for all to see. Look what happens on the roads: overtaking on the brow of a hill; ignoring double white lines; road rage races on the motorway: nine times out of ten the culprit is a man. Violent crime, war mongering, pub fights, domestic violence, overwhelmingly it is men that cause the trouble. Prison statistics bear it out by a ratio of more than twenty to one.

We are to believe that it is all to do with upbringing. Boys are given guns and girls are given dolls. And that explains it all. For sheer facile naivety that one must win some prizes. Many a feminist mother will have had the opportunity to find out for herself that it is not as simple as that. She would soon learn that (provided he is normally masculine) her Johnny would not be long in kicking Barbie into touch and wrenching the meccano set from little sister Mary, ready to beat her over the head with it, if necessary. Such inclinations, alas, are innate in the male of the species and no amount of gender bending or wishful thinking can eradicate it. Let those who doubt it take a walk in the country past a herd of cows, overseen by a strapping bull. Then let them interfere with any member of the herd and see what happens next. Whilst airborne they might just find time to protest that that bull's mummy should have made him play with dolls, but somehow it will lack conviction.

And no arguments please that we mustn't extrapolate from the animal world, we humans are very much part of it and cannot escape its rules. (When preparing for space travel NASA scientists used chimpanzees in order to predict the physical, psychological and task motor responses of human astronauts and these were subsequently proved completely accurate). The time is not far off when differences will be found in the brains of men and women which will establish beyond doubt that a tendency to aggression and derring do is inherent in the male. Then, not before time, we shall be free of the nonsense that is now being talked about the predominance of environmental influences on upbringing and we shall finally come to realise that these account for little in determining what makes men and women tick.

There is no question that the jungle with its emphasis on brute force from which the human race is trying to extricate itself has dealt women particularly a poor hand. In primitive societies might tends to be right and I am all for measures protecting women from the scourge of male aggression. But such attempts are not helped by a wrong diagnosis of the problem. Let's recognise that nature, not nurture, is the chief culprit and then decide how justice for all can be achieved.

My bête noir amongst the theories pushed by nurturists is that a lot of abused children within families subsequently become abusers themselves because of learned behaviour. *"You know, I really hated this cruel abuse I suffered and I would not wish it on my worst enemy but there is nothing for it; I have learnt how to do it so I will just have to go on doing it to others, unpleasant though it may be for all concerned"*. No, abused children often become abusers because, unfortunately, they have inherited the propensity through either parent and it is what they are inclined to do. Instinctive inherited behaviour is common-place in non-human animals. It's there for all to see. To assume that humans are not affected this way strikes me as deeply anthropomorphic.

Very few victims of non parental child abuse go on to become abusers in turn. I am making this statement without being able to refer to research because I don't think any has been done. But I am willing to challenge anyone to prove me wrong. Or take recidivism. We are told that habitual offenders re-offend because they haven't been taught the difference between right or wrong. The prisons and society do not treat them right. I am sure their ears must be buzzing from lectures handed out by magistrates and judges. Their heads must ache from probation officers' and social workers' loving ministrations; prison chaplains do their bit and still they keep knocking on the prison door. Ministry of Justice statistics for the year 2011 show that for sentences of less than twelve months duration the re-offending rate was 58 per cent.

If we then bear in mind that the crime detection rate generally is no higher than 30 per cent, we get a pretty good idea about the huge percentage of people unable to mend their ways. Rather than blaming the environment Dr. Robert Hare, a Canadian psychologist who has spent decades researching the subject, comes up with a better explanation. He says that there is a sizeable proportion of criminals who are sociopaths; in other words they are socially flawed insofar that they were born without a conscience. They are totally self-centred and do not know nor care what it is like to hurt others.

I once saw an example of this "non-conscience" in action on a TV show. A number of repeat burglars had been invited to take part in a discussion on crime.

Victims gave heartrending accounts of the horrors of finding their houses desecrated and their prize possessions stolen. The young offenders remained totally unmoved. They needed money to buy cigarettes and booze they said, other people have these things why not us. Ordinary people with a concern for others are unable to imagine that such sentiments are wholly absent in others and they keep on looking for different explanations.

Few people would deny that physical traits are inherited to predictable patterns: hair colour, shapes of ears, noses and so on. The evidence is overwhelming. But when it comes to the brain or personality suddenly all bets are off. It is as if the brain must be treated as an extraneous part of the body, not affected by the genetic determination so clearly noticeable elsewhere. But if you do not believe in the religious notion of dualism, i.e. a soul or 'ghost in the machine'; if you believe, like Humanists do, that the brain is just another, admittedly complex, ingredient making up the whole, then you must apply to the brain the same genetic ground rules that are applied elsewhere. Then it becomes difficult to escape the conclusion reached by the Harvard neuroscientist Edward Wilson that: "the brain is not born as a *tabula rasa* waiting to be filled by experience but an exposed negative, waiting to be slipped into developer fluid".

In his book 'The Blank Slate' cognitive scientist Steven Pinker expresses a similar sentiment. But the can of worms that this idea unleashes is too much to most people to swallow. Early pioneers in genetic research Sir Francis Galton and Sir Cyril Burt have been described as zealots who had fiddled their figures but in at least two studies, (Robert Joynson's *The Burt Affair* and Prof. Ronald Fletcher's *the Cyril Burt scandal*) Burt has been fully rehabilitated. There has since been further extensive research on identical twins, separated at birth, both here and in the US, the best known being the Minnesota twin study, and the evidence overwhelmingly points at inherited characteristics and intelligence. No other explanation can account for the remarkable correlations found in both physical and mental abilities.

If the environment and upbringing really did exert as much influence as is sometimes alleged, children growing up in orphanages under very uniform regimes, as used to be the case early in the century, would have shown great convergence in personality and intelligence but no such similarities have ever been found.

I have never understood why there has been this zealous search for sameness amongst the human race. Different does not mean inferior. The fact that I am good with my hands has always been much more use to me in my life than any intellectual assets I might possess. The very fact that it is acceptable for me to say that I am good with my hands and not that I have a good brain shows how hung up we have become about intelligence.

There is nothing wrong with diversity in people. Vive la difference! The trick is to identify and value individual talents, be they cerebral or manual and develop them to the full, without prejudice, in an open and free society. The great German poet and Humanist Goethe once expressed the influence of heredity powerfully in a poem, which sums up what most people, unaffected by political correctness, have many times observed for themselves. I quote the original German, followed by a loose translation:

Vom Vater hab ich die Statur,
das Lebens ernstes Führen,
Vom Mütterchen die Frohnatur
und Lust zu fabulieren.

Urahnherr war der Schönsten hold,
das spukt so hin und wieder;
Urahnfrau liebte Schmuck und Gold,
das zuckt wohl durch die Glieder.

Sind nun die Elemente nicht
aus dem Komplex zu trennen,
was ist denn an dem ganzen Wicht
original zu nennen?

(My posture comes from father's side along with a bent for earnest discussion. My mother gave me my easy nature and tendency to fantasise. My granddad had an eye for the ladies, that still rings a bell with me. Grandma loved pomp and circumstance, I can still feel that in my bones. If none of these features can be disregarded what can be said to be original in the child?)

MENACE OF RELIGION

*'All religions are ancient monuments to superstitions,
ignorance, ferocity and modern religions
are only ancient follies rejuvenated.'*
Baron d'Holbach 1772

*'All religions are founded on the fear of the many
and the cleverness of the few'*
Stendhal

*'Religion is what common people see as true,
wise people see as false and the rulers see as useful'*
Seneca

Why are humanists so worried about religion.
Why can't they leave it alone, why wrench away
religion from lonely old people who wear religion like a
comfort blanket? Put this way it seems indeed a wicked
thing to do. But it would be a gross mis-representation
of what worries humanists. Our objective is not to
undermine people's personal faith or take away their
hope of eternal life. When my father came to stay with
me for the last time in his nineties, I detected some
creeping uncertainty in his religious convictions. All his
life he had been devout but in latter years he had been

exposed to the slide in religiosity in Holland and he began to quiz me on what I thought. I don't subscribe to outright lies so my tact was sorely tested. I was determined not to shake his hope of meeting my mother again. A belief he had firmly expressed when standing at her graveside two years earlier. I kept on saying stick with your beliefs, it doesn't matter what I think.

No, humanists have bigger fish to fry, the ones that do the harm. The pacemakers behind organised religion: evangelists and politicians with nefarious agendas. People like prime minister Tony Blair, who promoted faith schools and his prayer pal George W. who stopped stem cell research and re-invented Christian crusades. Or his father who said that atheists should not be considered either citizens or patriots. Or the Rev. Ian Paisley, who for years stoked the fires of sectarian hatred in Northern Ireland with vocal chords highly developed by years of ranting. We are after Popes who piously intone: "let there be no hunger" and "let there be no more war" and then preach dogma and urge measures that ensure that such objectives are for ever out of reach. Or ayatollahs who try to have authors killed for writing the wrong books. Those are the egregious characters in our firing line.

All these people stand on the shoulders of a multitude of well meaning followers, affording them power and legitimacy. Humanists' antipathy to religion is not of equal strength. There is harmful, pernicious religion and there is the acceptable face. We all know which are the harmful ones. Unfortunately they are the most widespread. The gentler ones are much less known: Unitarians, Quakers, Shakers, Jaines, Buddhists, Mennonites.

If only all religions could be like them the world would be a better place.

How did religion manage to gain such a strong position in human affairs? A position exploited ever since by opportunists of every stripe. The obvious answer must be: fear and ignorance. When humans first took to their feet, almost two million years ago, they had little understanding of the natural world around them. Full of fear of the unknown, their fragile situation left them wide open to all forms of superstition. There were no explanations and answers for disease. Natural phenomena were mysterious and frightening. There wasn't the faintest comprehension of cosmology, geology, biology, meteorology to name but a few of modern scientific disciplines. They could only interpret floods, volcanic eruptions, lightning, pestilence within the primitive notions available to them as the doings of angry gods hidden from view.

This primitive heritage has proved extremely difficult to shake off. So God has become the product of an inherited human perception, the manifestation of an evolutionary adaptation, a coping mechanism that emerged in our species in order to enable us to survive our unique and otherwise debilitating awareness of death. It could be argued that make-belief has infiltrated the genes and mankind is stuck with it. Richard Dawkins calls it a virus of the mind. It is as if the human species has a schizoid nature - his feet implanted on the earth but his imaginative head soaring toward a heaven of magical unreality.

Over time this vulnerable state of affairs was taken advantage of by self-appointed opportunist priests, who have memorably been described in Andrew Marvell's poem as the first deluders of mankind. Or by others as the second oldest profession. Rather than pursue explanations by investigation, trial and error, these leaders invented an elaborate fairy tale and spend the rest of their days discussing and spreading the detail of their own inventions as god given fact. It is a truly remarkable example of human gullibility that the entire edifices of the main churches rest on the equivalent of the end product of a Chinese whispers story passed round a group of people as a party game.

Many belief systems were thus created all over the world and because most of them offered considerable advantages to the inventors, non-conformity was suppressed by dire threats of hell fire and if that didn't work there was always the rack and the stake. Having cowed their dupes into submission these leaders have been allowed to set up oppressive regimes in the form of churches and theocracies and to go to war with rival systems. This regrettable development has become the reason why Christopher Hitchens has said that religion poisons everything and why humanists must always be on guard against further encroachment.

Composing a comprehensive list of religious privileges and the harm caused by religion in the past and in the present would be hard to do but the following summary offers a good selection:

- Conduct of holy wars and crusades.
- Handicapping scientific progress for example delaying stem cell research
- Witch trials in Europe and America.
- Missionaries destroying/converting smaller, "heathen" cultures.

- The demonisation of other religions or secular life stances
- Persecution of heretics and scientists- e.g. Galileo and Bruno.
- Children dying because their parents refuse them medical treatment on religious grounds; relying instead on faith-healers and prayer.
- Slavery, supported by scripture ("Slaves, obey your earthly masters with respect and fear, just as you would obey Christ.", St. Paul, Ephesians 6:5)
- The destruction of great works of art considered to be pornographic/blasphemous, and the persecution of the artists.
- Censorship of speech, art, books, music, films, poetry, songs and, if possible, thought.
- Persecution/punishment of blasphemers (Salman Rushdie is still under death sentence) and blasphemy laws in general.
- Serial killers believing they are doing the work of God.
- Harmful exorcisms by priests believing they are destroying the work of Satan.
- Delusional behaviour: people suffering injury or death in the belief that their faith has made them invulnerable (e.g. religious serpent handling).
- Whole societies divided by differences in belief or doctrine, often resulting in violence.
- Mass suicides of cult-members following a charismatic leader.
- Sacrifices to appease the gods, or to ensure a good harvest.
- Forced marriages and 'honour' killings.
- The practice of FGM (female genital mutilation).

- The discouragement of rational, critical thought.
- Uncontrolled population growth caused or encouraged by natalist churches prohibiting birth-control and abortion.
- The spread of sexually transmitted diseases, most lethally AIDS, due to churches prohibiting the use of condoms.
- Unwanted pregnancies and pregnant teenagers condemned to a life in mental institutions to avoid embarrassing their church and families.
- Believers whipping, impaling, poisoning or crucifying themselves during religious festivals as a demonstration of their faith and piety.
- Suicide bombers taught to believe that martyrs go straight to Paradise.
- The indoctrination of children into the religion of their parents, giving them an arbitrary, life-long belief that is almost entirely dependent on their place of birth.
- Women treated as second-class citizens or the equivalent of livestock for breeding purposes
- Persecution of homosexuals
- Abuse of power, authority and trust by religious leaders (for financial gain or sexual abuse of followers and sometimes children).
- Creating false moral dilemmas, which causes the religious to suffer emotionally and inflict suffering on other people.
- Fostering an "us" and "them" mentality facilitating conflict.
- In Britain segregation of children in faith schools and compulsory worship in community schools.
- Opposition to assisted dying legislation

- Unelected religious leaders in parliament
- In America breaching Jefferson's wall of separation. One nation under God; in God we trust on coinage. Constant pressure to displace the teaching of evolution by creationism.
- Attacks on abortion clinics and doctors.

A very sorry list indeed. Towards the end of my book I have attempted to compile a list of the good things that come out of religion but try as I might I couldn't strike a balance.

Hitler/Stalin Counter Claim

When atheists confront believers with the extensive list of religious iniquity, including the actions of the murderous 'Taliban' or the horrors of the 'Inquisition', they counter with the accusation that atheists such as Hitler and Stalin were even worse. Because they consider this unfair slur a major trump card it calls for a strong rebuttal. My first point is so critical that I must put in another 'read my lips' request. I will say it slowly: *if Stalin was an atheist he did not pursue his appalling acts in the furtherance of atheism. He was a political thug. The atheism was purely incidental.* The Taliban and the Spanish inquisition, to name but two examples of dreadful religious persecution, are and were, exclusively concerned with spreading religious doctrine and crushing infidels.

As for Hitler he never was an atheist. He was born a Roman Catholic and remained so all his life. There are at least 30 well documented quotes from 'Mein Kampf', Reichstag speeches and other sources which confirm that, whilst not much of a friend of the church, which he saw as a rival, Hitler had a firm belief in God and frequently let it be known that he considered himself the custodian of the Almighty's mandate to carry out his great missions of establishing National Socialism (Fascism) and the extermination of the Jews.

A few samples will illustrate the point:

"I believe today that I am acting in the sense of the Almighty Creator.
By warding off the Jews I am fighting for the Lord's work."
[Adolf Hitler, Speech, Reichstag, 1936]
"I am now, as before, a Catholic and will always remain so".
[Adolf Hitler, to General Gerhard Engel, 1941]
"Anyone who dares to lay hands on the highest image of the Lord commits sacrilege against the benevolent creator of this miracle and contributes to the expulsion from paradise."
[Adolf Hitler, "Mein Kampf" Vol. 2 Chapter 1]
"A society aware person in particular has the sacred duty, each in their own denomination, of making people stop just talking superficially of God's will and actually fulfil God's will, and not let God's word be desecrated. For God's will gave men their form, their essence and their abilities. Anyone who destroys His work is declaring war on the Lord's creation, the Divine will."
[Adolf Hitler, "Mein Kampf" Vol. 2 Chapter 10]
'Almighty God, bless our arms when the time comes; be just as thou hast always been; judge now whether we be deserving of freedom; Lord, bless our battle!'
[Adolf Hitler's prayer, "Mein Kampf", Vol. 2 Chapter 13]

I think this should put paid to 'Hitler the atheist' and worryingly for Christians, manoeuvre him into the theist camp. Moreover it should be pointed out that there are elements in fascism that have a particular appeal to the religious mindset: belief in total certainty and total control; contempt for the independent mind and insistence on uncritical acceptance of authority from above; the belief that the world is decaying and must be rescued from nihilism and rootlessness; the emphasis on tradition, inequality, stern laws, warfare against decadence; appeal to the heroic; nationalism, patriotism; the appeal of security and stability in exchange for freedom and justice.

Nevertheless I am not going to argue that all Hitler did was motivated by his Christian beliefs. Although as far as the extermination of the Jews was concerned he claimed to do the Lord's work. (see top quote).

For atheists Stalin is a harder nut to crack. It would be much harder still had he been a humanist. Atheism, as argued before, is not a life stance or a world view it merely means not being a theist. By no stretch of the imagination was Stalin a humanist. That's why a comparison with Torquemada of the Spanish inquisition does not wash. Torquemada persecuted Jews and non-Catholics because they weren't Catholics and refused to convert. Stalin's reasons for his murderous campaigns were strictly political. He ordered his purges because he had corrupted the ideologies of communism not because he employed the rationalism of freethought.

If he was indeed a confessed atheist he certainly didn't behave like one. He was a paranoid and anti-intellectual maniac. He once answered a question about his most enjoyable hobby and said: "My greatest pleasure is to choose one's victim, exact vengeance and then go to bed." Stalin was virulently anti-Semitic which led to the execution of nineteen Jews in 1952 for being part of a supposed 'Zionist Conspiracy'. This could have been taken straight from Hitler's hymn sheet and his actions were odd for a man who was, through his dictatorship, ruling a society based on a corrupted version of the ideas of Marx, who was of course a Jew.

Like Hitler, Stalin fostered a personality cult, in his case that of 'Uncle Joe', presented as an avuncular, down to earth character. Russian historian Roy Medvedev made an interesting observation about Stalin. He wrote: "We cannot equate Stalinism with socialism, Marxism or Leninism – no matter how imperfect these doctrines might be in some respects. Stalinism is the sum total of the perversions he introduced into the theory and practice of scientific socialism". So as well as atheism Stalin also managed to give communism a bad name. Later in his regime he chose to appeal to the religious side of his people in order to unite them against Hitler. But like Hitler, he did see the church as a rival in his fight for total control. Stalin and his regime's antipathy towards religion is likely to have arisen from the churches' opposition to the revolution.

Most of the clergy reacted toward the Russian revolution with open hostility. During the Civil War, many representatives of the Russian orthodox clergy collaborated or had sympathies with the White Armies and foreign invading armies, hoping for a restoration of the pre-revolutionary regime. The church had expressed its support to General Kornilov's counter-revolutionary coup attempt. The church adopted the 'Enactment on Legal Status of the Church in Russia' which tried to vindicate the privileges that the church had enjoyed for centuries under the old regime. The Orthodox Church, said the document, "holds the pre-eminent public and legal position in the Russian State among other denominations" PatriachTikhon of Moscow anathematised the Soviet government and called on believers to fight against it and its decrees. The church leadership openly urged fighting against the Soviet Government in its appeal entitled *"To the Orthodox People"*. "It is better to shed one's blood and to be awarded a martyr's crown than to let the enemies desecrate Orthodox faith".

The church's opposition to the Soviet Government was part of a general counter-revolutionary movement. In the first days after the victory of the October armed uprising in Petrograd, the clergy assisted the rebellion of Kerensky and Krasnov as they attempted to overthrow Soviet power. The activity of the Local Council in Moscow supported the cadets who had revolted. When the rebels seized the Kremlin for a time, its cathedrals and bell-towers were placed at their disposal at once.

This brief historical context may go some way towards explaining Stalin's reign of terror. Regretful though it was that he carried the 'atheist' label, there is no way that a case can be made that his behaviour had anything in common with a humanist world view and none of his policies had the specific intent of forcing people to convert to atheism.

ATHEIST MILITANCY

*"If you turn on the news tonight and hear of suicide
bombers murdering civilians anywhere from Baghdad to
the London Underground, I can reassure you of one point:
the bombers will not be humanists".*

T.A.

Atheists/humanists have a dilemma encountered by all
non-believers in a religion dominated society. They
can choose to keep their heads down (they used to have
to not that long ago, if they wanted to keep them on) and
quietly put up with the liberties taken by the religious or
they can opt to be more militant and kick up a fuss when
confronted with religious presumptuousness. Putting
one's head above the parapet comes with the danger of
being accused of militancy. Historically the best way for
religious leaders was to eliminate troublemakers and
doubters, but now at least in the West, they are reduced
to arguing their case. Religion should be moribund by
now but its virus-like nature means it keeps spreading
unless humanists develop better immune systems. We
have no churches and must rely on word of mouth or
books like this as our ideological white blood cells.

The problem is humanists are generally not pro-active
in the defence of rationalism since it is not as gripping a

pursuit as all the fire and brimstone and eternal life stuff, because common sense is usually more mundane. Theists, finally on the back foot after two thousand years of dominance, now feel threatened by the turning atheist worm and the term 'aggressive atheism' is gaining currency. One does not need to puzzle long over why religionists dislike atheists so much. Atheists stir up the suppressed doubts of believers to the point of producing anguish. This is the anguish that prompted believers to burn heretics and atheists at the stake in bygone times to remove the source of the unsettling, disturbing doubts that plagued the believers.

What they tend to overlook is that our form of aggression tends to stop at words whereas theirs for centuries was expressed in oppression and bloody violence. There is a very important difference between feeling strongly, even passionately, about something we have given a lot of thought to and examined the evidence for, on the one hand, and feeling strongly about something because it has been revealed to us, or reputedly revealed to somebody else in ancient history and subsequently legitimised by tradition. Particularly if such beliefs are held with murderous conviction. Atheism doesn't make good people do bad things, that contradiction is left to religion. Let me just give a couple of dreadful examples: a mere three hundred years ago Thomas Aikenhead, a 20 year old Edinburgh university student was hanged, Bible in hand, for the crime of ridiculing the holy scriptures. The church refused a reprieve and urged "vigorous execution to curb the abounding of impiety in this land". In France in 1766 Francois de la Barre, a 21 year old French nobleman, was tortured and beheaded before his body was burnt on a pyre along with Voltaire's "Philosophical Dictionary" nailed to his torso. His crime had been refusing to doff his cap to a religious procession and damaging a wooden crucifix.

Go back another century or two and such ghastly scenes could have been witnessed a thousand fold. Even today some of our god-fearing citizens are aggressive enough to shoot people who carry out abortions, issue fatwas on authors who write what they don't want to hear, assassinate people on the streets of London and fly planes into buildings in New York. There are plenty of other, more minor issues atheists are entitled to be militant about. Unelected Bishops in the House of Lords, compulsory worship in schools, 'in God we trust' on American coins, unopposed religious propaganda on the BBC.

Centuries of oppression have taught rationalists that if vigilance is relaxed, religion will seize the opportunity to resume its innate bullying nature. Religion has a bullying nature for several reasons. It is of course in the interest of its leaders to cement a strong position in society giving them status, influence and wealth. Also, and more benignly, some religious people genuinely believe that heathens, the likes of humanists, are in mortal danger of missing out on heaven and they go to great lengths to make them see the error of their ways.

I must re-emphasise here that 'atheist aggression' is rarely directed at this second category of peaceful, privately religious individuals. Our beef is with the organ grinders, not the monkeys. The people at the top of the religious pyramid. The ones that manipulate and organise, using religion for their own ulterior motives.

Atheists are unpopular because they are upsetting the religious apple cart. That cart has rolled on untroubled for almost two thousand years but now the wheels are coming off and the apples are past their sell by date. Believers are stirred out of their complacency. Their certainties put to the test and found wanting. The religious underlings are being told that their emperors wear no clothes. That their magical castles are built on sand. They are not turning the other cheek as they are meant to, but are up in arms and go all out to demonise the foe.

But where is the evidence for our supposed demonic behaviour? Where are the atheists rioting in the streets. Where are the atheist holy books burning parties? Where are the prisons bulging with benighted infidels? Where are the atheist suicide bombers? Atheists want a quiet life but they are not going to get it unless they stop religion in its tracks. Since we are not the types to resort to violence we can only do it by making our rational voices heard. These messages no doubt will cause offence, particularly to those who secretly know that their sacred beliefs are poppycock. But nobody has a right not to be offended. You may offend my humanism to your heart's content. Sticks and stones and all that. Rather than act the offended victim I would relish the thought of a good debate, but please don't go burning my book.

Because he has written a best seller against religion Professor Richard Dawkins, a very mild mannered and civilised man, is now being vilified as aggressive atheist in chief. Forgotten are his brilliant books on evolution. Footballers and cyclists are made Knights of the realm and more incredibly still, characters such as Sir Iqbal

Sacranie, who once said that death perhaps is a bit too easy for Salman Rushdie and has described homosexuality as not acceptable. But there are no gongs for eminent scientists like Richard Dawkins, who bang the drums for rationalism

THE TABLES ARE TURNING - RELIGIOUS DISCRIMINATION ON TRIAL

Christians have ridden rough-shod over unbelievers' rights for centuries but in recent years the tables have been turning. Gradually people are no longer prepared to put up with Christians who believe that their precious beliefs trump the rights of others. What people do in their own homes is one thing but people who are in jobs dealing with the general public or run businesses offering open services, cannot impose their religious beliefs on others.

Two Bed & Breakfast operators who refused to let gay couples share a room lost their appeal against a court ruling and were ordered to pay thousands of pounds in compensation. The Supreme court told them that they were entitled to express their beliefs, but not if they were incompatible with the rights of gay people.

The couple said they thought that any sex outside marriage was "a sin" and denied discriminating against the complainants. They argued that their decision was founded on a "religiously-informed judgement of conscience". What such people don't seem to under-stand is that the days of 'No Blacks, no Irishmen, no Gays' are over.

A Christian nurse, moved to a desk job after refusing to remove her crucifix at work, lost a discrimination claim against her employers. The nurse had argued the cross 'ban' prevented her from expressing her religious beliefs. But an employment tribunal ruled that the Royal Devon and Exeter Hospitals NHS Trust, where she worked, had acted in a reasonable manner. The NHS trust's uniform and dress code prohibits front-line staff from wearing any type of necklace in case patients try to grab them. It offered the nurse the compromise of wearing her cross pinned inside a uniform lapel or pocket, but she said being asked to hide her faith was "disrespectful".

I have often wondered why people would want to go around wearing instruments of torture around their necks. If crucifixes complete with nailed on body are the fashion why not a gallows with a dangling victim. How about a guillotine complete with a basket for the head. An electric chair perhaps, with battery operated sparks? Humanists will have to come to terms with the fact that for a lot of people religion is a cross to bear.

In another case Appeal Court judges ruled that a registrar who refused to conduct civil partnership ceremonies because they were against her Christian beliefs broke the law. They said the right to express a strong Christian faith must take second place to the rights of homosexuals under equality laws. Lord Neuberger, the Master of the Rolls, said the rules meant the registrar had to stifle her religious principles to perform what she regarded as gay marriage – or give up her job.

The case was the most important legal test yet in the struggle between Christians and the gay rights lobby. Lord Neuberger, sitting with two other senior judges, said "the 2007 'Sexual Orientation Regulations' – which make it illegal to refuse to serve someone on grounds of their sexual orientation – outweigh the rights of religious believers. The prohibition of discrimination by the 2007 Regulations takes precedence over any right which a person would otherwise have by virtue of his or her religious belief or faith, to practise discrimination on the ground of sexual orientation'.

This meant that the registrar was faced with 'choosing between relinquishing a post she plainly appreciates or officiating at events which she considers to be contrary to her religious beliefs'.

A spokesman from the gay pressure group Stonewall said: "We are pleased that the Court of Appeal has upheld the right of lesbian and gay people to receive public services from public servants. When the rights of different groups clash, as they have in this case, surely there must be a proportionate attempt to balance those competing rights. In this case, one set of rights was trampled by another set of rights. That cannot be right in a free and democratic society".

Mike Judge, a spokesman for the Christian Institute, which helped fund the registrar's case, commented: "Christians will feel let down by this decision. It will only serve to reinforce the impression that Christians are being pushed to the sidelines of public life. Our nation's highest court has effectively told them their concerns are not of general public importance". Mr. Judge like many of his co-religionists seems to be unaware of the rule that their right to swing their religious fists, ends where secular noses begin.

Apart from the case examples given above there are an increasing number of instances where practitioners of religion are granted exemptions in the execution of their duties. A supermarket chain has allowed its Muslim staff to refuse to sell alcohol, or even stack it on shelves, if they don't want to. Another instance involved a woman being refused emergency contraception. Once this idea of religious exemptions on the provision of goods and services takes hold, there is almost no limit to how troublesome and disruptive it can become. The woman who was refused the morning after pill by a Muslim pharmacist joins the growing number of people who have found themselves confronted with religious objections to perfectly legal activities.

There have been cases of taxi drivers refusing to carry guide dogs in their cabs because of Koranic objections. We have had doctors refusing to prescribe contraception, a Muslim policeman refusing to guard the Israeli embassy and Jewish policemen demanding to be excused duties on Saturday. Now we have shop workers in supermarkets wanting to pick and choose what goods they will sell. A few years ago, a Jewish woman applied to Marks and Spencer for a job as a food taster. At the interview she said that she would not taste pork products on account of her "religious convictions". When the store declined to offer her the job, she took them to an industrial tribunal. She lost her case. But that was then, and this is now. If the idea gains ground that religious demands must trump all other considerations, the outcome of such cases might be very different.

Not all these problems are the fault of religious minorities, although there are plenty of religious activists pushing hard to get more and more religion into the workplace. Sometimes it is the fault of "diversity managers" who have been recruited by big companies to try to keep the peace among the many races and creeds that they employ. In their rush to be leaders in "diversity", companies are opening the door for a whole lot of problems. If you invite religion into the place of work, you can be sure that conflict will be riding on its back. Managers of diversity will rapidly find that they have become managers of divisiveness.

PRAYERS AT COUNCIL MEETINGS

A landmark legal ruling banning the tradition of saying prayers at council meetings was denounced as an 'assault on Britain's Christian heritage'.

The High Court backed a campaign to abolish official acts of worship as an integral part of council meetings. Christians and politicians reacted with dismay after a judge overturned centuries of custom by outlawing a town hall in Devon from putting prayers on the formal agenda. The ruling means prayers will not be allowed as a constituent part of council meetings across England and Wales, though they may still be said before the official start. Atheist former councillor Clive Bone started the case against Bideford town council in July 2010, claiming he had been 'disadvantaged and embarrassed' when religious prayers were recited at formal meetings.

Backed by the National Secular Society, he insisted that the 'inappropriate' practice breached the human right to freedom of conscience and discriminated against non-believers, making them feel 'uncomfortable'.

The society claimed council meetings should be "equally welcoming to everyone in the local community and should therefore be religiously-neutral".

Mr Justice Ouseley, sitting in London, ruled that formal prayers at council meetings were unlawful. He said local authorities had no power to "say prayers or to have any period of quiet reflection as part of the business of the council". Communities Secretary Eric Pickles described the ruling as 'very illiberal'. He said: "The ruling is surprising and disappointing. Christianity plays an important part in the culture, heritage and fabric of our nation". He vowed to override the High Court ruling by bringing in the Government's Localism Act, which would give councils the power to hold prayers at the start of meetings. Simon Calvert, of the Christian Institute agreed: "Prayers have been a part of council meetings for centuries, and many people, either for religious reasons or cultural reasons, see them as a positive part of our national life. It's a shame the courts have taken sides with those whose goal is to undermine our Christian heritage. It is high time Parliament put a stop to this assault upon our national heritage".

Harry Greenway, a former Tory MP and ex-chairman of the National Prayer Breakfast, said: "If people do not want to attend prayers of this nature, they can stay away instead of meddling and busybodying with other people's beliefs. Non-believers are not harassed in this way by believers. Why cannot the non-believers show the same kind of tolerance?" Mr Bone, who left Bideford council because of its "refusal to adjust" its prayers' policy, commented: "This has got nothing to do with intolerance towards religion. Religious freedom is an absolute right and so is freedom *from* religion an absolute right".

Religion nowadays in Britain is under closer scrutiny. Twenty first century modernity and updated laws are exposing it for what it is: an anachronism caught in the headlamps. Increasingly this is dawning on the theists and they don't like it. Victimhood for them is a new phenomenon. It used to belong to the despised infidel, a much better fit, their hides are thicker from years of battering.

TRANQUILLISING THE GRIZZLY BEAR

"Almost any sect, cult or religion will legislate its creed into law if it acquires the political power to do so".

Robert A. Heinlein

"Atheism deprives superstition of its stand ground and compels theism to reason for its existence".

[George Jacob Holyoake, "Origin and Nature of Secularism"]

Agitating against religion may be seen as a necessary anti-dote to indoctrination but also carries drawbacks. Vehement protest and ridicule enables the religious to adopt the hair shirt of persecution and there is little that a good god defender likes better than the thought of martyrdom. Strong counter arguments to the absurdities that religion preaches also force the purveyors of nonsense to present their nonsense in more subtle and plausible forms. Exposure of patently absurd or contradictory statements in the Bible and Koran enables apologists to justify them by presenting them as 'symbolic', 'metaphorical' or 'allegorical', three of the buzz words now favoured by religious obfuscators to get them out of jail.

Between them they strip scripture of any meaning it may have had and turn it into a smörgåsbord of hollow mystification to suit every taste. Even the blood of Christ at Catholic mass is conveniently symbolised as wine and not as something so boringly unalcoholic as apple juice. That is why I sometimes feel that the humanist movement is organised religion's greatest asset. It acts as religion's ever vigilant pilot fish, leading the great white shark into clear blue water, scraping away its barnacles and keeping it lean and fit to hunt. Religion is by nature conservative and reactionary, with an aversion to reform and always in danger of being left behind and rendered irrelevant.

It badly needs a think-tank to keep it abreast of modern times. This is where humanism comes to the rescue. Progressive, humane, creative, humanism develops universal, people-friendly ideals and standards which it then hands on a plate to religious leaders, enabling them to catch up with mainstream thinking, be it a little breathless and a little late and re-occupy the centre ground. It moves the spotlight from hard and unpalatable doctrine to the more sociable and enjoyable aspects of church membership. It is like teaching manners to a Grizzly bear. Rock bands in the aisles, happy-clappy congregations. A subtle shift to catch the zeitgeist, a slick PR campaign to take the credit and humanism is left protesting on the sidelines. Women's rights, gay rights, sex education, contraception, relaxed censorship, easier divorce, gay marriage, Sunday sport and shopping, humanist style funeral services; all benefits pioneered by humanists in the teeth of religious opposition and now stealthily adopted by religion as proof of their modernity.

Not only are they becoming more modern on earth it is encroaching on the afterlife. Yes, hell has been given a make-over. They have removed the brimstone, quelled the flames. Red Adair would have been impressed. No more bliss or blisters for the afterlife. From now on it's bliss or bleakness. But for those who cling to perdition like they cling to mangy old Teddies there is good news: hell has not been abolished altogether. It has merely been downgraded. It now is a place of neutral temperature and eternal quiet. I could warm to that idea, just the sort of environment I would wish for to write my book.

The problem for the Churches of course is that hell, like all its other past nasties, had become more of a hindrance than a help. Not the sort of thing that the Lord's spin doctors would recommend as good public relations these days. No longer able to scare people into line there was no option but to move the goal posts once again. The way they are going the C of E's goal posts will soon be off the pitch. It is amusing to hear the modern theist telling you how mild and rationalistic their religion really is, all the while ignoring the fact that all its mildness and reasonableness was gained over the dead bodies of heretics burned at the stake.. As life-styles have changed so has the theology of the churches. Manifest destiny has become social gospel with barely a backward glance.

By constantly countering religion's worst excesses in the Western world, humanism has hugely contributed to religion's survival well beyond its sell by date. Perhaps it is time that humanism called for a moratorium on this mission of mercy. As an experiment it should stop handing out the medicine and let the ailing patient recover. For be under no illusion; behind its politically correct façade **fundamentalist** religion still hides its ugly face. Its killjoy inclinations are still itching to be unchained. Its woman hostile nature, its hang-ups about sex and easy living are yearning to be freed again as does its pre-occupation with sin and self-abasement. It nourishes a secret longing to call the shots once more, to cajole, manipulate and regain control.

So perhaps we should allow them another run. Let them brush aside their mask and allow the true colours to show again. Let the preachers pontificate like the days of yore, let the ayatollahs of all persuasions fulminate against the iniquities of modern time. Let there be more prayer for pupils in state schools and creationism too. Allow the act of worship to be turned into an old fashioned hell and brimstone session. Make religious education concentrate on tales of gods, devils and the blood of Christ, all given to pupils as hard fact, as they were originally intended. Let them remove sex education from schools. Let them once more put priests in charge of women's bodies. Give them control over what we may see on TV and the internet, condemn premarital sex. Let them shut the shops on Sundays. Let them re-instate anti-gay legislation. Let Islam try to introduce Sharia law.

Then stand back and see what happens next. At last the young would quickly discover what untrammelled religion is capable of. Our sons and daughters who seem to think that contemporary religion is just a harmless comfort blanket that does no more than giving people a warm glow and who are scornful of our dead horse flogging, would soon feel their precious freedoms and liberal life-styles under threat. They would realise that stripped of its touchy-feely disguise, religion in the raw can be harsh, dogmatic and decidedly uncool. But this time round its tyranny would fail to conquer, for in today's society old fashioned religion cannot regain its ground. It can succeed only in a climate of ignorance and fear. That climate humanism has changed for good. Rocked out of their complacency the young would join humanist ranks in droves, up in arms in defence of their liberal way of life. Then almost overnight humanism would at last achieve its rightful place.

The danger of my shock and awe scheme might be that it is an over-reaction. That the battle is already being won the gentle way. Are we in enlightened Britain and other European Union countries not now so far beyond the reach of the medieval darkness that we can no longer be dragged back into its shadows? Aren't we now in an era where religion, like royalty has acquired the status of harmless light entertainment? As long as Lizzy, Phil, Charlie and Wills remain on the fringes for our amusement their continuing irrelevance will be assured. Banish them altogether and one day there will be a national clamour for King William to be anointed at Westminster Abbey on a wave of national nostalgia, in an attempt to recapture former glory.

So it could be with religion. Keep it as a source of anodyne homilies on BBC and it will retain its status of naff tedium. Eradicate it forcefully and before long Bibles will be traded behind the bike sheds along with fags, drugs and condoms. Look at what happened in the Soviet union following the fall of communism. Religion and rarity value; seemingly an irresistible cocktail.

MORALITY

*"Wherever morality is based on theology, wherever right
is made dependent on divine authority, the most immoral,
unjust, infamous aims can be established and justified.
If morality has no foundation in itself, there is no inherent
necessity for morality; morality is then surrendered to
the groundless arbitrariness of religion"*

Ludwig Feuerbach

Man creates systems of morality and with uncalled for humility attributes their authorship to his gods. For theists morality is based on holy scripture, the Bible the Torah or the Koran. Books, reportedly the unalterable word of God, all originating amongst primitive tribesmen in the Middle East. For modern present-day society to take these writings seriously may be likened to consulting a donkey cart's service manual to run an electronically guided combine harvester. Yet that is what many millions of people are prepared to do when it comes to looking for moral guidelines.

There is an obvious question here: by what celestial means were these precious words of wisdom transferred from God to Moses and Mohammed. Was it through wi-fi, blue tooth or telepathy? Whichever method it was, it certainly was a defective one. As there are a huge number of conflicting and confusing passages in these writings (whole books and websites have been devoted to pointing out these flaws) the question is how does one cherry pick the best and appropriate bits?

The answer is of course do what humanists have to do. Rely on your innate sense of morality. This inbuilt sense always trumps religious prescription and over the centuries, as religious influence receded, we have become more compassionate. Our attitude to criminals, the mentally ill, children and animals is more humane compared to a more devout age when prisons were more brutal, the insane were baited for fun, children and wives were beaten and there was no RSPCA.

One of the most infuriating questions a theist can ask a humanist is: "if you don't believe in God and the Bible, where do you get your morals from? Haven't people asking this question got any non-religious friends who lead perfectly moral lives? So much so that in the ordinary conduct of life it is impossible to tell whether somebody is religious or not. Yet the 'religion good, atheism bad' myth stubbornly persists. Atheism tends to be used as a negative benchmark against which the faithful can measure their virtue. But every reasonable person knows that there are good people who believe in gods and good people who don't believe in gods. Like most atheists/humanists, I do not rape, murder, or steal, I know right from wrong and don't need to follow a set of superstitious beliefs to live a moral life. The idea that only a religious person can be a good person is demonstrably false. In fact, it could be argued that it is the atheists/humanists who are the more moral people; we try to do what is right, not for the selfish reason of fear of some afterlife punishment, but because we know it is the right thing to do.

Yet those who like their principles founded in some unshakeable transcendental truth, see atheists as feckless and untrustworthy. We are assumed to be morally dubious, too weak and spineless to stand up for anything at all and certainly not worthy of respect. Religious leaders in Northern Ireland habitually refer to terrorists as 'those Godless people' even though they must know that both sides of the conflict are equally devout with slogans 'for God and the Republic' and 'for God and Ulster'.

First thing these people should do for a change is read their holy books from cover to cover. This would be an unnerving experience. The Church is careful to feed its flock the more palatable extracts from the Bible, that is why the more civilised bits have become so well known. But let us not forget that there are a large number of really vicious, cruel passages which since they are also the word of God should be accorded equal status. An example is the one that tells us about eternal hellfire: *"Depart from me, ye cursed, into everlasting fire, prepared for the devil and his angels!" (Matthew 25,41). Here is another taster from Deuteronomy (28:27): "If you do not obey the Lord your God then the Lord shall smite thee with a consumption and with a fever and with an inflammation and with an extreme burning and with the sword and with blasting and with mildew....The Lord shall make the rain of thy land powder and dust...... thy carcase shall be meat unto all fowls of the air and unto the beasts of the earth.... the Lord will smite thee with the botch of Egypt and with the emerods and with the scab and with the itch whereof thou cans't be healed"*. Funnily enough I can't recall having heard this nugget of Divine tenderness read out on Songs of Praise.

I must admit that I have a lot more sympathy with biblical fundamentalists like the Jehovah's witnesses who stick to their guns, come hell or high water. Whereas the revisionists treat the Bible like an à la carte menu from which they pick and choose, the fundamentalists swallow the whole fare, including the tripe. This tends to make them a damned nuisance and sometimes dangerous to boot. But it must never be forgotten they are the real McCoy.

So churches and mosques have to do a lot of selective quoting. Just stick with the good bits and hope that the faithful don't read any further. No wonder there was so much opposition to having the Bible rendered into an accessible form. In the middle ages when people genuinely believed that the Bible contained God's word, people were desperate to have the text available in their own language. But with the passing of time, church leaders adopted the view that it was dangerous for ordinary people to hear about the Scriptures without the clergy's supervision. They insisted it was safer for people to rely on priests to tell them what the Bible said and meant. Because of this attitude, translators found themselves engaged in an increasingly dangerous business. In some European countries the ban on vernacular Scriptures carried the death penalty.

THE BIBLE FOR THE COMMON PEOPLE

But it was in England that a major battle was fought and won for the right of the common people to have the

Word of God in their language. One of the first who sought to make Bibles available to the average person was John Wycliffe, Oxford theologian and 14th-century English reformer. Wycliffe was brought to trial several times in church courts, but his powerful and influential friends protected him. He died a natural death in 1384.

The Dutch scholar Erasmus served as professor of Greek at Cambridge University from 1511 to 1514. His great love for that language - and at the same time, his zealous advocacy of vernacular Scriptures - left an indelible mark. William Tyndale was profoundly influenced by Erasmus' Greek New Testament. He immersed himself in its study. That obsession opened the most decisive chapter in the entire story of the English Bible. Never had official religion been at a lower ebb than in Tyndale's day. Finding both clergy and laity ignorant of the Scriptures, Tyndale conceived, in 1522, the ambitious project of translating the New Testament directly from the Greek into English, bypassing the Latin Vulgate. To a critic of the plan, Tyndale announced: "if God spare my life, ere many years pass, I will cause a boy that driveth the plough shall know more of the Scriptures than thou dost." The project became his life's work.

Tyndale's proposal, however, met strong opposition from religious authorities in England. English translators had been banned since 1408. So in 1524 Tyndale fled to Germany to continue his work, never to return to his own country. There he forged ahead with his English translation, completing it in 1525. Copies of Tyndale's Testament were smuggled into England in barrels and bales of cloth. They were widely distributed and eagerly studied. But when church leaders discovered their existence, they ordered them gathered up for burning. So successful were they in destroying the Testaments that only two copies of the first edition survived. A master stylist, Tyndale had rendered the Greek into simple, fresh and vigorous English. The beauty and rhythm of his language fixed the style and tone of the English Bible for centuries to come. He may be considered the 'Father of the English Bible'.

In May 1535, Tyndale was betrayed, kidnapped and imprisoned by papal agents at Vilvoorde Castle near Brussels. After about 15 months' imprisonment, he was tried for heresy and condemned to death. A decade earlier they had burned the translation; now they resolved to burn the translator. Tyndale went boldly to the stake, still defending his belief that Englishmen should have a Bible in their own language. On 6th October 1536, he was tied to a post and strangled after which his body was burned to ashes. He died bravely, with his last breath crying out in a loud voice, "Lord, open the king of England's eyes!"

In 1603, King James I came to the throne following the death of Elizabeth I. A year later, an important conference was convened at Hampton Court Palace near London. The conference was a series of meetings between Anglican bishops and Puritan leaders, presided over by King James. Its purpose was to consider Puritan demands for reform in the church. Among the issues discussed was a Puritan request for a new translation of the Bible, to correct the imperfections of the current Bibles.

Some church leaders countered that there were already too many translations. King James replied that another translation was needed precisely because there were too many already.

He wanted one Bible for the nation, as accurately rendered as possible. To carry out the work, King James appointed 54 scholars, drawn from Oxford, Cambridge and Westminster, who were renowned for their Greek and Hebrew expertise. They worked in six groups, the work of each group being reviewed by the other groups. What distinguished the *King James Version* of the Bible was that is was produced by a committee of scholars, rather than by one man. Significantly, their New Testament was based largely on Tyndale's translation. It is estimated that 80 to 90 percent of Tyndale's wording passed into the *King James Version* of the New Testament. The King James translators' work was published in 1611. The *King James* or *Authorised Version*, soon took the place of all the other English versions.

It is remarkable that somebody like Tyndale should have wished to go to so much trouble and risk to render the Biblical texts into English. These texts, particularly the ones in the old testament are a collection of savage tales from a very primitive and often barbaric epoch. Although this is a chapter on morality I will resist trying to extract moral guidelines from the scriptures as this would involve a great deal of selective quoting. I will however spend a little time examining the ten commandments because they are often held up by theists as a good guide to ethical conduct.

THE TEN COMMANDMENTS

The ten commandments do not appear as a neat list of ten instructions and prohibitions. The first three are all variations on the same theme, in which god insists on his own primacy and exclusivity, forbids the making of graven images and prohibits the taking of his own name in vain. This self-important introduction is accompanied by some very stern admonitions including a dire warning that the sins of the fathers will be visited on their children "even unto the third and fourth generation". This goes against the moral and reasonable idea that children are innocent of their parent's wrongdoing. The fourth commandment insists on the observance of a holy Sabbath day and forbids all believers and their slaves and domestic servants- to perform any work in the course of it. The dictate then becomes more brusque. "Honour thy father and thy mother" (this not for its own sake but in order "that thy days may be long upon the land which the Lord thy God giveth thee"). Next in line are the four famous "shalt nots" which flatly prohibit killing, adultery, theft and false witness. With these we can all agree as they would hardly need pointing out to any semi-civilised human being.

Then there is a ban on covetousness, forbidding the desire for "thy neighbour's house, manservant, maidservant, ox, ass, wife and other property. The whole thing comes across much more as a man-made set of injunctions appropriate to the primitive society of the time rather than a timeless set of moral edicts that will keep their freshness. However little one may think of the Jewish era, it is surely insulting to the people of Moses to imagine that they had laboured all along under the impression that murder, adultery, theft and perjury were permissible. No society ever in history has failed to protect itself from self-evident crimes like those supposedly identified on Mount Sinai.

Finally, instead of the condemnation of evil actions, there is an oddly phrased condemnation of impure thoughts. One can tell that this too, is a man-made product of the alleged time and place because it throws in "wife" along with the other property, animal, human and material of the neighbour. What's more, it demands the impossible; a recurrent problem with all religious commands. One may be forcibly restrained from wicked actions, or barred from committing them, but to forbid people from merely contemplating them is a requirement too far. In particular it is absurd to hope to banish envy of other people's possessions or fortunes, if only because the spirit of envy can lead to emulation and ambition and have positive consequences.

It is important to notice what is left out of the commandments. The moral dogs that failed to bark. There is nothing about the protection of children from abuse, nothing about rape, nothing about slavery, nothing about genocide and no mention of cruelty to animals. Instead some of these offences are positively recommended in verse 2 of the immediately following chapter where God tells Moses to instruct his followers about the conditions under which they may buy or sell slaves and the rules governing the sale of their daughters.

Religious believers usually cite the Bible as an expression of ethical eloquence but they rarely submit these tenets to careful scrutiny or else they would become immediately aware that because of all the contradictions in their 'good book' and all the downright ugliness, they would have to employ their own judgement to extract suitable moral values. It follows that if people are able to mix and match they must possess an independent sense of what is moral. And of course that is what they do possess. It comes from evolution. Evolution of the mind. A quarter of a million years of Homo sapiens living within communities, of necessity have fine-tuned moral behaviour.

If murder and mayhem had been the norm, extinction would have been swift to follow. Animal and human societies will only function if the majority of participants are prepared to give and take. That kind of behaviour will result in mutual reward. There will always be a sociopathic minority who spoil things for other members of the group but these can be held in check by appropriate sanctions. The counter question to ask theists is this: do you think that if you were to lose your religion you would suddenly be able to take to crime? Would you be able to stalk an old lady, hit her on the head with a brick and run off with her handbag? Could you walk into a bank and demand money at gunpoint? Could you abduct and murder a child? I thought not. If you are moral only because of a fear of hell in the afterlife then your morality is bogus and you are a calculating cheat.

If godlessness made for crime, prisons would be full of humanists. In fact the opposite is true. Prisons are well stocked with believers and atheists/humanists are the proverbial needle in the haystack. The statistics leave one in no doubt. Extensive research carried out by Barnes and Teeters in the United States and published in their report 'New Horizons in Criminology' shows that there are surprisingly few non-believers in prison. Of 85,000 prison inmates polled, 60,000 or 80 per cent decisively expressed their preference as Christians. The proportion of avowed atheists was minuscule at 150. The study revealed that the proportion of religious affiliates among prisoners is significantly higher than among the general population. This is corroborated by similar findings among the UK prison population. 17 per cent of inmates are Roman Catholic, compared to 10 per cent in the general population. Over-representation for Muslims is even higher at 12 per cent of the prison population, compared to 4.8 per cent nation-wide.

If religion is such a force for good, keeping people on the straight and narrow, why is it that virtually all serial killers have been religious? Jeffrey Dahmer, Ted Bundy, David Berkowitz (the son of Sam), Wayne Gacy, Myra Hindley, the Kray brothers, Peter Sutcliffe, the list goes on and on. Mass killers too: David Koresh, Timothy McVeigh, the rev. Jim Jones, Anders Breivik. The Lee Rigby killers suffered the double religious whammy of first being Christians and then Muslims. Any Humanist killers anyone? Apart from committing murder and mayhem the religious haven't been exactly crime free in other areas either. Large scale priestly child abuse has already been mentioned and now we also have the recent revelation that the very Christian Sir Jimmy Savile set new records for paedophilia.

In defence of all these trespasses religious apologists invariably offer the 'one rotten apple' argument. Trouble is there are so many rotten apples that the baskets are overflowing. One would begin to worry about the orchard. Defenders of the faith are also keen to argue that it was not the religion that led to crimes being committed, but other factors such as poverty or political injustices, even though around the scenes of outrage shouts of 'Allahu Akbar' and 'God made me do it', are ringing in our ears. Although tempting, I am not going to suggest that these people's religious beliefs were solely responsible for their murderous and criminal behaviour but I will make the obvious point that their beliefs certainly didn't act as a deterrent.

Any such supposed deterrent is in any case undermined by the devices of repentance and forgiveness which both Christianity and Islam extend to their adherents. This convenient insurance policy means that they may trespass, wipe the slate clean and start sinning all over again. Not long ago there was a documentary on TV, featuring capital punishment in the U.S. where a double murderer was looking forward to going to heaven because "the Lord had forgiven him". There is no such easy let-off for the humanist. All actions must be measured against the strictures of the 'Golden Rule' and trespassing must be made good with the person trespassed against, or else the conscience won't rest. We shall know that Atheism has finally triumphed when prisoners qualify for early release on becoming newly-born unbelievers.

Religious people who are in the habit of misbehaving tend to be very good at coming up with excuses for their foibles, even to the point of stating that they heard God's voice, telling them to do it. Peter Sutcliffe, the Yorkshire Ripper, is one example, Yigal Amir, who assassinated Israeli Prime Minister Yitzak Rabin, is another: "I acted alone on God's orders". There is an interesting psychiatric question here: if Sutcliffe is now in Broadmoor, diagnosed a paranoid schizophrenic because he got messages *from* God, should people who communicate in the other direction, sending messages *to* God through prayer, not be viewed in a similarly light?

All of this confirms what has long been known to some of us that people tend to keep their religion and moral code quite firmly separate. Friedrich Nietzsche once said: "You say you believe in the necessity of religion; be honest! You believe in the necessity of the police". Apart from the police people are wary of their neighbours. They would do lots of things so long there is no chance of their neighbours finding out. Nosy neighbours have been responsible for more straight living than all the great religions of the world combined. Also evolution has equipped the large majority of people with a social conscience which strongly disposes them towards fair play.

There is also a strong sympathetic instinct. In wars many men, not specially selected or high-minded men, risk their lives readily to save a companion wounded in No Man's Land. Some may claim that they did it from a religious motive, a desire for medals or promotion, but the basic incentive was probably more or less the same all through; that instinctively they could not see a mate lying there wounded and not try to help him. The act of coming to the aid of somebody or some animal in apparent distress is therapeutic, it resolves the tension which has determined the action, just as eating and drinking resolve the tension of hunger and thirst. This innate moral code induces people to be sympathetic to others much more naturally than as a result of dubious promises of reward in a dubious hereafter.

Conversely the same natural inclination is what keeps most people, including the religious, from causing hurt to others much more effectively than any hellfire sanctions contained in their holy scriptures or sermons preached at them in their places of worship. As for the more lethal moral exhortations spread throughout Bible and Koran anybody wishing to follow these to the letter ought to be locked up double quick before they do any major damage. Much better to stick with modern man-made laws that govern social behaviour. This is because, unlike rigid scriptural law, man-made law has moved with the times, is much more detailed and appropriate and subject to revision should it no longer reflect changing conditions in society. That way it will stay relevant and deter people from taking the law into their own hands.

It can readily be seen that on a personal level religion does not make for improved individual behaviour. When it comes to the collective influence of organised religion at a national level the picture is even clearer. We need look no further than Northern Ireland, the Balkans, the Middle East and other troubled religious heartlands to see the enormous damage done.

The ten god given biblical commandments can be readily improved by any decent person with a well developed social conscience. It is morality that has modified religion, not religion that has modified morality. Here I am listing A.C. Grayling's suggestions, admirable in their brevity, yet covering the full range of social conduct:

Love well
Seek the good in all things
Harm no others
Think for yourself
Take responsibility
Respect nature
Do your utmost
Be informed
Be kind
Be courageous

RELIGION, SCIENCE AND POLITICS

"The whole thing is so patently infantile, so foreign to reality, that to anyone with a friendly attitude to humanity it is painful to think that the great majority of mortals will never be able to rise above this view of life".

Sigmund Freud

Today, as of old, we face the same conflict within the human psyche: science versus doctrinaire religion. The empirical world of verification versus the world of fantasy, knowledge of fact versus romantic superstition. In the debate about the roles of religion and of science the late Stephen Jay Gould argued that science and religion each have "a legitimate magisterium, or domain of teaching authority," and these two domains do not overlap. He stated that science can tell us about one aspect of world affairs and religion another. The magisterium of science covers the empirical realm: what the universe is made of and why it works the way it does. The magisterium of religion extends over questions of ultimate meaning and moral value. According to Gould these two domains have separate concerns; science studies how the heavens go, religion how to go to heaven.

This I fear is arrant nonsense. Science is concerned with all facets of human conduct and existence. So is religion. The two are fully intertwined. The difference is that unlike religion science is wholly focused on getting at the facts. If religion has no role in telling us about the nature of the universe and its operation why does it spend so much time doing exactly that? Most religions offer a cosmology and a biology, a theory of life, a theory of origins and reasons for existence. In doing so they acknowledge that religion is active in the science business; however badly.

A quick perusal of the internet will show any number of religious sites explaining why evolution is a lie, that there is no such thing as the big bang. Geology shows that fossils are of different ages. Palaeontology shows a fossil sequence, the list of species represent changes through time. Taxonomy shows biological relationships among species. Evolution is the explanation that threads it all together. Creationism is the practice of closing one's eyes and shouting "No, it doesn't!" I will not stoop in this book to countering their curious notions of 'Intelligent Design'. (Other than perhaps suggest that apes evolved from creationists). That has been done unanswerably by many leading biologists. When J.B.S. Haldane was challenged in a public lecture by a woman who doubted that even in millions of years a single cell could not develop into a complicated body with bones, heart, eyes and brain, he famously replied: "but Madam you did it yourself in just nine months".

Also arguing that science has nothing to tell us about morality and meaning is obviously false. Is morality the same across all cultures? How much of it is innate how much learned. Human behaviour is an evolutionary process like all animal behaviour. Empirical evidence can tell us how and why it evolved. Psychology is the science of the mind. Religion is also in the mind. Very much an overlapping magisterium. The existence or absence of a cosmic super-intelligence is doubtless a matter for scientific investigation. So are enquiries about the nature of alleged miracles. Was it physiologically possible for Jesus to come back to life, days after being crucified? Surely all legitimate scientific questions.

As for the magisterium of 'ultimate meaning and moral values' supposedly the exclusive religious domain of awe and wonder; science can readily compete. And it does so beyond the wildest dreams of any mystics or holy men. The fact that the supernatural has no place in a rationalist's approach to the enigmas of the universe and life doesn't diminish the wonderment. The merest glance through a telescope at a distant galaxy of a billion stars, easily out-marvels the wondrous abstruseness offered by religion.

The two pursuits of religion and politics are not supposed to mix either. If you were to ask a politician what religion they subscribe to, which I have done on several occasions, you are definitely not going to get a straight answer. Invariably you are going to be fobbed of with a standard reply from one of their aides, stating that their bosses' religious beliefs are a strictly private matter. Religion, apparently, is an innocuous personal hobby, like stamp collecting, that doesn't intrude in any way on a politician's judgement, ambitions or policies. The reason for this non-committal stance is only too obvious. If they confess to a particular brand of religion, particularly if it is a minority one, they are going to alienate a large number of potential voters. So the religious cards are going to be held very closely to the chest.

If you give this pat reply a mere few seconds thought it is immediately clear that it just won't do. There is no other field of interest where this reticence applies. Politicians are quite happy, indeed are expected, to hold forth on any other subjects. Be they the economy, the environment, education, defence and every other sphere of public concern. Since religion permeates all aspects of a politician's thinking it must colour his opinions on all matters of state policy. This means that religious convictions cannot possibly be seen as someone's harmless pursuit, of no concern to others.

Someone's religion is a big deal. It determines one's whole outlook on life and affects all decisions taken. As is the case for science and religion, there is no such thing as non-overlapping magisteria between religious belief and political convictions. They go together like motherhood and apple pie.

There are no special qualifications necessary to become a politician. Most trades and professions must pass exams before they are allowed to carry out their work. With teachers, doctors, nurses, policemen you may expect certain standards. Yet politicians, the people whose decisions will inevitably affect people's lives for generations, are not expected to have any special qualifications or knowledge before they are let loose on society. They don't have to be qualified scientists, economists or even lawyers; they don't necessarily have experience in international relations, military history, resource management, civil engineering or any other field of knowledge that may come in useful for running a country. All they need to be is expert fund raisers, self publicists, accomplished soothsayers and public speakers.

All qualities not dissimilar from the clergy. If holding bizarre religious beliefs were to become a disqualifier for holding public office then at a stroke there would be vacancies for large numbers of key positions right across the country, including that of the Prime Minister and most of his cabinet. There is absolutely no reason to believe that such people would be endowed with a surplus of integrity or a superior moral compass that would enable them to conduct public affairs without letting a personal bias intrude.

If George Bush and Tony Blair see Islam as an errant religion that is likely to be hostile to Christianity, then they are going to be more inclined to embark on a crusade. If they think faith is a good thing then they are likely to try and push religion into schools. If they think abortion is a sin, or even if their wives think abortion is a sin, they will do their darndest to promote legislation to curtail it. Never mind that religion is a private matter; any number of policies are going to be influenced by the religious mindset of the politician concerned. I'll be honest here. I would be just as partisan.

If I were Prime Minister a few humanist concerns would be near the top of my agenda. Bishops would be out of the Lords faster than a popemobile. I would work towards dis-establishment of the Church of England. The faith school policy would go into reverse. Assisted dying provisions would soon reflect the wishes of the voters. You may well argue here that I am just a prejudiced fanatic. That other people, particularly politicians, are able to rise above such personal priorities and strictly act in accordance with general opinion. Believe that if you must, but keep a close watch on their secret doings.

Prime Minister David Cameron is happy to play the religious card. He still believes it is what most voters want to hear. But the latest British social attitudes survey shows that three out of five of the population are not Christian - and that proportion is growing fast. The Prime Minister's message should therefore be to stress cohesion rather than to trumpet baseless Christian triumphalism. The non-religious becoming the majority should be a signal to treat them with more respect, but instead he seems intent on marginalising them. At an Easter reception for religious dignitaries held at Downing Street, he said religion had brought him his greatest moments of peace and claimed Jesus invented the big society 2000 years ago.

He also released a videoed Easter message for the country, in which he talked about the "countless acts of kindness carried out by those who believe in and follow Christ". In a separate article for the Church Times, he argued that some atheists and agnostics did not understand that faith could be a guide or a helpful prod in the right direction towards morality. While acknowledging many non-believers have a moral code and some Christians do not, he added: "People who advocate some sort of secular neutrality fail to grasp the consequences of that neutrality, or the role that faith can play in helping people to have a moral code. I believe we should be more confident about our status as a Christian country, more ambitious about expanding the role of faith-based organisations, and, frankly, more evangelical about a faith that compels us to get out there and make a difference to people's lives."

It is of course the familiar 'Christianity makes you a better person' message. Despite all evidence to the contrary its constant repetition has cemented the thought into people's brains.

Nick Clegg and Ed Miliband both are atheists and this will no doubt condemn them to never becoming Prime Minister. The UK has never had an openly atheist PM. Their atheism stopped Michael Foote, Dennis Healey and Neil Kinnock in their tracks and it will have the same effect on other non-religious candidates. All very similar to the US where a 2006 study, carried out by University of Minnesota sociologist Penny Edgel, found that atheists were the most mistrusted minority in the U.S. and a godless politician is the least likely candidate to win votes in a presidential election. Even pot smokers and philanderers are viewed more favourably than atheists. No wonder Barack Obama must keep piously intoning "God bless the United States of America".

Assisted Dying - Euthanasia

Whose life is it anyway?

Humanists believe that life is precious. Theists believe that life is sacred. Whereas the religious have surrendered control of their life's ending to a higher power, humanists prefer to remain masters of their own destiny. Apart from an aversion to religion and other forms of superstition, humanism has little in the way of specific precepts, rules or policies. A possible exception is the availability of euthanasia. Most, if not all, humanists feel that human dignity dictates that the option of an assisted death should be available to those who wish for it. The rational choice of one's own time, place and manner of death so as to round off one's life appropriately, completing its unique pattern with dignity and good sense, neither prematurely nor belatedly, could be seen as a sort of art form. We speak about the art of living, so why not also the art of dying?

The religious claim that human lives are a 'gift from God' but sometimes gifts can be unwanted, particularly when they are past their 'sell by date' and become burdensome. According to them God alone may determine our time of death; humans must not tamper with God's will. If that were so, then it would surely also be wrong to intervene to save life, as well as to hasten death. But the humanist case is primarily that what we want is merely permissive. We uphold the right of others to decide against euthanasia for themselves but not for us.

The religious have no moral rights to make laws that impose their views on those who may not even share the religious beliefs on which those views are based. Believers who always insist on complete 'freedom *of* religion' often fail to see that in all logic this must include 'freedom *from* religion'. Christians often talk about a 'merciful release' when a distressing terminal illness ends in death. Supporters of voluntary euthanasia simply want the merciful release to occur before the suffering has been uselessly prolonged, if that is the patient's wish.

Illogically enough, most religious believers contrive to make a moral distinction between active and passive euthanasia, as does the present law, though no moral distinction is made in any non-theological system of ethics between acts of commission and acts of omission, in other words, between assisted death and letting die, always assuming the same intent and same motive. Leading moral philosophers are agreed that there is no such moral distinction

This subject affects people deeply at the most vulnerable time in their life. Polls in Britain consistently show that some form of assisted dying is supported by almost 80 per cent of people. It is clearly a topic of great concern and I am reserving an extensive chapter for its discussion.

As one grows older the unappetising prospect of one's demise hoves slowly into view. It's a difficult thought to come to terms with. I can't imagine that one day the show will go on without me. But gradually realism is kicking in. There have been some warning signs. I have lost a good chunk of short term memory. Only the other day I gave my daughter all my passwords and showed her where the money is hidden.

From another perspective too the subject of euthanasia is rather highly charged. Mostly courtesy of a certain Herr H. The word derives from the Greek for 'good death' (eu = good; thanatos = death). To suggest that what Hitler's regime got up to in exterminating human life, unwanted by the Nazis, had anything to do with euthanasia, i.e. a good death, is a grotesque distortion. But ignorant opponents of euthanasia will persist in making the odious link.

The other day we were listening to a debate on Premier Christian Radio between Sarah Wootton, CEO of Dignity in Dying and Anglican priest George Pitcher. One or two things in that debate got my goat. Ministers of the cloth usually get my goat but this man got a whole herd of them. He was rude and bullying throughout; all very unchristian.

He also claimed that he had evolved from atheism to Christianity. A good example of topsy-turvy evolution. When people making that claim refer to atheism, they do not mean deeply thought through, card carrying rationalism, resulting in membership of the BHA or the National Secular Society. What they are referring to is the transformation from rebellious youth, too preoccupied with having a good time and too lazy to get out of bed to go to church, to the settling down phase of life, career, family and rediscovery of Christian traditions. They never really left; for a while, footloose and fancy free, they guiltily took time out. That's what they consider their brush with atheism. They use this pretence to rationalism as evidence of a searching inquiring mind, on a par with their Godless opponents.

Ironically early in the debate the Rev. Pitcher gave the game away by admitting that he had begged a nurse to administer an overdose of morphine to his dying mother. He didn't seem to think that this somewhat undermined his anti-euthanasia stance. It is interesting how people change their tune when adversity strikes near to home. But praise the Lord he had bounced back from his momentary weakness so that his poor mother could linger a little longer.

The 1961 suicide act decriminalised suicide in England and Wales but still calls for a prison sentence not exceeding 14 years for any person who aids, abets, counsels or procures the suicide of another. This complicity in suicide is unparalleled in law as there is no other instance in which an accessory can incur liability when the principal does not commit a criminal offence. It is a bit like my mowing the lawn is not a criminal offence but if you help me do it the police will feel your collar.

Because no form of euthanasia or assisted dying is acceptable in the UK, people are forced to travel to Switzerland (More than 180 have done so in the last 10 years). Otherwise compassionate relatives who offer help are hauled into court as suspected criminals. Because the general public recognises the dilemma that caring relatives find themselves in (up to 80per cent of polls favour euthanasia) very few juries have returned guilty verdicts.

There have been a few recent attempts at legislation but all have been defeated. The House of Lords has seen the most debate with Lord Joel Joffe introducing several private members bills proposing assisted suicide in highly restricted circumstances. Another initiative came in July 2009 from Lord Falconer whose amendment to the Coroner's and Justice Bill had the purpose of decriminalising assisted dying in Switzerland. But even this 'not in our backyard' solution was defeated by 194 to 141. However a few weeks later, in a case brought by MS (Multiple Sclerosis) sufferer Debbie Purdy, against the Department of Public Prosecution the Law Lords agreed that the law on assisted suicide was unclear and ordered the Crown Prosecution Service to issue clarification.

These guidelines were duly published by the Director of Public Prosecutions Keir Starmer in Feb 2010. They made it clear that prosecution would be unlikely if:

- The victim reached a clear, voluntary decision to commit suicide.
- The suspect was wholly motivated by compassion.
- The suspect reported the suicide to the police and fully assisted inquiries.

But the clarification shied well clear of giving assisted suicide the green light.

In fact the opportunity was taken to give precise details of aspects which were likely to lead to prosecution. So whilst the subject was foggy and open to interpretation before, it now gives clear guidelines to the CPS as to when to prosecute. One of the key changes is the removal of any reference to the condition of the 'victim' – whether they are terminally ill, have an incurable physical disability or are near death – as a mitigating factor. Instead the focus has switched to examining the motivation of a suspect when considering whether to prosecute anyone for assisted suicide.

The DPP emphasised that he is not a one man law maker and that it is up to parliament to bring new legislation if that is what is required.

To this end Lord Falconer is making another attempt with a new Assisted Dying Bill which was debated in the House of Lords on 18th July 2014. It advocates a change in law where terminally ill adults who meet strict up-front safeguards would have the option to take life-ending medication. A record number of 130 peers spoke in the debate which was finely balanced for and against, with a small majority in favour. The Bill was passed to the committee stage but being a private member's bill has little chance of becoming law.

It became clear from the individual contributions that those who had personal experience of the distress associated with unassisted dying spoke in favour of the bill. This even included past Archbishop of Canterbury Lord Carey, who in other matters has a strongly conservative reputation. It proves that there is no substitute for personal exposure, it truly concentrates the mind. All other Bishops spoke against. Prior to the debate Catholic Bishops had been issuing press releases, claiming that any such legislation will 'lead to the deaths of large numbers of vulnerable people'. This, despite the fact that no such deaths have occurred in Oregon where very similar legislation has been in place for more than twenty years. Nor in the Netherlands where Euthanasia has been available for even longer.

The British medical establishment is still largely opposed to any form of assisted dying. The BMA particularly is a conservative body but it should be borne in mind that in the past they also strongly opposed contraceptives and abortion. However the Royal College of Nursing has recently dropped its opposition and has adopted a neutral stance.

As things stand in the UK end of life care is largely in the hands of hospices and palliative care. The impression tends to be given that palliative care is now of such high quality that it has made the need for euthanasia redundant. Whereas there certainly has been progress, pain cannot always be alleviated by drugs. Morphine, which is most widely used, is a depressant, associated with unpleasant hallucinations. It also has some troublesome side effects such as severe constipation. In any case what seriously ill people fear most, apart from pain, is loss of dignity and independence.

Doctors aren't robots, most of them care for their patients and are compassionate. So in the absence of an open and above board system such as in the Netherlands, they often practise assisted dying by stealth. In his research Professor Clive Seale of Brunel University has found that on average there are 8 assisted deaths performed by doctors in the UK every single day.

Apart from Dignity in Dying, which used to be known as the Voluntary Euthanasia Society, there is another campaign known as SOARS (Society for Old Age Rational Suicide) set up by Dr. Michael Irwin in Brighton. This is specifically aimed at the 1.3 million people in the UK aged 85 or over. Their aim is to campaign for the right of very elderly people suffering from a variety of health problems, but not terminally ill, to have the right to say enough is enough, I have had a good innings let's call it a day. This is an example of the so called 'Slippery Slope' argument but what is wrong with giving people what they want in that irreversible, terminal stage in life.

Scotland traditionally has been able to enact different laws from the rest of the UK and this has continued despite the Act of Union in 1707. In 2005 Lib Dem MSP Jeremy Purvis attempted to table a 'Right to Die' bill in the Holyrood parliament but few other MSPs were willing to support it. A new attempt was made in 2010 by the independent MSP Margo McDonald whose *End of Life, Scotland Bill'* would have allowed people whose lives become intolerable through a progressive degenerative condition, a trauma or terminal illness, to seek a doctor's help in dying. It also proposed a series of safeguards, similar to those applying in other countries, which would prevent abuse of the legislation. But the bill was defeated 85 votes to 16 with 2 abstentions.

Scottish public opinion regarding assisted dying closely resembles that elsewhere. A YouGov survey (May 2006) asked the question: "Do you think the law should be changed to allow competent terminally ill patients to receive a prescription from their doctor to end their suffering, subject to a range of safeguards?" 76 per cent of all respondents agreed, whilst the Scottish figure was 78 per cent.

When it comes to issues of major interest to humanists such as integrated non-denominational education and assisted dying, there is overwhelming public support, but remarkably this support is not reflected in the opinions of our elected politicians. It suggests to me that a lot of politicians share the holier than thou approach and outlook of religious leaders. They live in ivory towers and are out of touch with the developing zeitgeist amongst the electorate. They parrot the 'slippery slope' argument suggesting that old people might be made to feel a burden to their families and be talked into an assisted death. This silly notion crops up time and again without any evidence to back it up. Auntie is supposed to lay down her life prematurely because her nephew needs her money for a new car or to take his girlfriend to see the Taj Mahal.

If I am still OK with life no amount of prompting from those around me would induce me to opt for an early exit. I suspect the same applies to everybody else. People's lives are precious and they will not surrender them until all other options have run out. Besides, all proposed and existing assisted dying legislation includes cast iron safeguards against all potential abuse of this kind. The red herring 'bumping off' argument is trotted out by theists because they daren't own up to their belief that human life is in the gift of God.

Some forms of euthanasia are now permissible in five countries in the world:

Switzerland, the Netherlands, Belgium, Luxembourg and three states in the USA : Oregon, Washington and Montana. Switzerland was the first country in the world where some form of assisted dying was legally condoned. Under Swiss law assisted suicide is not a criminal act if it is motivated by altruistic considerations. It is legally permitted and can be performed by non-doctors. The law does not allow any direct help, only the means to commit suicide are provided.

The relevant article of the Swiss penal code came into effect in 1942 but it wasn't until half a century later that the article was interpreted as legal permission for organisations to administer life ending medication.

The main organisation providing this service is Dignitas, a non-profit organisation based in Zurich. The Dignitas logo is: To live with Dignity – To die with Dignity. In total the clinic has helped more than 1000 people to die.

There are substantial safeguards. People have to be Dignitas registered members of whom there are some 6000 world-wide. They have to send in medical records and doctors' statements as well as their own justifications. These are scrutinised by one of the clinic's doctors. The suicide procedure is filmed and subsequently viewed by police. To date no prosecutions have been deemed necessary.

EUTHANASIA IN THE NETHERLANDS

The Netherlands was the first country to permit doctor assisted suicide.

Starting in the 1970s there has been incremental legislation liberalising euthanasia. Under the latest Dutch law which came into force in 2002, euthanasia is still considered illegal but is protected from prosecution provided strict safeguards are observed. The safeguards are many and are carefully supervised:

- There must be an established doctor patient relationship
- There must be physical or mental suffering which the sufferer finds unbearable.
- The suffering and the desire to die must be lasting and not temporary.
- The decision to die must be the patient's own decision.
- The patient must have a correct and clear understanding of his or her condition and prognosis.

He or she must be capable of assessing the available options and must have done so.

- There must be no other solution that is acceptable to the patient.
- The time and the way the patient dies must not cause unavoidable misery to others (for example, if possible the next of kin should be informed and the patients should put their affairs in order).
- The decision to help a patient die must be made by more than one person. The doctor involved must consult another independent medical professional who also sees the patient. If the patient is suffering from depression or has a psychiatric disorder the doctor must ask for the patient to be examined by at least two further doctors, one of whom must be a psychiatrist.

These are just the qualifying conditions. Afterwards further strict procedures have to be followed: When a doctor has terminated the life of a patient on request or has assisted a suicide, the supervisory doctor must submit a report in writing. A local pathologist must be called in. The pathologist carries out an autopsy, checks the conduct of the procedures used and writes up the findings in a report. Both reports, along with other relevant documentation such as the patient's medical file and advance directive, are then submitted to a regional review committee. There are five such committees located throughout the Netherlands. Committees consist of three members, including a lawyer (who doubles as chairman), a doctor and an expert on ethical issues.

Members are appointed by the ministry of Justice in conjunction with the ministry of Health and Social

Services for a 6 year period. The committees consider whether the doctor has observed all legal requirements. If they agree the doctor is exonerated. If the committee expresses reservations the case must be discussed with all five committees. If it is found that a case has been handled 'without due care' this opinion is passed to the Public Prosecution Service and the Health Care Inspectorate who decide whether or not to prosecute the doctor concerned. To date there have been no such prosecutions.

It is clear that the safeguards used are draconian yet opponents of euthanasia, particularly abroad, will insist on talking about 'the thin end of the wedge', where soon vulnerable people feeling a burden to family and society will be arm twisted into suicide. In reality euthanasia remains very much a last resort. Of the 140 000 annual deaths in the Netherlands only some 4000 die by means of euthanasia. As in the UK a much larger number of terminally ill people die following palliative care. Palliative care is seen as part of standard medical procedure and is not considered illegal and is not governed by the Euthanasia law.

ADVANCE DIRECTIVE

Contrary to popular belief the Dutch Euthanasia Act does not require an 'Advance Directive' to be drawn up. The Act requires the doctor to be satisfied that the patient has made a voluntary and deliberate request. The initial request is almost always made during a conversation between the doctor and the patient. By recording details of any general discussion of a patient's wish for euthanasia and the decision-making process concerning the end of life in the patient's records, the doctor can also help eliminate any uncertainty.

This may, for example, be useful to locums and others involved in reaching a decision. What matters most is that the doctor and the patient should be in no doubt about the patient's intention. In practice the existence of an advance directive makes it easier to assess the case but it is not mandatory, if only to ensure that people are not put under unnecessary pressure to draw up such a directive, sometimes very shortly before they die. Although the existence of an advance directive does not entitle a patient to euthanasia or assisted suicide, especially in cases where the patient is unable to make decisions, it is advisable to write a directive in good time, update it at regular intervals and, where possible, describe the specific circumstances in which the person wishes to have his/her life terminated. The clearer and more specific the directive, the firmer the basis it provides for the doctor's decision.

Dementia in itself is not a condition qualifying for assisted death. However developing dementia may be considered a condition of unbearable suffering.

Requests for euthanasia from patients suffering from dementia are normally treated with great caution. A key issue is whether dementia patients can be said to be suffering unbearably. In the early onset stages, being aware of the disease and the prognosis may cause the patient great distress. At a more advanced stage patients will rarely be considered competent to make decisions. In all cases involving elements of dementia doctors must consult one or more experts in addition to the statutory second opinion. Because of these difficulties there are very few recorded cases of active euthanasia where dementia has been a factor.

A further area of difficulty is whether comatose patients can be said to be suffering unbearably. The general medical opinion is that deeply comatose patients are not conscious, do not suffer and hence do not suffer unbearably. Patients are able to ask for an assisted suicide from the age of 12. But up to the age of 16 such decisions must be taken in conjunction with the parents or guardians. Sixteen year olds may in principle take such decisions for themselves but parents must be informed and consulted. As in other cases of assisted death, suffering must be unbearable and deemed incurable.

An overwhelming majority of the Dutch population is in favour of doctor assisted suicide. Polls repeatedly show that over 80per cent of the public support the practice. About 200,000 Dutch people carry documents declaring that they wish to die quickly and painlessly if physical or mental illness strikes and prevents them from leading a tolerable life. The Dutch equivalent of the UK's Dignity in Dying, the NVVE, has 110,000 members. Euthanasia takes place mostly in people's own homes, sometimes in hospitals and rarely in nursing homes. Patients suffering from cancer make up 90 per cent of all euthanasia cases. Due to the close doctor/patient relationship requirement people from outside the Netherlands do not qualify for help in assisted suicide.

BELGIUM AND AMERICA

In May 2002 the Belgian parliament passed an assisted suicide bill with conditions virtually identical to the ones applicable in the Netherlands.

Luxembourg followed suit in 2008.

As in the UK and many other countries, public opinion in America is strongly in favour of some form of assisted dying. In a 2002 Gallup poll 72 per cent of Americans approved. The 50 states have wide ranging autonomy to pass their own laws. That's why it has been possible for the state of Oregon in 1994, following a state-wide referendum, to pass the 'Death with Dignity' law allowing PAS (Physician Assisted Suicide) to Oregon residents under strict conditions:

- Patient must be terminally ill, with 6 months or less to live
- There must be at least 2 consecutive oral requests and 1 written request, witnessed by 2 independent witnesses who do not stand to gain.
- At least 2 doctors must be convinced
- Patient must not suffer from depression
- Patient must be made fully aware of alternatives such as palliative care
- There must be a waiting period of at least 15 days

Once these conditions are judged to have been satisfactorily met the patient's doctor may prescribe a lethal medication which must be taken by the patient supervised by the doctor. The number of suicides under this scheme have averaged approx. 50 per year. Following Oregon, assisted dying is now possible in 2 further states. In Washington state after a state-wide referendum in 2008 and in Montana as a result of a court ruling on a test case in 2009. The Montana judges majority verdict read: *"Competent, terminally ill patients have the right to self administer lethal doses of medication as prescribed by a doctor. Prescribing doctors will not face prosecution".*

In many other states there is constant pressure for similar provisions. No doubt in due course more states will follow suit, but it will be a long road to travel. Between 1994 and 2010 there have been in excess of 75 legislative bills to legalise PAS in at least 21 states. All have failed to become law.

My concluding thoughts on the assisted dying controversy are that it boils down to a struggle between the authoritarian lobby who believe in the sanctity of human life, regardless of suffering, and those of us who feel that people should have full autonomy to decide when life is no longer worth prolonging. When good, life is precious but when no longer good, with no improvement in prospect, people should be allowed to be masters of their own destiny.

HAPPINESS

"The fact that a believer is happier than a sceptic is no more to the point than the fact that a drunken man is happier than a sober one"

George Bernard Shaw

The Humanist emblem is the Happy Human. There s(he) is on my book cover, arms joyfully aloft. But are humanists really happier than anybody else? And another thing: how do you measure happiness? If I claim that I am a fast runner and so do you, then the matter is easily settled. On your marks, get set, go and a few seconds later all is revealed. Our relative speediness there to see for everyone. But happiness is a much more difficult concept to pin down. If two people, even in the same household, were able to swap their sense of happiness, they would likely be in for quite a jolt. What one of them had thought of as contentment is shown up as comparative misery.

It is often suggested that religious people, thanks to a comforting faith, are ahead in the happiness stakes. Recent American research has tried to throw some light on the matter. According to a Barna Research poll nine out of ten Americans are happy with their lives and say their religious faith has a lot to do with it. Those with an active Christian faith - who attend church, read the Bible and pray during a typical week - were more likely than other adults to say that they are very happy with their lives, that their faith is growing deeper and that they are in good physical condition.

Respondents in the "non-faith" group were least likely to feel very happy or connected with others and most likely to feel that their lives are increasingly stressful and complex, according to the study. Non-practising Christians and adults affiliated with other faith groups fell between the two extremes on the happiness scale.

But George Barna, who directed the study and provided an analysis, said that many of the happy respondents are also the most affluent and that happiness doesn't mean that religion is being practised properly, especially a Christian faith that puts service to God before material comforts. When discussing the survey on Radio 4's *Sunday* programme, one commentator made clear that Americans who claim to be religious actually know very little about their religion. They are ignorant of its theology and indifferent to its teachings, and treat religion as a kind of social support and a means of self-congratulation.

Religion has been associated with happiness for other reasons. For instance, religion often gives people social support and contact. People meet other like-minded people at church, and in many instances can count on them when they need help. Another reason that some religions might enhance subjective well-being is that they provide optimism for an afterlife. These religions solve the "terror" associated with death by promising a better life in the hereafter. Whereas for humanists all the pies are in the earthly kitchen, for the religious they are mostly in the sky.

One of the best-known claims is that religion supposedly protects people against depression. According to a 2003 meta analysis, that combined the results of 147 different studies, religiosity explains less than 1 per cent of the differences in vulnerability to depression. It could be argued that if religion has such a marginal correlation with depression, it may not be a huge factor in happiness either.

Such doubt emerges most strongly from comparisons between countries. Much of the research linking religiosity and happiness was conducted in the U.S. where more religious people appear slightly happier. Researchers saw this as evidence for the universal benefits of religion yet there is no association between religiosity and happiness in either Denmark or the Netherlands.

Why the difference? Religious people are in the majority in the U.S., but in a minority in Denmark and the Netherlands. Feeling part of the mainstream may be comforting whereas being in the minority is potentially stressful. If religion contributes to happiness, then the most religious countries should be happiest. Yet, the opposite is true. According to Gallup findings for 2010, the happiest nations were Denmark, Norway, Sweden, and the Netherlands. The Gallup data also showed that Sweden, Denmark and Norway were the second, third, and fourth least religious states, being exceeded only by Estonia in their atheism.

Why are these European countries so happy? Their happiness is explainable in terms of a combination of national wealth and redistribution of resources via high taxation and a well-developed welfare state. So paying taxes can make people happy after all! Of course it's not the actual payment of taxes that cheers citizens, but the end result of good government which is to say a secure standard of living for everyone. It's the starting point for a lot of other benefits, particularly a superior education and sophisticated media. In the jargon of social studies, the European social democracies provide existential security. No one has to worry about being arbitrarily dismissed from their job and running out of money for basic necessities.

The principle source of European happiness is also the main reason for their unprecedented level of atheism. When countries become more affluent and their people acquire greater material security plus better education, their religious temperature takes a nose dive. So perhaps George Smith is right when in his book 'Atheism, the Case against God' he says: *'Just as Christianity must destroy reason before it can introduce faith, so it must destroy happiness before it can introduce salvation'.* Another great American, Robert Ingersoll, puts it this way: *'The clergy must show that misery fits the good for heaven, while happiness prepares the bad for hell; that the wicked get all their good things in this life and the good all the evil; that in this world God punishes the people he loves and in the next one the ones he hates; that happiness makes us bad here, but not in heaven; that pain makes us good here, but not in hell'.*

My own, necessarily limited experience, inclines me to conclude that the credulous and simple religious mind makes for a less troubled existence. The focus is on self-centred, atavistic entertainment with less concern for the broader picture. When walking the village streets at night as an earnest adolescent, discussing the world's woes with my equally studious friend, we were often struck by the sounds of relentless happiness cascading from the local tavern, where following the Evensong service church folk had gathered for an evening of mirth. Similarly, many decades later, when I lived in London, next door to a Salvation Army house, I was a long suffering recipient of happy titterings and gigglings passing through the party wall. Not a care in the world apparently and there was me agonising over the Holocaust in episode twelve of the 'World at War'.

The great pull of religion and one of the reasons why it will not go away, is the fact that it exempts its followers from the need to torment themselves over worldly affairs. Such worries may be delegated to the Almighty. So for me the happiness contest remains undecided. In the end it's up to the individual. Personally it makes me happy that humanism exempts me from having to spend time in church and at prayer. It also releases me from worry about Heaven or Hell in an afterlife. On the minus side I am concerned about population growth and conflict, a lot of it religion related. We Humanists, without the Lord to provide, must face the world as it is, the good, as well as the bad. And often the bad can be pretty depressing. The dilemma was summed up by the famous Ecuadorian painter Guayasamin who, when asked if he was happy, replied: "As happy, I suppose, as anyone has a right to be in a world with so much injustice".

HUMANIST UTOPIA

"Imagine there's no countries
It isn't hard to do
Nothing to kill or die for
And no religion too".

John Lennon

What would the world be like if religion disappeared from the face of the earth? A very interesting question and a proposition that humanists would dearly love to experiment with. Although many people derive comfort from religion and others do good things in the name of God, these acts pale in comparison to the atrocities committed to please an invisible, supernatural deity. Most (if not all) of the good things done in the name of religion could be and have been done in the course of helping one's fellow human beings. Religion enforces the status quo and fights against scientific and social evolution. It has been responsible for wars, mass suicides and bigotry and it is used as an excuse to do horrible things with an air of righteousness. In exchange for providing negligible benefits to society, religion holds humanity back from accomplishing its potential, fettering it with superstition and myth. As Bertrand Russell said, "It is possible that mankind is on the threshold of a golden age; but, if so, it will be necessary first to slay the dragon that guards the door, and this dragon is religion.

Even if this dragon finally bites the dust, there can't of course be an expectation that an instant utopia would ensue. There would still be crime. Unfortunately there will always be a small proportion of people with sociopathic tendencies who tend to spoil things for everybody else. For some of these there can never be a cure and so it will be impossible to arrive at a perfect world. However one category of crime that would disappear is the one where good people do bad things because of their religion.

Elsewhere vast improvement could also be achieved. For starters most wars would be eliminated. Conditions for women everywhere would massively improve. Finance that is now applied to religious buildings and institutions would be much better applied elsewhere. The cost of a single mosque, temple or cathedral could finance a whole new housing estate where now there is a shanty town. Homosexuals would no longer be persecuted. Tax payers would no longer have to pay for the indoctrination of other people's children. All speech, not inciting crime, would be free. Censorship for adults would be a thing of the past. Religious morality police would be made redundant. Animals would suffer less. There would be no more genital mutilation. Women would be in full charge of their own bodies without men telling them what to do. Population growth would be drastically curtailed. Children would be able to choose their own philosophy. Gullible poor people would no longer be fleeced by devious faith healers and televangelists. Without religious restrictions placed on research, science could make more rapid progress. Sex would lose its repugnant status. Clerics would start to do more useful jobs. The United Nations and Unicef would become much more influential.

In a post-superstitious society people would get into the habit of requiring evidence before jumping to conclusions. They would start thinking for themselves rather than expect to be spoon-fed by their supposed betters. Must I go on? The list is almost endless. Without religion, we would know just as well that we must live according to the golden rule: behave towards others as we would want them to behave towards us. We can be good without God. If religion is needed for good, theists should be able to answer Christopher Hitchens' challenge, "Name one moral action or statement that a religious person can make that can't be made by a non-believer."

I must be fair and look for some negative results that would flow from the eradication of religion. The first is a patronising one: we morally upstanding humanists might not need religion to live a crime-free life but some of our less principled companions might need the strictures of religion to stay on the straight and narrow. It is not a theory I subscribe to and I have explained elsewhere why. Others might think it valid.

Some more plausible advantages offered by religion to some people could be these: People like the authority figures and moral absolutes of religion to guide them so they can know the right path to tread in a very confusing world. They like to feel that they are walking on the solid rock of infallible religion rather than on the shifting sands of tentative science and moral relativity. People also like the warm, loving acceptance of religious groups, and emotional fulfilment that gives them a closer feeling to God and their church. And mysticism just by itself seems to satisfy a deep, primitive emotional need for most humans.

Another benefit of religion is the raising of one's self-esteem, the feeling that one is superior to soulless lower animals as well as superior to non-believers because one is saved and chosen for eternity. It makes dying easier for a lot of people, with a promise for a glorious reunion to come. It helps one feel less alone in the world; it can promote positive social activity. It gives people with troubled lives a reason to keep going. As discussed in the 'afterlife' chapter, I am not convinced that many people genuinely believe in the existence of paradise, but for those that do there is no doubt that it offers a sizeable chunk of consolation. And for those wronged on this earth it offers a sweet come-uppance for their tormentors in the next life. The religious are active in charities. Religion has inspired beautiful works of art and music. It makes for interesting and animated debates. It has given rise to national holidays. It can be as addictive as drugs or alcohol and addiction can provide inspiration. It provides excellent material for programmes like the 'Vicar of Dibley' and last but not least: monks brew excellent beer!

My Humanist Wish List

As a child each year I had a wish list for Santa Claus. Mostly my wishes came true. As an adult the items on my wish list for humanity are a good deal more ambitious and seeing them fulfilled will probably be a forlorn hope. But here it is nevertheless:

*I **wish** that never again people would throw away their only life in the service of some pointless superstition.*

*I **wish** that all egregious religious doctrine would regress to the primeval depths from which it sprang.*

*I **wish** that people would learn not to accept 'truths' without examining them independently*

*I **wish** that the human race would treat the animal world more kindly*

*I **wish** that male aggression could be eliminated from the human psyche*

*I **wish** that people would be allowed to make decisions about their own bodies*

*I **wish** that censorship would be restricted to advocating direct harm to others*

*I **wish** that parents would allow their children to develop their own life stances*

*I **wish** that people would be less inclined to take offence*

The pinnacle of religious wishful thinking is the existence of an afterlife. The above wish list is my humanist equivalent. Where we differ is that mine could be achieved in the here and now on our beloved blue planet. It is up to future generations to put them into practice. If they fail the planet will continue to be blue but mankind's future will be black.

 **Tony Akkermans** was born in the Netherlands at the start of the war. He trained in engineering, modern languages and commerce. He settled in England in 1966, lived in Canada and finished his career as Head of Marketing at the Netherlands-British Chamber of Commerce in London.

He retired to live in Shropshire where for seven years he was Chairman of a local Humanist group.

Lightning Source UK Ltd.
Milton Keynes UK
UKOW03f0302270914

239256UK00001B/4/P